T0366859

Horace Greeley

HORACE GREELEY

Print, Politics, and the Failure of American Nationhood

James M. Lundberg

Johns Hopkins University Press
Baltimore

© 2019 Johns Hopkins University Press
All rights reserved. Published 2019
Printed in the United States of America on acid-free paper

2   4   6   8   9   7   5   3   1

Johns Hopkins University Press
2715 North Charles Street
Baltimore, Maryland 21218-4363
www.press.jhu.edu

Library of Congress Cataloging-in-Publication Data

Names: Lundberg, James M., author.
Title: Horace Greeley : print, politics, and the failure of American nationhood /
James M. Lundberg.
Description: Baltimore : Johns Hopkins University Press, 2019. | Includes
bibliographical references and index.
Identifiers: LCCN 2019005190 | ISBN 9781421432878 (hardcover : alk. paper) |
ISBN 9781421432885 (electronic) | ISBN 1421432870 (hardcover : alk. paper) |
ISBN 1421432889 (electronic)
Subjects: LCSH: Greeley, Horace, 1811–1872. | Presidential candidates—United
States—Biography. | Newspaper editors—New York (State)—New York—
Biography. | Politicians—United States—Biography. | United States—Politics
and government—1849–1877.
Classification: LCC E415.9.G8 L86 2019 | DDC 070.92 [B] —dc23
LC record available at https://lccn.loc.gov/2019005190

A catalog record for this book is available from the British Library.

*Special discounts are available for bulk purchases of this book. For more
information, please contact Special Sales at 410-516-6936 or specialsales@press
.jhu.edu.*

Johns Hopkins University Press uses environmentally friendly book materials,
including recycled text paper that is composed of at least 30 percent post-
consumer waste, whenever possible.

For Rebecca, and for Delaney and Winifred

CONTENTS

I initially went to graduate school to study early America, but my interests quickly moved forward through time. My collected seminar papers and prospectuses track me moving from seventeenth-century writing on colonial settlement, to eighteenth-century book history, to Revolutionary print culture. I might well have made it to the twentieth century by the end of my second year but for the intervention of three professors who stopped me firmly in the nineteenth.

Joanne Freeman and David Blight have shaped me and this book in countless ways. Any faults with either product are the result of my imperfect emulation of Joanne and David as scholars, writers, and teachers. Both encouraged me to take on and stick with this project; both picked me up in moments of doubt; both bought me too many lunches at Yorkside Pizza.

Joanne's teaching and scholarship opened my eyes to the early American republic and political culture, and I've seen the past in a new light ever since. When I returned to this project after some years in the teaching swamps, Joanne helped give it new life, as her own research had moved into the antebellum period. I was energized by my conversations with her about the content, fortified by her advice about the process. She generously showed me chapters of her brilliant manuscript as working models of research and writing.

David's refrain through this process was always, "Greeley is important." My work with him has helped me explain why. After any conversation we've had about this project, I've always found a note in my inbox from David with some additional words of encouragement, some new lead, some fuller reflection on something we'd discussed. Like Joanne, David is such a brilliant scholar and electrifying teacher because he has both an insatiable curiosity about the past and a keen sense of its moral stakes.

Frank Turner introduced me to the history of ideas, the curiosities of the Victorians, and the virtues of the Whigs. Most importantly, though, he became a great friend and dogged ally through trials and triumphs alike. Since his sudden passing, I have missed his good humor, his unfailing support, and his midwestern decency every day. His spirit lives on in my work as a teacher and, I hope, as a scholar, too. Most of all, I hope this book would make him proud. Imagining him here to see it only makes me miss him more.

Work colleagues have been indispensable, particularly in the second phase of this project's life. In coming to Notre Dame to direct the undergraduate program in history, I took on new and daunting responsibilities—and also gained a remarkable collection of friends and colleagues. My chairs Patrick Griffin and Jon Coleman have been great mentors. Both remained active scholars under the administrative deluge and thus robbed me of the excuse of having too much work to write. At the same time, both have taught me how to juggle it all. Jon read substantial portions of the manuscript, as did Felipe Fernandez-Armesto. Both gave me feedback that has made this book better. John Deak, Korey Garibaldi, Dan Graff, Nikhil Menon, Paul Ocobock, Emily Remus, Christina Ryan, Sarah Shortall, and Kevin Vaughn have been great pals along the way.

Generous people across the historical profession have helped this project with their insights, conversation, and feedback. They are Susan-Mary Grant, Tim Mennel, Peter Onuf, Benjamin Park, K. Stephen Prince, Ariel Ron, and Adam Tuchinsky.

I'm immensely grateful to the many people at Johns Hopkins University Press who have helped make this book a reality. Elizabeth Demers first saw merit in the project. Laura Davulis has shepherded it through peer review, revisions, and into production; she has shepherded me, a first-time author, through what was an opaque and daunting process. Her great expertise and insight—always administered with patience and good humor—has helped make a better book and, hopefully, a better author for future projects. Copyeditor Kathleen Capels has been a delight to work with. She has smoothed out the rough edges, and, with any luck, has helped me begin unlearning the arbitrary capitalization habits picked up in reading too many eighteenth- and nineteenth-century texts.

Many great friends have sustained me through this process. Those from graduate school are Gerry Cadava, Helen Curry, KC (Kay-Cee) Harrison, Dan Gilbert, Blake Gilpin, Charles Keith, Bob Morrissey, Lindsay O'Neill, Isaac Reed, Jake Ruddiman, Sam Schaffer, Helen Veit, and Wendy Warren. As much as they have enriched me intellectually, these friends have kept me laughing. The untold hours that Gerry, Blake, and Bob spent talking me through the hard parts spared me the cost of a life coach. For that, and much more, I'm in their debt forever. In college, Minor Myers III physically wrested my senior thesis from my hands and turned it in when I insisted it wasn't good enough to submit. He was my best friend and most trusted consigliere then, and so he remains now. I have learned much over the years from John Swansburg's writing, editing, and voracious curiosity. I thank him for his feedback on the introduction, and for his belief in and encouragement on this book and much else.

Great teachers along the way nurtured my love of learning about the past, beginning with Ms. Morales, my seventh grade social studies teacher, and "Coachie" Roberts, who taught me US history in high school. In college, George Willauer taught me that intellectual curiosity is a virtue; Michael Burlingame, Tony Crubaugh, Alexis Dudden, Marc Forster, and Lisa Wilson did their best to rein in my wild energies and teach me how to do it right as a historian.

My parents, Dee and Bruce Lundberg, were the first people to awaken my love for the past and for the written word. My mother, an English teacher by trade, taught me more about writing than anyone else. A single book she gave me in fourth grade—a children's historical novel about Revolutionary War spies plying the waters of Long Island Sound—made me see the past all around me and made me want to write about it. My father's relentless hunt for undiscovered daguerreotypes, which took us into nearly every antique store in New England, was its own historical awakening. So, too, was growing up among the saltboxes and salt marshes of Guilford, Connecticut. My mother-in-law, Aïda Tinio McKenna, has become a third parent. Her wisdom and experiences open my eyes to the world; her patience with her too loud son-in-law is a marvel; her unbreakable love for our children is as inspiring as it is indispensable to our working lives.

Finally, nothing is possible without my wife, Rebecca Tinio McKenna. No one has lived with this book longer, and believed in its author more, than Rebecca. All of the book's merits, and none of its faults, are owing to her love, support, perspective, encouragement, insights, suggestions, and edits. I am ever in awe of her brilliant work as a historian, her dedication as a teacher, and her commitment as a colleague. More importantly, though, I love her as my wife, my partner, and the mother to our daughters, Laney and Freddie. Our girls might not know or care much now about Horace Greeley or newspapers or nations, but in ways I can't define, they have made my work better because they have made me better. It is to them, along with Rebecca, that I dedicate this book.

Horace Greeley

Print and Legends

In March of 1849, on the final day of his brief, rollicking turn as a United States congressman, Horace Greeley rose to the floor to address the problem of his country's name. "'THE UNITED STATES OF AMERICA,'" he said, "is at once inconveniently cumbrous and palpably indefinite." The founder and editor of the *New-York Tribune* had a solution: a new name. "Columbia," he said, was more fitting, more precise, and more historically rooted. The bitter sectional wrangling over the results of the US-Mexican War that had marked the session no doubt brought the issue to mind, but the concept of the name change was not new for Greeley. His *Tribune* had first put forward "Columbia" three years earlier, after members of the New-York Historical Society had mounted a failed campaign for "Alleghania." Where "Alleghania" was regional and broadly unfamiliar, "Columbia" was a truly "National name." It was also available, albeit as a secondhand, slightly damaged commodity. As Greeley reported in 1846, "The obstacle which at one time existed in the Republic of Colombia, South America, has been removed by the severance of that Republic into three distinct nations, no one of them bearing the name under which they were united." Greeley's legislative resolution, which "was read twice, and went over among the unfinished business," made little impression. The name stood, and the nation itself was to remain "inconveniently cumbrous and palpably indefinite," only becoming more so over the ensuing decade. In 1861, the republic would suffer the same fate as Colombia, with its "severance" into "distinct nations."[1]

The problem of American nationhood could not be solved by words alone, though Horace Greeley never gave up trying. Over his four decades in journalism, he pursued an American consensus that would break through rival sectional identities, persistent localism, divergent expressions of republicanism, and contested definitions of the nation itself. Greeley's efforts made him one of the most famous men in America, but they did not yield a unified or coherent American nation. If nations were made in print, few people were better positioned than Greeley to solve the riddle of America. During the 1860 presidential election, his *Tribune* reached nearly 300,000 subscribers and many more readers. The following year, the Civil War tore the nation asunder, and over the final decade of his life, Greeley himself would be reduced to a rubble of irreconcilable contradictions. When he died in 1872, utterly humiliated and roundly drubbed by Ulysses S. Grant in that year's presidential election, Greeley had become as disjointed as the nation he sought to embody and unify. He began his career wishing to be America's oracle; he ended it as America's prism.[2]

Greeley has been eluding his biographers since 1854. Raking the soils of northern New England that year for details on Greeley's early life, James Parton found his informants as likely to obscure as to illuminate his subject. Among them, Parton noted what he described to Greeley as a tendency "to make you into the primmest, dullest little Moral Philosopher that ever went to church." Greeley understood the complaint. A decade earlier, the *Tribune* editor had noted in a short autobiographical sketch that many of his youthful accomplishments had already become "modern fables," subject to the most "monstrous exaggerations."[3]

Parton wasn't terribly troubled. He went to New Hampshire and Vermont to print the legend, not to dispel it. He began his work with a deep admiration for Greeley and the solemn conviction that his story "ought to be told" to "subserve the interests of the country." In his pitch to publishers, Parton promised a book as useful and engaging as Benjamin Franklin's *Autobiography*. What was Greeley, after all, but a latter-day incarnation of that great American personage? Those who had known the young Horace Greeley were happy to help. Their recollections had already been shaped by

Greeley's celebrity and the larger American characteristics it exemplified. If, as Parton lamented, several of his "best stories" turned out to be untrue, the book didn't suffer.[4]

The Life of Horace Greeley, Editor of the New-York Tribune was both a particular account of its subject and a journey through the American national imagination. Parton's tale of a young printer who wrests fame and influence from poverty and obscurity ended up as a kind of textual collage: Greeley improves himself through exhaustive reading by firelight; he sets upon a prized fruit tree with a hatchet (in this case pear, not cherry); he enters a great American city to make a name for himself with nothing but his tireless habits of industry. Greeley emulated the great models of American life who came before him. Now, readers of Parton's book could emulate Greeley, and the republic would endure.[5]

Though separated by several geologic ages of historiography from James Parton's work, this volume shares at least one thing in common with *The Life of Horace Greeley, Editor of the New-York Tribune*—it considers its subject as both person and personage, an individual as well as an idea. My book is not a quest for a real man waiting to be revealed, if only we can peel away the layers of newsprint. Instead, it takes Greeley as we find him—as an uneasy hybrid of a living, breathing individual and the persona he and others created in printed texts. If this understanding makes Greeley a slippery figure for the biographer, it also makes him a rich register of the conflicts and tensions of his age. Greeley shaped his public persona, defined his work, and crafted his journalism according to the print culture that made him, underscoring his broader aspirations for national consensus. In public discourse, he was constantly received and always depicted as a symbol for a broader set of constituencies, from America itself, to the North, to the Republican Party, to a radical fringe of reformers and abolitionists.[6]

Many Horace Greeleys lived between 1811 and 1872; as many more have lived in biographical and historical literature since. The *Tribune* editor has been, among other things, a fearless crusader limited by his irrepressible ambitions for public office; a political propagandist who helped blunder the nation into the Civil War; an exemplar of reformist Whig politics; a champion of American liberty; an intellectual impresario at the center of

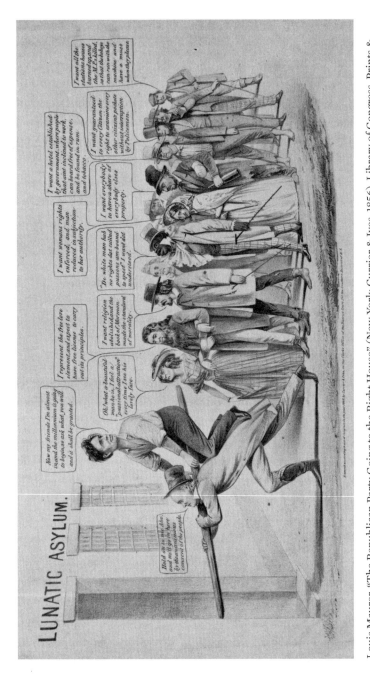

Louis Maurer, "The Republican Party Going to the Right House" (New York: Currier & Ives, 1856). Library of Congress, Prints & Photographs Division

nineteenth-century debates over labor, liberalism, and capitalism. Meanwhile, the Greeley who appears in political histories of the nineteenth century emerges as an often-cartoonish figure, known mostly for his unaccountable inconsistencies, apparent authorship of every word in the *Tribune*, and a certain directional imperative to young men.[7]

None of these characterizations of Greeley are wrong; it's just hard to believe they all describe the same person. In narrating the story of the man in dialogue with the shifting public persona who lived in print—in capturing Greeley in his many guises—this book seeks to understand him and his many contradictions. Orienting Greeley around three core beliefs, it finds a more capacious figure whose inconsistencies are less bewildering than they have often appeared. At base, Greeley believed in the American nation, print, and himself. That is, he believed in his own special calling to help realize an American national consensus through the power of print. Whether working on the page or walking off the page as a public figure, Greeley was consistent on these points across his tortuous, often-tortured career. The young Whig who founded the *New-York Tribune*, made it a forum for radical ideas, and later became the face of Republican anti-slavery, wasn't as far removed as it might seem from the one who paid Jefferson Davis's bail and ran for president against Ulysses S. Grant in 1872. In each of his guises, Greeley worked with the broad faith that printed texts and their fabled creator could elevate the people and bring them to reconcile their great differences.

Greeley's dreams of national harmony and consensus existed within a particular cultural and intellectual framework: he was an American Whig. The culture of nationalism taking shape in Europe and the United States gave Greeley typical ideas about the nation as a mystical and transcendent historical entity. Whig ideology aligned those beliefs rife with a positive nation-building program that would strengthen the bonds of union, eliminate sectionalism, and create conditions for individual uplift. Whig economic policies, such as protective tariffs and internal improvement projects to facilitate transportation and commerce, would knit the nation together into a single, harmonious whole. Whig moral beliefs linked individual improvement and cultivation (which were facilitated by economic opportunities) to the good of the "common country." For Greeley, editors and newspapers were essential to this Whig project of nation building. What he called

"Intelligence" had the power not only to bind together—to create "a community of thought and feeling"—but also to prepare the people within it for harmonious citizenship.[8]

〜

If James Parton's biography portrayed Greeley more as an ideal American type than a flesh-and-blood individual, it still captured something essential in its subject: Horace Greeley, editor of the *New-York Tribune*, was a creature of print. Born in New Hampshire in 1811, Greeley was the product of a Protestant American culture that accorded great power to printed texts and the reading practices that brought them to life. In the long shadow of the Revolutionary period, white Americans turned to print in the midst of an ongoing nation-building project. Common ideas of the nation needed to be fixed, and young people needed to be stamped with the virtue and character that would sustain the republic. Used correctly, printed texts would meet these needs, forming individuals, binding them to the national community, and forging consensus across space.[9]

Such assumptions were written into the books and printed ephemera that made up Greeley's formal and informal education. As a child, he consumed, as Parton put it, "every readable book" in a seven-mile radius, filling his head with vast stores of information and a chapter-and-verse knowledge of the Bible. One of Parton's informants—a fellow apprentice at the print shop in Vermont where Greeley learned the trade—remembered the boy settling factual matters in arguments "as a dictionary settles a dispute respecting the spelling of a word."[10] But the inheritance went beyond information alone. Noah Webster's *American Speller*, Jedidiah Morse's *American Geography*, Caleb Bingham's *Columbian Orator*, Benjamin Franklin's *Autobiography*, M. L. Weems's *Life of George Washington*, Lindley Murray's *English Reader*, and the sleepy country newspapers he devoured—these texts established the contours of individual effort and national belonging to which Greeley would shape himself as a private man and a public editor. When Greeley arrived in New York City in 1831 as a penniless youth with the whole of his scant patrimony stuffed into his proverbial knapsack, he carried in his head the inheritance that would guide his entire career: printed texts and exemplary white men were essential to the nation's well-being.[11]

Producing printed texts in New York after 1834, Greeley quickly estab-

Young Greeley's arrival in New York. From James Parton, *The Life of Horace Greeley, Editor of the New-York Tribune* (New York: 1854). Courtesy, American Antiquarian Society

lished himself as an exemplary white man, ready to harmonize the nation through information. He did not merely conform to the familiar American storylines of self-made men; he also shaped himself to a new ideal type emerging in the 1830s: the editor. Parton's epigraph from one of Greeley's intellectual heroes, Thomas Carlyle, captured the grandeur of this aspiration in 1831: "The journalists are now the true kings and clergy." Amid the diffusion of the United States, Carlyle's observation seemed all the more relevant—and urgent. Information, gathered and disseminated by the editor, would form and maintain the bonds of community and nation. As Alexis de Tocqueville noted in *Democracy in America*, "when men are no longer united in any firm or lasting way, it is impossible to persuade any great number of them to act in cooperation." Under such circumstances, newspapers and their editors took on immense importance; they alone could "place the same thought at the same moment into a thousand minds." As Greeley knew well, those newspapers were far from being impersonal, disembodied instruments. They required the labor, discernment, and vision of an individual—some heroic soul capable of condensing, compiling, and interpreting volumes of information and transmitting all of it to the public.[12]

The fame Greeley quickly won as an editor was rooted in established ideas about the uses of print and magnified by perceptions of its ever-expanding influence in an age of steam-powered presses. In Parton's account, Greeley was important not only as a model American self-made man, but as a man who moved the world through the printed word. With the *Tribune*, he "addressed a larger number of persons than any other editor or man" and "influenced a greater amount of thought and a greater number of characters than any other individual who has lived in this land." Indeed, the "Cheap Press," of which Greeley was the great genius, was the "great leveler, elevator, and democratizer" of the age. "[The Cheap Press] makes this huge Commonwealth, else so heterogeneous and disunited, think with one mind, feel with one heart, and talk with one tongue," Parton continued. "Dissolve the Union into a hundred petty States, and the Press will still keep us in heart and soul and habit, One People."[13]

It was hard to exaggerate Greeley's reach, even if Parton tried. In 1855, the *Tribune* invested in the world's largest and fastest steam-powered printing press—the better to reach the nearly 200,000 subscribers to all of its editions. When the paper predicted growth to 250,000 by the end of 1856, it was wrong; the number reached over 278,000 by October of that year. Calculating that each subscription copy reached five readers, an editorial crowed that the *Tribune* was "read by a million and a quarter of intelligent, upright, and substantial people" at a moment when the national population was just over 23 million. The centerpiece of the *Tribune*'s masthead—an image of a rotary steam press sending forth rays of light—expressed Greeley's audacious mission: mass intelligence, enlightenment, and consensus.

Masthead of the *New-York Daily Tribune*, December 25, 1855. Courtesy, American Antiquarian Society

Never mind that the *Tribune* was an industrial-scale operation with armies of subeditors, correspondents, compositors, pressmen, and distributors.[14] Most believed—and Greeley did little to discourage—the notion that he wrote the copy, set the type, and manned the presses himself. The result was a remarkable sense of intimacy that carried from Down East to the Far West. In the still localized world of nineteenth-century America, "Horace Greeley" was everywhere.[15]

Testimonies to the editor's great power abounded. In the spring of 1854, Ralph Waldo Emerson wrote to Thomas Carlyle, astonished at Greeley's hold on his followers. Following the editor on a western lecture tour, Emerson marveled at the scores of men and women "flocking" over great distances to see their "spiritual father." "As was right," Emerson joked, for "[Greeley] does all their thinking & theory for them, for two dollars a year." Recalling his travels in the West in *Roughing It*, Mark Twain complained bitterly of hearing the same word-for-word account "four hundred and eighty-one or eighty-two times" of Horace Greeley being pitched through the roof of a stagecoach going over a rough road in Nevada. The dreadful story was always precisely the same, but everyone recounted it with the same sense of warmth and possession. "Spare me just this once," Twain pleaded to the final raconteur, "and tell me about young George Washington and his little hatchet for a change."[16]

There was no single Horace Greeley, however, Twain's facsimile version notwithstanding. It was fitting that the *Tribune* editor should have been the inspiration for one of the guises of Herman Melville's *Confidence-Man* (1857)—the man from the P.I.O. (Philosophical Intelligence Office). As an imagined figure among enemies and even a good number of allies, he was a shape-shifting menace: a fanatical abolitionist and champion of a hundred other "isms"; a prudish and disappointing conservative; a terrible liar; an office-hungry megalomaniac.[17]

~

As Parton wrote of Greeley, "the click of the types that set up his name is seldom hushed." But what of Greeley himself? Amid the deluge of print, Greeley the man maintained a steadfast belief in his own rare powers. From his beginnings in New York journalism in 1834 through his ill-fated presidential run and death in 1872, Greeley sought to inhabit a national character. In that role, he understood himself as an indispensable figure in achieving national consensus. He would illuminate and connect the dark corners of the land. The *Tribune*, forged in his battles against the new penny newspapers and upstart radical abolitionists in the 1830s, embodied the promise of "Intelligence": informing, enlightening, elevating the people to exercise correct and uniform political judgments.[18] Greeley rose to great national prominence in the 1840s and '50s in the service of this mission, becoming synonymous with his paper of ever-expanding circulation and visibility. Even when inescapably embroiled in the sectional politics of the 1850s and the Civil War, Greeley did not abandon his hopes. Though he used the *Tribune* to help build the Republican Party by forging a sense of Northern unity, he understood the new coalition as the truest embodiment of the nation. Though the Civil War militarized rival national identities, his journalism and his massive two-volume history, *The American Conflict*, captured it in print as a struggle for the nation's truest expression.[19]

In 1872, when Greeley walked off the page and into the political battles of Reconstruction, he did so in the name of national consensus. Though no longer working in print, Greeley's faith that he could contain and reconcile the nation's great differences always remained. A pro-Greeley cartoon in *Frank Leslie's Illustrated Newspaper* that summer captured the whole conceit. Greeley towers over Grant, rendered as a diminutive and ridiculous Napoleonic figure swinging a sword that's gone limp. Greeley wields a giant quill pen in one hand and a printed broadside with his famous call for unity and reconciliation—"the North & South are eager to clasp hands across the bloody chasm"—in the other. "Take away the sword," the caption reads, "bring the pen." Only Greeley, his pen, and the great printed texts that came from it could make the nation whole—or so Greeley and his allies maintained.[20]

For Greeley, though, there was a bitter truth to 1872 and, indeed, to his entire career: he was not the figure of national consensus he imagined. Sizing up the second volume of Greeley's *American Conflict*, one reviewer diagnosed the problem. Greeley had an "unfortunate habit of mistaking his opinions and sentiments for those of the nation." Greeley rarely succeeded in his aspirations to speak for the nation. Instead, amid the mounting sectional tensions of the antebellum years, the violent fracture of the Civil War itself, and the bitter conflicts of Reconstruction, Greeley was more often a figure who embodied the inherent problems of American nationhood, rather than its transcendent harmony.[21]

This tension came to a head in the great traumas of the 1850s and '60s, when Greeley rose to the height of his powers, not as symbol of national unity, but as one of irreconcilable sectional divide. His own newspaper shaped a narrative of national politics as sectional conflict, and Greeley embodied all of the ambiguities of "the Yankee," awkwardly poised between a regional and a national symbolism (tellingly, Parton dedicated his story of Greeley as a national hero "to the young men of the free states"). To admirers, Greeley was "our later Franklin," a celebrity whose wisdom, vision, and feats of self-creation made him a representative Yankee in the national sense. To critics, Greeley's influence in New England and its midwestern satellites made him the sum of all that was wrong with Northern culture and its hegemonic aspirations.

Greeley's efforts at consensus still came to naught when he embraced reconciliation at the close of the Civil War. As some white Southerners accepted his plea to "clasp hands across the bloody chasm," Northern allies abandoned him. After Greeley paid Jefferson Davis's bail in 1867, subscribers to his crowning work of national history, *The American Conflict*, cancelled in droves, and he was ejected from the New York Chapter of the Union League. In 1872, when his reconciliationist vision won him the Liberal Republican nomination to challenge Grant, Greeley's failure was complete. Thomas Nast's iconic *Harper's Weekly* cartoons from the campaign signaled the end to his claims as a representative figure capable of reconciling the nation's differences. Where Greeley had once been taken as a symbol for larger constituencies—of Northerners, reformers, radicals, Republicans—Nast's images captured him now in his abject singularity. For Greeley, the reckoning was too hard to bear. He died just weeks after his defeat, in December of 1872. He was the Civil War's most peculiar casualty.

⤳

The present volume also tells a larger story about the problems of American nationhood that neither print nor politics could reconcile. Greeley was not wrong in his assumptions about the power of print, nor was he wrong about the broader culture he expressed. Printed communication had indeed been essential to the work of nation building in the new United States. American Revolutionaries and their heirs among Greeley's generation hardly needed modern students of nationalism to tell them that print helped people imagine national communities—to bind citizens together across space around shared information, ideas, culture, and history.[22]

But Greeley's career as both a wildly successful editor and an otherwise failed nation builder shows that print could just as powerfully divide as it could unite. When a Washington, DC, newspaper early in 1861 called Greeley "a bad man . . . if not the worst man in America" and claimed that *he* had been responsible for secession, it did so with at least a small grain of truth. The massive expansion of journalism and printed communication that Greeley embodied drove the narratives of sectional conflict that made the Civil War possible. In the context of an American nationalism that was fragile, contradictory, and regionally inflected, print and the languages of American nationhood it circulated magnified differences and widened divides.[23]

Indeed, the turns of Greeley's fortunes highlight the near impossibility of the consensus nationalism for which he yearned. Nowhere could this be seen more clearly than in the 1850s, when Greeley played an instrumental role in forging the Republican Party around a coherent Northern identity. The coalition of white men who elected Abraham Lincoln in 1860 certainly saw themselves as the heirs of the nation's founders. Yet their abiding faith in Free Labor and strident opposition to slavery were inextricable from conceptions of inherent Northern virtue within a larger story of sectional strife. Nothing, meanwhile, did more to encourage and consolidate expressions of Southern nationalism and distinctiveness, a dynamic only encouraged by Southern perceptions of the expansive power of Northern print.[24]

The Civil War did not resolve the problems of American nationalism, contrary to the notion that the war somehow transformed a union of states into a consolidated nation and made the United States whole. This was certainly Greeley's most earnest hope, one embodied not just in his account of the war as an "American Conflict," but also in his conduct during the postwar years and the election of 1872.[25] To his utter humiliation, though, and to the financial detriment of his two-volume history, his version of the war and his vision for national reconciliation found little traction. Greeley did help establish a language of "race and reunion" that reoriented the story of the war away from emancipation and toward a shared white nationalism. Yet in the short run, the sectional categories Greeley helped harden before the war were simply too strong and too enduring.[26]

Chapter 1 follows Greeley from his country printer's apprenticeship into the maze of Manhattan's streets and the jangling politics of the 1830s and early 1840s. Amid explosive developments in urban journalism and the rise of radical abolition, Greeley constructed a theory of newspaper "Intelligence" around the ideal of an oracular editor. Blending enlightened republican beliefs in a connected citizenry with Romantic notions of individual genius, Greeley argued that the editor bore the noble burden of uplifting and unifying the public through information. Newspapers, guided by rare and special souls, were not to be sources of entertainment, but instruments of instruction and consensus. Greeley sharpened his craft and shaped his editorial persona at the head of a series of Whig political and literary weeklies before founding the *New-York Daily Tribune* in 1841. The *Tribune* was to stand as a guardian of public interest, agent of reform, and vehicle for the nation's great harmonization.

The 1840s, however, proved an inopportune decade for a would-be newsprint oracle to shape the nation through "Intelligence." Chapter 2 finds Greeley straining to maintain his grand visions of national consensus amid growing sectional divisions wrought by territorial expansion. Beginning with an undying loyalty to Henry Clay and his American System, Greeley believed that a reformist Whig Party could carry the nation through rancorous debates over slavery, war, and revolutions abroad. When political developments in 1848 offered Greeley the possibility of becoming a sectional oracle to the North, rather than a national one, he stayed with his idea of the nation. His fealty to the Whig Party and national principles earned him a three-month stint in the House of Representatives. As sectional rage shook the House to the rafters, Greeley waged a quixotic, losing fight for national principles. Few people in the whole history of Congress have ever made themselves so unwelcome in so short a time.

In the political battles of the 1850s, Greeley became the sectional oracle he had not wanted to be. After declaring political independence from the Whig Party, Greeley reentered the political fray with renewed purpose following the passage of the Kansas-Nebraska Act in 1854. Chapter 3 finds him at the height of his powers, abandoning his compromise-oriented Whig nationalism and reenvisioning American nationalism through a Northern lens. Free of his former political obligations, Greeley used his prodigious influence to help imagine a North united against slavery and its spread—a Yankee nation that became the foundation of the emerging Republican Party. As the *Tribune* framed the sectional and political narrative of that decade, Greeley himself became a symbol not of national unity, but of regional divide—a fact made vivid by his brutal caning at the hands of an Arkansas Democrat in 1856.

As sectional conflict slid into disunion and war, there was seemingly no one better suited than Horace Greeley to give voice and meaning to the Northern struggle for the nation. In practice, however, Greeley turned out to be an unreliable narrator, both as an editorial interpreter and as one of the war's earliest historians. Chapter 4 traces what one critic of Greeley's massive history, *The American Conflict*, called his "criminal vagaries." Greeley's insistence that the war must not merely preserve the Union, but also redeem and deliver the nation, led him into startling inconsistencies. After a string of contradictions and reversals, ranging from apparent acceptance of secession, to full-throated calls for conquest and emancipation, to blathering pleas for peace on any terms, Abraham Lincoln summed up the attitudes of many by the end of the war: Greeley had become "an old shoe, good for nothing now, whatever he has been."

In the postwar years, Greeley still had enough influence to appear in one final persona: as a reconciliationist celebrity. Chapter 5 reorients Greeley's nationalism southward and follows his course out of the Republican Party and into his climactic fight with Ulysses S. Grant in the presidential election of 1872. Immediately following the war, Greeley returned to his early oracular self-assurance and designated himself as healer of the nation. Though he pledged his support for both "impartial suffrage" for freed slaves and "universal amnesty" for former Confederates, his quest for a middle ground took him deep into Dixie, both in person and in spirit. The stentorian figure who had once urged conquering Yankee armies "on to Richmond!" visited the Confederate capital in 1867, not to revel in Northern triumph, but to pay Jefferson Davis's bail. By the time of his presidential run against Grant in 1872, Greeley was calling for an end to Reconstruction and voicing his sympathies for men who had once been his bitterest enemies. With a torrent of mockery, Greeley's old Republican allies turned a bizarre spectacle into a national circus.

⌒

Greely wrote in a notoriously illegible hand. What he called his "Egyptian characters" tormented both his contemporaries and subsequent chroniclers. In his time, many found a reliable vein of humor in comparing what Greeley wrote by hand versus what the compositor set in type. In another episode of *Roughing It*, Twain has a young man write to Greeley for advice on how to grow cucumbers, only to be driven to madness as he tries to decipher the letter he gets in return. Every student of Greeley is faced with the opposite problem of the compositor or the recipient of the letter. In the absence of much of Greeley's original correspondence, we are left to work largely from the printed texts back to the handwriting and the person who created them. We begin that work in New York City.

Greeley to Richard T. Jones, January 17, 1860. Horace Greeley Papers, New York Public Library; used with permission

CHAPTER ONE

Oracle

Perfect strangers took the liberty of writing to Horace Greeley, vaunted editor of the *New-York Tribune*. They wrote to scold him about editorials, to invite him to invest in their new mining concerns, to seek guidance on career choices and crop yields, to beg for letters of recommendation for their nephews, or just to get an autograph. If they were fortunate to hear back and able to decipher the scrawl that Greeley called his "Egyptian characters," they were usually staring at a piece of harsh advice. "If you live to be considerably older and wiser," Greeley told an autograph hunter in 1860, "I am sure you will realize that collecting other persons' autographs is not the way to make your own worth possessing."[1]

Greeley reserved the coldest water to douse young men's literary and journalistic ambitions. Those like Harvey Hubbard, who wrote from the canal district of New York State in 1844, might sooner "rush on suicide" than seek "what is called a Literary Life" in the city. Aspirants to fame could not expect to succeed on "the mere talent of writing well." There was "no school for Editorial Knowledge," but writers and editors needed vast stores of it. This meant assessing the "general political character" of each county, of each state. They also had to learn about about "thousands of little and great men"—the governor of Alabama, the chief US marshal in Missouri, the editor of the Democratic paper in Portland, Maine. Greeley knew these things, but only after "years of affliction." "I have been fortunate here," Greeley told Hubbard, "But how? I need money badly and I am an assemblage of pains. I cannot bear five years longer with my present work." Not even the aid of eager young supplicants like Hubbard could alleviate the strain: "Why not have more help? you will ask—Because no one can see through my eyes, compose present facts with my best knowledge . . . nor write out my thoughts. In a word, no other man can do my work. The laws of the Universe forbid."[2]

Through the 1830s and '40s, Horace Greeley's name stood atop the mastheads of a series of publications that marked his rise in journalism: a literary weekly called the *New-Yorker*; two Whig campaign sheets, the *Jeffersonian* and the *Log Cabin*; and, beginning in 1841, the *New-York Tribune*. Each was a notable contribution to the torrent of print flooding the United States in those years, but no less a creation was the editorial persona behind them. That Horace Greeley—the one who could invite the intimate correspondence of strangers and bluster on in response about the terrible burdens of the editor's calling—was part Romantic genius, part folk character.

It was not an accidental concoction. Greeley's Romantic genius persona was a newsprint version of Scottish Romantic Thomas Carlyle's "Man-of-Letters Hero," who stripped away the world's false appearances to reveal things as they really were. He possessed a commanding knowledge of politics and affairs and a progressive vision for reform and social unity. As Greeley told a friend, the editor should feel "the grave importance of our vocation, and the necessity of throwing earnestness, power into every thing."[3] Greeley's folk character was rooted in antebellum popular culture. His notoriously disheveled appearance—flowing coat, crooked top hat, muddy boots—had a studied air about it that bore a resemblance to the day's popular stage Yankees and Brother Jonathans. Though a more intellectual version of those characters, this folk Greeley played much the same role of the wise New England rustic critically sizing up a changing world. While the *Tribune* rapidly became a starkly modern, even industrial-scale operation, Greeley appeared to many readers as the village printer who wrote every word, set the type, and worked the press all by himself. He did little to discourage such impressions. "For whatever is distinctive in the views or doctrines of The Tribune," he huffed in 1847, "there is but *one* person responsible." Greeley was the *Tribune*, and the *Tribune* was Greeley. The editor reigned.[4]

This mythic Greeley—part self-made, part creature of popular fancy—

strode out from a lively passage in the history of American journalism. Arriving in New York City as a journeyman printer in 1831 and then founding the *Tribune* in 1841, Greeley achieved his rise amid a revolution in the popular press. Older paradigms had kept newspaper circulation within the tight bounds of the business community and political parties. In the early 1830s, editors embraced a new model. Rather than relying on expensive subscription fees, political patronage, and elite clientele, they would sell papers on the street to anyone able to part with a penny; rather than addressing narrow groups, they would appeal to the broad public with gripping, sensational coverage of local events. The new penny papers, led by Benjamin Day's *New-York Sun* and James Gordon Bennett's *New-York Herald*, seemed perfectly tuned to the democratic ideals of Andrew Jackson's America. They were liberating information from the grip of the few and delivering it to the many, all for a pittance. Amid a wider profusion of printed media, the penny papers were leading what the *Sun* called "a march of intelligence."[5]

Or were they? For all the promise of the penny press and an expanded print marketplace, there were also many perils. Soon after Greeley launched his weekly *New-Yorker* in 1834, a rival publication placed a mock classified in its own pages: "Wanted: a machine for reading newspapers—to sift the chaff from the wheat . . . the useful facts from the idle fictions—the counterfeit coin from the unadulterated metal." Amid such a profusion of information, fundamental questions arose about its veracity, value, and purpose. It was not clear what might be real and what might be "humbug," nor was it apparent whether the purpose of information was to empower and instruct, or simply to entertain. There were also questions about the role of information in constituting the community and the public. Ideas going back to the nation's founding had held up the press as a great engine of unity and consensus. Yet the jangling politics, the explosive social and economic changes, the increasingly radical ideas about slavery in the 1830s suggested a different possibility: the press could just as easily widen the fissures within American society as bridge them.[6]

These questions defined Greeley's early work: his editorial identity, the content of his journalism, and his struggles to survive in the marketplace. For the young Whig Greeley, the popular press expressed the diffusion of cultural authority, social antagonisms, and political disorder that ailed Jackson's America. But as much as newspapers threatened to worsen these problems, Greeley believed that they also contained solutions, if only they were operated correctly. He constructed a theory of journalism with himself at the center—one that was geared toward the instruction and unification of the public, rather than its entertainment. His mission, he said in 1835, "was to elevate the character [of the press] and [to] extend the sphere of its influence." The editor would lead the people, create a "unity of thought and feeling" among them, and teach them to see "the right and wrong of politics." In the crowded metropolis, who was better suited to the work than a rough genius, a Yankee printer too busy to shake off the dust of the countryside?[7]

March of Intelligence, or March of Humbug?

"In civilization," George Foster would write in Greeley's *Tribune* in 1848, "every powerful nation must have one intellectual center, as every individual must have a brain, whose motions and conceptions govern the entire system. In the United States, New York is that center and that brain."[8] Horace Greeley never loved New York City, but he needed it. As a journeyman printer, he needed the work afforded by its expansive print marketplace; as a would-be newsprint oracle, he needed it as a platform for visibility and influence; and as a self-made man, he needed it as a backdrop for his rise from penniless hayseed to towering eminence.

Greeley arrived in Gotham late in the summer of 1831, poised precariously between a Franklinian success story and the common cautionary tale of the rustic innocent who is ruined by the city and its evils. His origins in what he called "poverty of the manly American sort" set the stage for either possibility. Greeley was born in southern New Hampshire in 1811 to a downwardly mobile farm family. His father Zaccheus and his brothers Benjamin, John, Isaac, Gilbert, and Parker had inherited names befitting New England farmers, but not the land to go with them. Zac, as Mr. Greeley was called, purchased a small holding near Amherst two years before Horace's birth. By the son's account, Zac was a "bad manager," a shiftless worker prone to drink and debt. Zac's wife, the former Mary Woodburn, was a New Hampshirite of Scots-Irish stock. She was said to have brought brains and a severe Presbyterian inclination for industry to the operation, but this was not enough to redeem Zac or save the family farm. In the wake of the Panic of

1819, Zac was $1,000 in debt, and the family fled their creditors. In the root-less period that followed, the Greeleys lived on rented farms across Vermont and New York State. Horace peeled off in 1826 to begin his apprenticeship as a printer at the age of fifteen.[9]

For all of Greeley's future rhapsodies on farming—"I should have been a farmer" was a favorite refrain, beginning in middle age—the printing trade suited him.[10] The legendary schoolboy attainments recalled by biographer James Parton's informants were rooted in an uncommon aptitude for reading, language, and information. As a child, he'd devoured any piece of print he could get his hands on, beginning with the first book he ever owned, Caleb Bingham's *Columbian Orator*. In the tiny town of East Poultney, Vermont, where he served his apprenticeship, Greeley luxuriated in exchange newspapers coming into the office of the weekly *Northern Spectator* and plowed through the collection of a local lending library. By the time he left that state, Greeley was a thoroughgoing product of an American print culture, with its Protestant textual practices, Enlightenment ideals of improvement, republican morality, and nationalism. These all mingled together to give Greeley a profound sense of the power of print to shape individuals and forge the bonds of community.[11]

Two small items that Greeley himself would have set in type and then put into print as an apprentice at the *Northern Spectator* condensed much of what he knew and believed as he entered New York City. First, in 1826, a piece reprinted from *Niles' Weekly Register* heralded newspapers as "the great engine that moves the moral and political world," instruments that must "establish the character of a people, as well as to preserve their liberties." Two years later, in 1828, the *Spectator* filled part of a column with another reprinted item, this one a brief tribute to the life and accomplishments of "Dr. Franklin." Beyond his reputation as a model of self-denial, frugality, and temperance, Franklin was notable as "an editor and publisher" whose work "had a prodigious influence on the temper of his countrymen." Greeley could scarcely have imagined that his efforts would attain the reach of *Niles' Weekly Register* or achieve the status of Franklin, but he would need both exemplars as he navigated New York City and its expansive trade in print.[12]

New York was well on the way to achieving its status as the "center and brain" of American communications when Greeley arrived there in 1831. In scarcely a generation, the city had expanded from a midsized port town to an American answer to the great cities of Europe. The marketplace for print grew accordingly. Evangelical societies had begun to embrace the possibilities of mass publication in the 1820s, churning out Bibles and tracts for free distribution to needy souls. The secular press, already robust thanks to cheap postage and limited governmental restriction, was not far behind. Though smaller communities would retain their local papers, New York was rapidly becoming a national hub of information. In 1830, the city's presses put out forty-seven newspapers, eleven of which were dailies. Their influence was growing rapidly. Some 160,000 papers had gone out of New York's post office in 1828. The number would be close to a million in 1833.[13]

Amid the explosive growth, Greeley found plenty of work but not much of the guidance or community he had known in Vermont. Under a hard-driving boss who mocked him as a "green Yankee, just hatched," Greeley fell back on the model of Franklinian industry ("[the boss] knows that I can set any manuscript, however abominable, and make a cleaner proof than almost anyone else"), but that did not make the experience any less alienating. "I am heartsick of this working out among strangers and living on sour looks, solitude, and salt pork," he told a friend after three months in town. At odds with the well-lubricated drinking culture of urban shops and boardinghouses, Greeley found refuge in the severe dietary practices of Sylvester Graham. An orator who spoke with the fire of a camp-meeting Jeremiah, Graham exhorted his followers to adopt a program of consuming raw vegetables, cold water, and wholesome bread and foreswearing coffee, tea, alcohol, and sex. By the summer of 1832, Greeley had taken up residence in a Graham boardinghouse, where inmates maintained a strict adherence to the diet and a precise daily schedule that began with a 5 AM bell for exercise. As a correspondent to a rural Connecticut paper noted in 1832, "a Graham Boarding House is a Bangup place for Yankees" in New York.[14]

There was no journalistic refuge in the city comparable to a Graham boardinghouse. When Greeley arrived, the preeminent New York newspapers were the sixpenny "blanket sheets," known for their massive size and high cost. Their editors were keenly aware of the growing value of information in the commercial metropolis, and competition among them to provide it was stiff. Although news could travel only as fast as it could physically be carried, the sixpenny editors did all they could to obtain the "freshest advices" for their papers. Express riders galloped along the roads from Washington, DC; speedy "news schooners" plied the waters off Sandy Hook (at the entrance to Lower New York Bay) to get the latest from ships arriving from Europe; even carrier pigeons were employed. The papers themselves had ample room to contain the information. Editors outdid one another with ever-larger formats, to the point where these "blanket sheets" could cover nearly five feet of a merchant's breakfast table or desk. Whatever space editors could not fill with news and advertisements, they dedicated to vicious personal attacks on one another. The disputes often tumbled from the columns into the streets, where editors were known to wield a cane or cowhide whip when honor demanded it.[15]

For all their commercial utility and occasional color, the blanket sheets had limited appeal to the broad public. As eventual *New-York Herald* founder James Gordon Bennett bellowed in 1832, the immense blanket sheets were not just expensive, they were also "the pine barrens of intelligence and taste," "the reservoirs of crude thoughts from different persons who were continually knocking their heads against each other, without knocking anything remarkably good out of them." The moment beckoned for someone to come along and offer a new way to make and sell a newspaper. Both Bennett and Greeley tried. After Bennett's *New-York Globe* failed in 1832, Greeley served as the printer for the city's first penny daily, the *Morning Post*. The paper was launched on New Year's Day in 1833 and did not last a month. As Greeley said later, the *Post* was remarkable for its low cost and "also for the absence of any other desirable quality." The paper's chief backer, a young doctor, had failed to grasp that people would not part with even a penny for a paper that had nothing worth reading.[16]

The trick, a young printer named Benjamin Day showed, lay in capturing the drama continually unfolding in the city's crowded streets. Day made September 3, 1833, a signature date in the history of American journalism with the launch of his *New-York Sun*. Though tiny in comparison with the blanket sheets—just 7-5/8 by 10-1/4 inches—the *Sun*'s brand of journalism illuminated the city and its dark corners. Newspapers had traditionally shunned local reportage as an unnecessary rehearsal of what everyone in town knew already. But the *Sun* and its imitators gave readers a compelling narrative of urban life with reports scraped from the city's underbelly. "Fires, theatrical performances, elephants escaping from the circus, women trampled by hogs"—these would sell papers. "We newspaper people thrive on the calamities of others," Day confessed in the *Sun*'s first week. Should crime scenes and the smoldering ruins of buildings offer up no compelling copy, the *Sun* could also manufacture news by other means. In the summer of 1835, the paper perpetrated the famous "moon hoax" with a series of faked articles about lunar life forms, seen through a new telescope. The gambit worked. As readers rushed to sort fact from fiction in the columns of the *Sun*, they made it the best-selling newspaper in the world—surpassing even the *Times* of London.[17]

Benjamin Day pioneered the cheap newspaper, but James Gordon Bennett perfected it. A cross-eyed Scot who had been working in American newspapers for more than a decade, Bennett founded the *New-York Herald* in May of 1835 and quickly improved upon the *Sun*'s model. The *Herald* covered the same beat—fires, accidents, murders—but Bennett made himself a character in his paper's coverage. He filtered the stories through his all-knowing, all-seeing persona as "an editor on public duty"—something akin to the wise and crafty detectives then emerging in the popular urban literature of the day. Most famously, he was granted (or granted himself) exclusive access to the scene of prostitute Helen Jewett's murder in the spring of 1836, to give a lurid first-person narrative of seeing the young woman's corpse. When news got slow, Bennett picked fights with other editors or took extreme positions on local affairs. Through all of this, he applauded himself. In 1837, he took full credit for transforming the newspaper, once "a mere organ of dry detail," and infusing it with "life, glowing eloquence, philosophy, taste, sentiment, wit, and humor." If "Shakespeare is the great genius of drama—Scott of the novel—Milton and Byron of the poem," Bennett laid claim to being "the genius of the daily newspaper press." Though Greeley despised Bennett, the two shared a vision of the heroic editor.[18]

To subsequent historians and critics, Day and Bennett were successful because they gave form, order, and a daily narrative to the inherently disordered world of the city. The mastery of this complex urban environment represented in an editor's ability to organize it into a newspaper's neat, orderly columns—stood as a model and guide for readers trying to navigate through the bedlam of urban life. In the process, popular journalism—however sensational it may have been—helped forge some feelings of community and create a modern sense of a "public" out of the city's "motley population." The humbug style, far from being a nefarious perversion of the truth, invited this new public into the process of sorting out fact from fiction, plain dealer from swindler, honest exchange from scam. The penny press was a necessary corollary to the novelties of an urban, democratic, and capitalist society.[19]

But for the cold-water crowd in the Graham boardinghouse where Greeley lived, the penny press was a troubling expression of a society losing its moorings. Day promised that the *Sun* would begin a "march of intelligence" —the enlightening of the masses, especially among "the operative classes of society." Greeley feared that something else was happening. The penny press, "a force for evil in its savage infancy," had produced newspapers with "striking defects in their content and character." Between "1. Light stories; 2. Funny anecdotes and scraps; [and] 3. Shocking murders," the cheap dailies did nothing "to interweave intelligence of a moral, practical, and instructive cast." The great potential of the press was being squandered in a contest for the lowest common denominator amid a rude and chaotic urban culture. An instrument of mass instruction had become just another of the city's dangerous temptations that might swindle a young man out of his wages and virtue. "It seemed to us," Greeley said, that these tendencies "could not exist . . . and imperatively called for resistance and correction."[20]

Initially, resistance and correction came not in the form of another cheap daily, but instead as the *New-Yorker*, a "weekly journal of politics and intelligence" that debuted on March 22, 1834. Greeley was too much in debt from other failed ventures to hazard another daily paper (he had tried and failed with one the previous year), and a weekly format—reminiscent of the country papers of his youth and apprenticeship—better suited his vision for a reformed popular press. Absent the daily demand for sensational content that could sell papers on Manhattan's Park Row, Greeley could concentrate on accurate reportage and sober reflection. This, he promised, was "a measure of public utility." Gone from the pages of the *New-Yorker* would be the usual "rigmarole of preposterous and charlatan pretensions," the "captivating claptraps," and the "experiments on the gullibility of the public." Instead, Greeley would provide fair and judicious political news and uplifting literary content. Above all, he would do this "without humbug." To those who said this was impossible, he vowed, *"we shall try."*[21]

The word "humbug" typically calls up associations with either P. T. Barnum (who raised it to an art form) or Charles Dickens's Scrooge (who reduced it to a catchphrase). To Greeley, the word was essential to explain the mysterious and deceptive workings of 1830s New York and the media problems it spawned. What Noah Webster had defined as "an imposition" or deception (*"a low word"*), Greeley called the most important "single combination of letters" with which to characterize the "spirit of the times"; it was "an age of humbug—emphatically, preeminently, audaciously so." As Dr. David Meredith Reese wrote in his 1838 book, *Humbugs of New York*, the city itself was the preeminent "theatre of humbugs, the chosen arena of mountebanks." The penny papers' playful coverage of the city seemed to reinforce and exaggerate these dangerous tendencies in this new society, rather than seeking to expose and correct them.[22]

The most prominent crime in 1830s New York—the murder of prostitute Helen Jewett—offered an object lesson in the perils of sensationalist, humbug journalism. As the case unfolded in the spring of 1836, Greeley was as captivated as anyone else. He speculated privately that the suspect, Richard Robinson, was "atrociously guilty and ought to walk up the ladder" and lamented the fact that Robinson would most likely "cheat the gallows" (which he did). But, tellingly, Greeley limited his public commentary on the case in the *New-Yorker* to the implications of the overheated press coverage in papers like the *Herald* and the *Sun*. In a tirade editorial on "The Morals of Our City," Greeley reminded readers that "the press owes a stern duty to the country and the cause of public morals." As long as the newspapers flogged every "nine-days' sensation" like the Jewett murder, New York was hopelessly destined to remain, "after New Orleans, the most profligate city of the Union." Filled with "countless temples of infamy," draped in the "hideous mantle of beastly intemperance," it was nothing more than a moral quagmire: "Shall the boisterous revels of lewdness break upon the startled ear of the stranger among us, in his first evening ramble in our city—and this from whole blocks, and streets, and neighborhoods? Shall the thousands of youth who are annually thrown upon the exciting tide of city novelty, with no efficient guardianship, no matured principles, and too often fitted by their very ignorance of evil to become easy victims of its snares, be still beset on every side by seductive though meretricious allurements to ruin?"[23]

For Greeley, all of these questions would be answered in the affirmative as long as the press appealed to the base interests of the untutored masses and stoked the fires of vice. The press, Greeley claimed in an earlier editorial on "The March of Humbug," was "in some measure the guardian of public taste." Using it any other way made him shudder: "We know nothing more completely destructive of all just ideas of propriety and decorum . . . we deprecate this course . . . for the depravation of public taste which must inevitably follow the unchecked indulgence of this vaporing propensity." As a devotee of Sylvester Graham's dietary program, Greeley might well have noted that the humbug served up in the popular press was tasty, but it was hardly nourishing fare.[24]

Greeley was certainly not alone in his moral condemnation of the penny press. In 1840, the more established papers went so far as to launch a "Moral War" against Bennett in an attempt to put the *Herald* out of business. Even the young Walt Whitman, who would later revel in being "one of the roughs," denounced the low tone and sensational quality in his early days in the New York newspaper business. But Greeley's early work at the *New-Yorker* and his responses to the cheap press suggest the roots of the broader vision for journalism and the role of the editor that would define much of his career. Above all, Greeley's *New-Yorker* reveals his emerging belief that the press, properly operated, could be a force for social harmony, consensus, reform, and even mass instruction. If the great task of the day was, as he said, "the elevation of the character and the increase of the happiness of the many," the popular editor was uniquely positioned to carry it out.[25]

In an expansive 1835 essay on "The Literature of the Age," Greeley laid out his vision for the editor in a world increasingly defined by its unprecedented profusion of information. With so many outlets of intelligence emerging in New York City and beyond, a great danger lurked—especially if people neglected the "nobler" ones "in the headstrong pursuit of the ephemera of the day" found in the columns of the cheap press. But here also was great opportunity, for information formed the "firmest as well as most endearing bonds which link mankind in social brotherhood." In a remarkable, heady vision, Greeley imagined a "train of thought awakened in the bosom of the resident by our Hudson" traveling to each corner of the land so that people would "echo the same sentiments, and respond to the same oracles." If Greeley's implicit self-designation as one of these oracles was a bold one, so, too, was his characterization of the oracles' work: "[To] exert a potent and resistless influence over public opinion, to which they conjointly give form and consistency; but they are not less beneficent in simply creating a community of thought and feeling than in giving the right direction to it." The editor was not merely an informer; he was an oracle who instructed and directed the people toward unity through the power of "Intelligence."[26]

Dark Forebodings of Peril: Slavery and Abolition

There was one glaring obstacle to consensus in the United States, however. Growing disagreements over slavery in the 1830s only added to the complexity of the editor's job—and to its consequence. In particular, the emergence of radical abolitionism early in the decade roiled the public sphere. Led by William Lloyd Garrison—himself a former printer's apprentice, with newspaper experience going back to the 1810s—abolitionists rooted their crusade in publicity and the power of the press. When he famously promised, in his very first *Liberator* editorial, "*I will be heard*," Garrison was not speaking in the abstract. He and other abolitionists were determined to make their ideas audible, not just with the force of their passionate rhetoric, but also through the sheer volume of its distribution. Garrison wrote in the American Anti-Slavery Society's 1833 *Declaration of Sentiments*, "We shall circulate, unsparingly and extensively, anti-slavery tracts and periodicals." By 1837, abolitionists were churning out nearly a million publications each year.[27]

Quickly, the views of a small group took on large importance. Abolitionists' efforts raised fundamental questions about the boundaries of public discourse and the viability of a national community held together by information. Could white Americans stand to hear one another's views on the institution of slavery—in particular, radical views in opposition to it? Indications in the 1830s were that they could not. Backlash against abolitionist speech was rampant. Anti-abolition violence was common in Greeley's New York and other cities, as well as in small communities like Alton, Illinois, where a mob murdered the abolitionist editor Elijah Lovejoy in 1837. In official spheres, Southerners succeeded in effectively barring the movement from public discourse in Washington, DC, and throughout the South. The first congressional "gag rule," passed in 1836, prohibited all anti-slavery petitions from being read or discussed. While that same session of Congress failed to pass legislation banning abolitionist literature from the mails, Southern postmasters effectively enacted such a ban by destroying or refusing to deliver it.[28]

Try though he did, Greeley could not avoid the issues of slavery and abolition—and the questions they raised for newspapers and their editors. The *New-Yorker*'s debut in the spring of 1834 came amid tensions in the city over rising abolitionist activism and the approach of emancipation in the British Empire on August 1. As other elements of the New York press reacted with varying degrees of hysteria, Greeley largely kept mum. The few statements he did make betrayed both his conservative temper and a fear that radical discussions of slavery posed a grave danger to the nation at large. In his first known editorial treatment of what he called "The Question," Greeley intervened less to disparage the horrors of slavery than to condemn the actions of those fighting against it. Groups "with the leading and avowed purpose of effecting the overthrow of the internal economy of the South by vehemence and intimidations" were outside the realm of acceptable public discourse. Should they continue, Greeley said, "we have dark forebodings of peril, not merely to the tranquility but to the continuance of our Union, with its measureless and unnumbered blessings."[29]

Opponents of slavery should try a different tack, Greeley argued. The institution was an evil—indeed, "at the bottom of most of the evils which afflict the South"—but the problem required a cautious approach and measured discourse, led by the press. Editors should give voice neither to radical abolitionists nor their hysterical detractors. Reasoned public discussion and "Intelligence" would gradually eradicate the problem. If only "objections to slavery, drawn from correct and Enlightened political economy, were once fairly placed before the Southern public," Greeley said, "they would need no further inducements to impel them to enter upon an immediate and effective course . . . to the ultimate extinction of the evil."[30]

Events through the summer of 1834 and beyond suggested the difficulties of establishing an "enlightened"—or "enlightening"—public discourse on the subject of slavery. First, there was the basic question of whether the institution should even be discussed. Greeley's first editorial generated at least one angry letter from a reader vowing to cancel his subscription should the *New-Yorker* ever print the word "slavery" again. Greeley's response demonstrated his already stubborn faith in the powers of the press and its more civilized operators. In a lengthy essay on "The Freedom of the Press," he asserted the virtue and necessity of fearless yet reasoned discourse on even the most controversial of topics. The people must understand that the proper role of the press was to reveal "truth with which they are not yet acquainted" and to "unlearn our errors." They must further see that the editor who "combats . . . cherished prejudices does not necessarily impugn their honesty and intelligence."[31]

If knowledge, enlightenment, and collective advancement were the editor's proper brief, danger loomed when they worked toward other ends. All too frequently for Greeley, they did just that. After tensions surrounding slavery and abolition in New York City erupted into a series of riots in July of 1834, Greeley laid the blame squarely at the feet of his fellow editors. Spirited rhetoric was to be expected from "the gladiators of the political arena," but editors must be aware of their unique power and the "incendiary" results of its abuse. Half the New York press, Greeley said, had "instigat[ed] a lawless rabble to the violation of the public peace and the destruction of private property" and then greeted the events with "open approval" in the aftermath. Beyond this critique, Greeley would say no more. There was "no occasion for multiplying words" on the subject. But for the "ferocious declamation with which the press teemed at the crisis, the riots of July would never had been heard of." Wise editors knew when to inform, and when not to.[32]

The caution, conservatism, and even the silence that Greeley urged on other editors with respect to slavery characterized the *New-Yorker*'s own coverage through the remainder of the decade. "Our readers will credit us for a long and thorough abstinence from the discussion of the delicate and exciting topics involved in the existence of slavery in this country," Greeley began, in a relatively rare editorial on slavery in 1835.[33]

When forced to confront slavery, however, Greeley returned to his assertion that the editor was an instrument of consensus and a guardian of the public sphere. Amid mounting abolitionist activism and often violent efforts to silence it, Greeley played both sides. He defended abolitionists' freedoms of speech and the press, but he also condemned their arguments and approach as ultimately damaging to productive and enlightened public discussion. Following the murder of Elijah Lovejoy in 1837, Greeley published an impassioned editorial defending the freedom of expression and denouncing the tyranny of violent mob rule. But he could not resist an oblique reference in the same piece to "Mr. Lovejoy's errors, or those of Abolitionists generally." Riot and arson surrounding an abolitionist meeting the following year brought forth a clearer expression of Greeley's dark, underlying sentiment. Abolitionists' provocations were at least partly to blame—and perhaps were even deliberate incitements to violence: "[They], we doubt not, would like the fun of having their Hall burnt every year . . . and their chance to make ten or twenty thousand converts out of the outrages and excitements." Extreme opinions bred extreme responses.[34]

Ultimately, it fell to the editor to police public discussion and maintain its moderation. Following the Lovejoy killing, Greeley urged Southern editors to condemn the murder less as a moral outrage than as a threat to the public sphere. "This tragedy, if its effect be not thus counteracted, is calculated to give a fearful impetus to the cause of Abolition," he warned. "It will immediately add thousands to the unwelcome petitions with which the halls of Congress are now crowded."[35]

Editors must take on this work. If they didn't, officials might well close off the national public sphere altogether. In 1836, Amos Kendall, postmaster general under Andrew Jackson, moved to restrict the cheap passage of newspapers through the mails. Kendall argued that it was unnecessary that "large quantities of newspapers should be transported from one end of the Union to the other as a means of instructing and enlightening the public mind. . . . That office can be as well performed by local presses." Kendall couched his proposed rate increases in a concern for local editors being crowded out by metropolitan papers, but the move came out of a longer effort by the Jackson administration to keep abolitionist publications out of the mails altogether. Greeley called the move a "pitiful clap-trap of checking the circulation of Northern papers at the South." It was entirely antithetical to the project of creating consensus and enlightenment through a shared body of "Intelligence." Editors should be left to themselves in an open marketplace of free- (or cheaply) flowing ideas. If each kept to his responsibility of guarding the public sphere from extremism in all forms, restriction would be unnecessary. Greeley himself claimed to be a model of this kind of caution. Earlier in 1836, he defended a *New-Yorker* article on abolitionism to an angry reader as the kind of "cool, accurate, and impartial" coverage that the movement required. This was in stark contrast to pro-slavery papers in the South that gave "ten times the space" to abolitionist ravings, thereby initiating equally extreme responses.[36]

Greeley never imagined these cautious, genteel Northern editorial guardians as anything other than white men. White men would build consensus within the political community of other white men. Others would simply have to follow. Through the 1830s, Greeley did not recognize black voices and actors in the public sphere, and it was telling that most of his commentary relating to slavery dealt with the political and cultural implications of abolitionism, rather than slavery itself. Further, abolitionists were dangerous not just because of their Union-threatening radical immediatism, but also because of their egalitarian views on race. As Greeley explained during the tense summer of 1834, the colonization movement was preferable to abolitionism, because the differences between the races were too great to imagine an integrated society.[37]

No less threatening to the public (as Greeley envisioned it) were those women who presumed to speak in the name of abolition. Like many critics of abolitionism, Greeley condemned radical anti-slavery activists' belief in sexual equality and the prominent public roles given to women within the movement. Greeley reprinted a small item undermining an 1837 speech by the Southerner-turned-abolitionist Angelina Grimké: "The eloquence, pleasing address, and apparent sincerity of that bright-eyed Carolinian will *make more slaves* than she will ever emancipate." An editorial notice regarding minister Hubbard Winslow's book, *Woman as She Should Be*, likewise suggested the boundaries for keeping women out of the public sphere. The piece applauded the notion that "the gentler sex of our day can find much better business than forming anti-slavery societies" and commended the book to women readers: "If some damsels should read one novel less and give an evening to his admonitions, they would have no cause to regret it." If Greeley would allow that women might be more than ornamental, literary contributors to public life, they still could not serve as its guardians or gatekeepers.[38]

Closely Scrutinized and Fearlessly Discussed

The increasingly complex and mystifying workings of economic and social life in Jacksonian America also called for editorial genius and vision. The need appeared most clearly during the economic crisis that culminated in the Panic of 1837, when the press stood at the center of a fierce and novel contest of interpretation. A new kind of press was taking on a new kind of society. Multiple factors related to an increasingly intricate economic order had conspired to create this panic and its ensuing depression. Sorting through the wreckage wrought by frighteningly large and impersonal economic forces, New York City's editors raised their usual pitch to the level of pandemonium. As Greeley noted in a March editorial, there was nothing new in the experience of hard times; it was the explosion of the press over the preceding decade that made the Panic of 1837 different. A babel of voices arose from the columns of the city's papers seeking to explain who or what was to blame for such widespread misery. Wall Street bankers and speculators, or Andrew Jackson and Martin Van Buren, or the riotous lower orders—all came under fire for having brought on the crisis. Editors themselves, meanwhile, lofted volleys across their columns, blaming their rivals for creating this panic through willful misrepresentation. James Gordon Bennett concluded in the *Herald* that "the greater part of the terrible evils that now afflict society has been produced by the want of a free, talented, energetic, clear, and fearless press."[39]

Here was a point on which Greeley could agree with Bennett: the fracturing of meaning that came with so many voices in the print marketplace had created great confusion about what was happening and why. Under such circumstances, information regarding the Panic of 1837 was like the paper money many believed to be at its center: there were too many variants of it, and no one knew what any of it was worth. Though Greeley's name stood atop the masthead of a weekly newspaper with a circulation of 9,000 rather than a daily of 20,000, he hoped to preach reason, understanding, and caution from his modest perch. Amid "the Pressure" of 1836 that preceded the following year's panic, he was already urging his readers to consider the situation before taking in "the melancholy bodings of the prophets of evil who throng the land." It was a moment for sober analysis and reflection, and who better to provide it than judicious oracles of the press: "The present condition of the country and aspects of the future are in the highest degree critical; so much more the need, then, that they be closely scrutinized and fearlessly discussed." Perhaps the whole crisis could have been averted if the oracles of the press had tutored the masses.[40]

When pressure became panic, Greeley followed through on his promise to closely scrutinize and fearlessly discuss it. The *New-Yorker's* columns became laden with disquisitions on the dynamics of currency, banking policy, and the principles of political economy. By June of 1837, there was evidence that readers were groaning under the weight. A minor treatise on the problems of specie currency began with the disclaimer that "the prominence now given in our columns to the statement of facts and opinions relating to the currency of the country and the great commercial revulsion now approaching its consummation is not particularly relished by a considerable portion of our readers." Those among that segment were duly shamed and urged, as it were, to eat their vegetables: "To those who read solely to be amused, an essay savoring of political economy or aiming at the advancement of public welfare is but a tax on their patience or a waste of the column. . . . But while striving to suit the tastes of these, we shall not forget that there are others to whom . . . practical information [is] more acceptable than simple amusement." And so Greeley proceeded forthwith to enlarge upon the deleterious effects of the Democrats' monetary policy.[41]

As the course of the Panic of 1837 demonstrated, this was a quixotic fight. When a run on funds forced city banks to stop payments, Greeley knew precisely where to place blame. "We do not know but this suspension was . . . inevitable, but we do know that it has been precipitated by an unmanly panic in the community . . . which [was] mainly excited by the influence and untiring exertions of our penny and two-penny press, the most profligate and ruin-loving engine of mischief that ever curses a community." The public's misunderstanding of events had come from the cheap press. Rather than carefully explaining its dynamics, these penny papers and their "third-rate barroom oracles" only "minister to the blind prejudices of the ignorant, and . . . strive for the applause of the multitude."[42]

If there was a measure of desperation in Greeley's response to this panic, it was because he and the *New-Yorker* were nearly swept away in it. Greeley had previously built a solid base of 9,000 subscribers, only to lose more than a quarter of them in 1837. Though the paper had never been an immensely profitable concern (having subscribers and having subscribers who paid were different things), it had held its own. Now Greeley was losing $100 just to publish each week. He confessed in 1838 that he "would gladly give away the whole concern to-morrow." "I have had some eighteen months of perpetual horrors," he said, "which I would not live again for a dukedom." Worst of all, Greeley's financial woes were an expression of a harder truth: success without humbug looked like an illusion. "I essay too much to be useful and practical," he told a friend, and "there is nothing that loses people like instruction. It implies that they do not know every thing already, which is very humiliating." If a paper was to provide instruction, it needed to administer small doses—shorter political articles, less preaching—with plenty of "sweetmeats and pepper sauce" to make it palatable.[43]

Clear principles and good intentions could not make the *New-Yorker* pay, and Greeley's letters through the end of the paper's run in 1841 tell a story of continued frustration and financial loss. As the paper continued to flounder, it became clear to Greeley that only two things could ensure survival in the print marketplace: humbug, or the patronage of a political party. No match for penny editors and barroom oracles, Greeley stayed afloat as a Whig.[44]

The March of Truth Is Onward

The *New-Yorker* was never "calculated to enlist partisanship or excite enthusiasm," but anyone who picked it up could not have missed the Whiggish drift of its editorial content. The paper and the Whig Party had more or less come into being at the same time, and Greeley held to what were becoming its articles of faith from the start. With equal parts enthusiasm for Henry Clay and abhorrence of Andrew Jackson, Greeley endorsed the party's nationalist vision under Clay's "American System": economic development and opportunity built on government-sponsored internal improvements, strong central banking, a sound paper currency, and a tariff to protect domestic industry. But beyond a set of policies, allegiance to the Whigs also amounted to a sensibility, which Greeley also amply possessed. Taking more than a few remnants of the old Federalism, Whigs imagined an ideal society as an organic unity, bound together by a "harmony of interests" up and down the social ladder. They rejected the divisive, class-bound politicking of Jacksonian Democrats that pitted these interests against one another. Though more egalitarian than their Federalist forebears, Whigs shared their assumption that liberty was best maintained through order, restraint, and deference to leaders. Greeley's whole vision of the press and its relation to society—especially as exhibited in the midst of the Panic of 1837—carried more than a whiff of these Whig assumptions. The fact that his work caught the eye of Thurlow Weed that year was a fortuitous turn of events.[45]

Thurlow Weed knew how to make a living from political parties. Fourteen years Greeley's senior, he, too, had been a printer by trade and had known the hardships of being a journeyman. The difference was that Weed had learned early on to never get too far from party purse strings. His first editorial position had come through friends of New York governor DeWitt Clinton in 1818. From there, he ascended to the editorship of the *Rochester (NY) Telegraph* by proving his worth to that Erie Canal boomtown's business leaders. But the ultimate prize awaited in Albany, where backers of the short-lived Anti–Masonic Party furnished the funds for the *Albany Evening Journal* in 1829. As the editor of what was destined to become the official organ of the Whig Party in the state capital, Weed emerged as a master of party organization and political communication in New York and national politics.[46]

Though more of a shrewd and ruthless powerbroker than the younger Greeley, Weed recognized a kindred spirit behind the columns of the *New-Yorker*. Thus, when Weed mounted the stairs of Greeley's "rude editorial attic" in December of 1837, he did so to offer Greeley a job. Weed and the Albany Whig machine were putting forward the bushy-browed, beak-nosed

redhead William Henry Seward for governor. The dim economic circumstances associated with the Panic of 1837 had tilted political fortunes in
New York toward the Whigs in the fall elections that year, and Weed was
orchestrating what he called "a vigorous campaign . . . to maintain and
confirm the Whig ascendancy." As Weed told Seward, "We are getting up
. . . a Weekly paper for <u>general</u> circulation. Twenty thousand copies of such
a paper, in the right hands, could do immense good." Greeley accepted what
seemed a king's ransom—a payment of $1,000—to edit the new sheet, and
the *Jeffersonian* was born in February of 1838. Greeley edited it out of Albany while still turning out the *New-Yorker*. Dividing his time between Albany, New York City, and the steamboats that ferried him up and down the
Hudson River, Greeley's life became more harried and hectic than ever.
After helping Seward win the governorship, he again became Weed's chosen man to run an even more ambitious campaign paper, the *Log Cabin*, a
sheet at the center of the "Tippecanoe and Tyler Too" presidential campaign of 1840. In these ventures, "the Political Firm of Seward, Weed &
Greeley," a partnership that would last for the better part of two decades,
came to life. Though Greeley was the unappreciated "junior partner," the
alliance more or less saved his career. When he advised his friend Obadiah
Bowe in 1840 to "make your politicians support you," he was speaking from
experience.[47]

Political life suited Greeley. Complain as he did to Seward of the "boiling
sea of politics," it nonetheless focused his energies as a writer and editor.
Taking on "the Democracy" (as his full reference to the rival party went) in
New York State and beyond gave him a taste for the hurly-burly of politics
that he would savor for the remainder of his career. His most spirited editorials always came amid moments of great political crisis or opportunity.
And politics also brought him identity and fellowship. Given the rootless-
ness of his youth and the atomized, anonymous experience of life in New
York City, this surely had great appeal for him. His letters to political allies
during this period and beyond crackle with a lively informality and intimacy that suggest as much zeal for the simple act of belonging as for the
political cause itself.[48]

According to a long tradition, Greeley's early Whig journalism was an
integral piece of a larger party program of deception that culminated in the

1840 "Log Cabin" presidential campaign for William Henry Harrison. When Whig boss Richard Smith Elliott copped to the idea that "passion and prejudice, properly aroused and directed, would do about as well as principle and reason in a party contest," he wrote the epigraph to an unfortunate chapter in American political history. Tired of losing elections to the Democrats, Whigs cloaked their paternalist and pro-business affinities in the language and style of their more populist rivals. As Arthur M. Schlesinger Jr. memorably had it, "the Whigs soft-pedaled their diehard aims and began to borrow the Jacksonian phrases." Led by "cynical bosses" orchestrating "a great commotion," they rode an "omnibus of lies" to victory and thus "marked a change of American politics from a respectable profession into a circus."[49]

Greeley could rightfully be called one of the ringmasters of that circus. In both 1838 and 1840, Greeley's work often fell somewhere below his lofty visions for humbug-free journalism and intelligence. The very name of his 1838 pro-Seward paper—the *Jeffersonian*—was an initial indicator of the political sleight-of-hand that was to come, since Thomas Jefferson was the acknowledged progenitor of "the Democracy," not the Whig party. In the midst of Seward's campaign, Greeley brimmed with excitement when he received the transcript of a speech by William Key Bond, an otherwise undistinguished Whig backbencher from Ohio. Though it was a lengthy and tedious account of the hypocrisy of Andrew Jackson and his party, dating back to 1828, Greeley plumped it as a thrilling philippic. He wrung weeks of content from the speech through the summer of 1838, including a special separate issue of the *Jeffersonian* exclusively dedicated to it. As he told Bowe, "We are going to publish 100,000 copies of Bond's speech . . . [which] ought to be crammed down the throat of every Tory till he pukes up the whole humbug in a fit of awful sickness and choking [sic]." Urging Bowe to use his *Herkimer (NY) Gazette* to broadcast the speech locally, he cautioned, "Don't die of modesty. It's a shocking disease for a political Editor."[50]

But the *Jeffersonian* was just a dress rehearsal for the *Log Cabin*, a sheet very much at the center of the ballyhoo for the 1840 presidential contest. Beginning with a modest run of 30,000 papers, Greeley crowed over its mounting circulation week by week until it peaked at 80,000, just before the election. Hunting for bigger game before a national audience, Greeley built on the work he had done for Seward. The *Log Cabin* took its name from a Democratic newspaper correspondent's jab at Whig candidate William Henry Harrison and his advanced age of 67. The suggestion that Harrison, an old veteran of military conflicts going back to the 1790s, would be better off retiring to a log cabin with a barrel of hard cider became the hook for the entire Whig campaign. Greeley played it to the hilt. "The Log Cabin," he announced in the paper's prospectus, "will . . . vindicate the Character of the Farmers, Mechanics, and Laborers of our Country—the dwellers in rude and humble cottages as well as those who are enabled to live in more convenient and elegant structures."[51]

He reserved no such delicacy for Democratic incumbent Martin Van Buren and his supporters: "Wherever you find a bitter, blasphemous Atheist and an enemy of Marriage, Morality, and Social Order, there you may be certain of one vote for Van Buren." Though Old Kinderhook was the humble son of a tavernkeeper, Greeley used the *Log Cabin* to propagate the smear that he was actually a silk-stocking aristocrat. Reprising his use of Bond's speech in 1838, Greeley proudly reprinted the wildly popular—and wildly inaccurate—harangue of Pennsylvania congressman Charles Ogle on "The Regal Splendor of the Presidential Palace." Quite far from Van Buren's actually shabby executive accommodations, Ogle described unmatched luxury in stark contrast to the privations of humble Americans and William Henry Harrison's (nonexistent) log cabin. What, Ogle wondered, would people say about "Mr. Van Buren . . . spending the People's cash on FOREIGN FANNY KEMBLE GREEN FINGER CUPS, in which to wash his pretty, tapering, soft, white lily-fingers, after dining on frincandeau de veau and omelette soufflé?"[52]

But these distractions and deceptions only tell part of the story. A closer look at Greeley's political work reveals something more than a cynical party insider manipulating the masses to victory. Though Greeley undoubtedly had broken his promise to "succeed without humbug," both the *Jeffersonian* and the *Log Cabin* retained something of his original faith in the transformative power of journalism and "Intelligence." Like many of his fellow partisans, Greeley believed deeply in the correctness of Whig principles as a simple matter of right and wrong. That Democrats wielded so much power nationally was merely because of the incomplete dissemination of those

Whig principles. In politics, as in the realm of general news, the people were misled by easy forms of misinformation, entertainment, and flattery. Democrats' misty invocations of the sovereign and infallible "People" were cynical forms of manipulation that bespoke contempt rather than faith: "Men are frail, fallible, imperfect in knowledge and judgment, and corruptible, whether singularly or in masses. . . . He . . . who assures the People that he believes them infallible tells them that he deems them fools, and is certain enough of the fact to treat them as such without ceremony." True respect for the people thus lay not in empty blandishments, but in earnest, good faith efforts to mend the imperfections in their knowledge and judgment.[53]

Here again the editor had a critical role to play, even over and above that of a political leader. For all the cynicism of Greeley's journalism in these elections, he worked on the optimistic belief that a Whig ascendancy would bring all its promised progress when information and instruction had created "an intelligent people." This began with the press itself. As Greeley wrote in the *Jeffersonian* prospectus, the people wanted only the "ample diffusion of correct political intelligence" and "correct and reliable information." Through the work of the editor, "many thousands will hereafter be enabled to approach the ballot-boxes with a more clear and perfect understanding and appreciation of the great questions which they are called to decide." For all the humbug that lit up the columns of the *Jeffersonian* and the *Log Cabin*, both were also full of meaty explanations of Whig ideas and their political applications. Readers of the *Log Cabin* were weekly implored to "CIRCULATE THE DOCUMENTS"—to pass on their copies of the paper and disseminate as far as possible key pamphlets explaining Whig positions. Watching subscriptions to the *Log Cabin* roll in during the summer of 1840, Greeley bragged to Seward that they were growing "by platoons" and crowed in the paper that "THE MARCH OF TRUTH IS ONWARD!" Such popularity and extended circulation were evidence not that deceptive tactics were working, but that the goal of "an intelligent people" was being realized.[54]

In some cases, humbug and substance could merge. Each week's edition of the *Log Cabin* included a new Whig campaign song, all of which Greeley collected into a Whig songbook. The songs are remembered mostly for their frivolity and have stood as classic examples of the mindlessness of the

1840 campaign. Yet some less memorable numbers also waded into more complex matters of policy and principle, however awkwardly. A Whig song-ster from the Toledo Tippecanoe Club set the lyrics of "The Currency Song" to the tune of "Hunters of Kentucky" and touched upon the "famed sub-treasury scheme," the "safety fund," and "wildcat banks." Though not the most penetrating analysis of banking and currency, the song nonetheless goes a bit deeper than the famous refrain of "Tippecanoe and Tyler Too": "Van, Van, He's a used up man." The "Baltimore Hymn" took on the eco-nomic policies of Van Buren and "the Democracy" to the rousing strains of France's "Marseillaise," imploring listeners,

> Will ye behold a sinking nation
> Her commerce crush'd and credit gone
> Her manufactures undone
> And pamper tyrants in their station.
>
> Arise! Arise! Ye Wise!

If just given the right information, whether in song or in prose, the people would become wise enough to exercise the correct political judgment.[55]

This belief in the power of information and intelligence could also work in other directions, with Greeley actively encouraging the broadcast of rival Democratic ideas. Such impoverished thinking just needed the proper air-ing, and the people would come running into the Whig ranks. With the pres-idential race heating up in the summer of 1840, firebrand Orestes Brownson produced what Greeley believed to be a gilt-edged opportunity to expose the "ultra" tendencies within the radical "Loco-Foco" wing of the Demo-cratic Party. Though ostensibly writing a review of Thomas Carlyle's slim volume on Chartism, Brownson produced a militant indictment of America's emerging market and industrial society. Brownson's essay, which became the famous pamphlet *The Laboring Classes*, included radical prescriptions, like the abolition of inheritance laws, along with a bitter polemic against the country's effete clergy. Greeley laid into the article in the columns of the *Log Cabin*, but beyond merely condemning the piece, he urged the Whigs to also give it as wide a circulation as possible. With an investment of no more than $100, he suggested to Seward that copies of the pamphlet be sent to ministers across the country, in hopes of capturing "votes that would not otherwise be cast." "It must not be a Whig paraphrase of Brownson's views," however, "but his own naked article just as he wrote it."[56]

Greeley's efforts in the *Jeffersonian* and the *Log Cabin* were part of two resounding victories for the Whigs. In 1838, Seward swept into the governorship and the party retained control of the state legislature. On the national stage in 1840, the Whigs took control of Congress and the White House. Harrison swept the Electoral College, 234 votes to 60, and the Whigs were alive with a sense of mandate. Greeley hailed the victory as nothing short of a "political revolution" and a "triumph of Right Reason and Public Good over Error and Sinister Ambition." "Arise! Arise! Ye Wise!"—an intelligent people had spoken.[57]

A Newspaper, in the Higher Sense of the Term

The *Log Cabin*, with its 80,000 subscribers, marked the pinnacle of Greeley's work as a Whig Party editor and opened up avenues to a career as a party operative. Amid the scrap for spoils after the election, Greeley had a strong claim to a plum post. After all, the bulk of the *Log Cabin*'s subscriber base was in New York, a state that had tilted dramatically from Van Buren to Harrison over the years 1836 to 1840. Given his exploits, some whispered Greeley's name as a possible postmaster general. He disavowed the unpleasant "hard elbowing" and "wretched" clawing needed to secure the position, however. The editorial reins of a Whig paper in Harrisburg—close to party purses in the Pennsylvania capital—could be had for less trouble but was no more appealing to Greeley. Its vices aside, New York City still had much to offer. There, he had $1,000 worth of printing equipment, nearly a decade's worth of experience, and a platform for a new kind of daily newspaper.[58]

As Greeley wrote a month before he rolled out his *New-York Tribune*, the press needed to be "purified and elevated, its independence asserted, and its influence extended." The *Tribune* would be the practical application of Greeley's informal education in journalism. Combining all of his previous ventures into a single daily organ, the *Tribune* was, Greeley said in his memoirs, "a newspaper, in the higher sense of the term." It would correct the abuses of the urban press: here was a cheap daily more fit for "the family fireside" than a Five Points barroom. Its columns would be expurgated of the "immoral and degrading Police Reports" and vulgar advertisements that "disgrace[d]" the penny papers. The *Tribune* would be broadly Whiggish in its sensibilities and informed by Whig notions of collective progress and national destiny, but it would not be a mere party rag. Instead, the paper would thread the needle between "servile partisanship on the one hand, and . . . gagged, mincing neutrality on the other." It would also encompass Greeley's notion of "Intelligence," a version of journalism that went beyond reporting news. As a vehicle for the best ideas, literature, and criticism, the *Tribune* would enlighten the people, even as it informed them. It was, in short, the realization of his editorial vision and the stage for his editorial persona. But could it survive?[59]

The *Tribune* debuted to bad weather (snow and sleet) and worse omens (the funeral for the late Whig president William Henry Harrison) on April 10, 1841. Barely 500 of its 5,000 copies sold, and the concern lost nearly $500 by the end of its first week. Relief was nowhere in sight. The *Tribune*'s political independence and principled opposition to immoral advertisements was bold, but it was also bad business. In the absence of revenue, Greeley would have to either beg for party support or run unsavory ads. He tried the Whigs first but found himself caught between two different streams of party patronage. Whereas city Whigs identified Greeley with the Weed-Seward axis in Albany, Weed and Seward balked at Greeley's troubling displays of independence. "I could have begged patronage," Greeley complained to Seward in June, "and done better. Now it seems all begged away, while I was getting down to the begging point." Help came the following month, when Greeley took on a lawyer named Thomas McElrath as a partner. McElrath steadied the operation with an infusion of $2,000 and the business acumen that Greeley lacked. For the first time in his career, Greeley could focus exclusively on editorial duties, while leaving the management to someone equal to the task. The perfect fitness of the partnership threw James Parton into an aphoristic turn of phrase in his biography fourteen years later: "Oh! that every Greeley could find his McElrath! and blessed is the McElrath that finds his Greeley!"[60]

By the end of 1841, the *Tribune* was "before the wind" with a healthy subscriber base, a daily circulation nearing 15,000, and a more realistic approach. With the help of his partner, Greeley found a formula that awakened him to the value in advertisers' cash payments. While the editorial page could rail against the "horrible prostitution" of other papers' columns, *Tribune* readers could keep themselves apprised of the latest performances at city theaters, as well as the benefits of Dr. Allen's Balsam, Dr. Fleming's Worm Candy, and Dinneford's Patent Improved Electrical Flesh Gloves and Straps. Shocking murders and vile seductions, meanwhile, were deemed fit for public consumption, so long as they were expressly denounced and not covered with too much zeal.[61] Meanwhile, lessons gleaned from campaign seasons and urban humbugs taught Greeley that moralism could be its own form of showmanship. In particular, he saw that jabs at other newspapers and their editors were good for business. The Democratic-leaning penny dailies, against which Greeley had defined himself and his publications, were the easiest targets. The *Sun* was a "depraved and filthy sheet," infusing "deadly venom . . . into the veins of the body politic." Bennett's *Herald*, meanwhile, presented "a reservoir of scoffing infidelity and moral putrefaction," "a horrid medley of profanity, ribaldry, blasphemy, and indecency."[62]

Greeley's editor persona as an uncouth, ink-stained Yankee truth teller took shape in the scuffles that ensued. Bennett led the way, mocking Greeley as a prudish bumpkin and cracker-barrel "philosopher" who deemed it too "naughty" to publish any news at all. "Galvanize a large New England squash," Bennett wrote in 1841, "and it would make as capable an editor as Horace Greeley." By 1844, Greeley seemed to have embraced the pose of the oddball rustic intellectual. Though Greeley disclaimed any overt calculation, there was a studied air to his signature getup: the old white coat that became a metonym for his very identity, the broad-brimmed country hat, the spectacles, the muddy boots with a single pant leg tucked in on one side, the spectacles, and the pockets stuffed with letters and clippings.[63]

The conservative Whig editor James Watson Webb wasn't fooled, suggesting that Greeley "lays claim to greatness" in his disheveled aspect and "seeks for notoriety in the strangeness of his theories and practices." Ever the editor, Greeley had just one amendment for Webb—he'd forgotten to add that Greeley was a *self-made* rustic oddball. "The Editor of the Tribune," Greeley began a familiar refrain, "is the son of a poor humble farmer; came to New York a minor . . . less than ten dollars in his pocket, and precious little besides." When another fussy conservative—an aging James Fenimore

Cooper—sued Greeley for libel, Greeley described himself in the manner of a Yankee humorist: "tow-headed, and half-bald at that . . . slouching in dress; goes bent like a hoop, and so rocking in his gait that he walks down both sides of the street at once." That description, like his perfectly slipshod clothing, succeeded in fixing an image of Greeley in the public's mind and making him thoroughly identified with his newspaper.[64]

The founding and spectacular growth of the *New-York Weekly Tribune* ensured that Greeley's persona became known well beyond the intramural quarrels of New York City editors. In the fall of 1841, Greeley consolidated the *Log Cabin* and the "poor old" *New-Yorker* into a carefully curated digest of the *Daily Tribune*—a "sheet of mammoth size, excluding all matter of local and transitory interest, and calculated mainly for Country circulation." While Greeley would remain an important figure in New York City journalism, he would never be a dominant one, along the lines of Bennett. It would be the *Weekly*, with its growing subscriber base extending from New England to the Yankee regions of the Midwest, that would make Greeley a national figure. By 1854, the *Weekly*'s reach would allow Ralph Waldo Emerson to report to Thomas Carlyle that Greeley was the "spiritual father" of the Midwest, doing his readers' "thinking & theory for them, for two dollars a year." Two decades after his start in journalism, Greeley was approaching his dream of becoming an oracle on the banks of the Hudson.[65]

If Greeley was a singular editor, his *Tribune* was a singular organ. The *Herald* had better newsgathering operations and a superior city circulation, but Greeley's paper had an editorial voice and perspective that reflected his carefully honed ideas of journalism. Where Bennett "disclaim[ed] all principle, as it is called" in the *Herald*, Greeley declared himself a "public teacher" who would "shape public opinion" and "direct it, not reflect it."[66] *Tribune* editorials thrummed with the assurance that they were doing just that. The line attributed to Greeley—that he could "write better slang than any editor in America"—may well be apocryphal, but it contains a grain of truth. A lively, democratic idiom infused the *Tribune*'s columns and obscured the high Whig moralism lurking behind them. Greeley's writing was, in managing editor Charles A. Dana's assessment, "plain, clear, striking." Though wordy by modern standards, Greeley spoke with a force, clarity, and "homely" style that grabbed a reader by the lapels. "We have preached ourselves hoarse in entreating the mass of young men," a piece began in 1841, "to resist that insane craving for city life by which the happiness of so many is shipwrecked." The editorials were formulaic—identify a problem, explain why it was intolerable, eviscerate those who were responsible, and propose a solution—but it was fitting for a "public teacher," as Greeley liked to call himself.[67]

The *Tribune*'s quest for the improvement of individuals and the advancement of collective destiny went beyond its editorials; the paper's ideal of "Intelligence" encompassed the diffusion of literature and ideas. Thus, for all of Greeley's bluster as the sole genius behind the *Tribune*, he was also a curator of talent, and the paper was a forum for intellectual life. From its first days, when future *New-York Times* founder Henry Raymond served as its managing editor, the *Tribune* offered a home to a notable collection of journalists, writers, and thinkers. Following Raymond's departure in 1844, Greeley hired George Ripley and Charles A. Dana, late of the Massachusetts utopian intellectual community Brook Farm, to serve as subeditors. Other notable lights would follow. Margaret Fuller left behind one journal, the *Dial*, to become the *Tribune*'s literary editor late in 1844, and the paper's columns would be a kind of newsprint salon filled with an impressive collection of voices, including those of Bayard Taylor, George Foster, Albert Brisbane, Stephen Pearl Andrews, and Henry James Sr.

Let Them Be Sea-Captains [and Editors?], If They Will

Greeley's *Tribune*—the newspaper and the editorial persona behind it—assumed a reading public that was almost exclusively white, and also exclusively male. In Greeley's eyes, women could be intellectual and literary figures, just not with the same kind of symbolic public role that he and other guardians of the press and public life must play. Greeley's beliefs emerged most clearly in his complex relationship with Margaret Fuller, the brilliant Massachusetts-bred feminist and Transcendentalist who served as literary editor of and correspondent to the *Tribune* from 1844 until her death in 1850. Greeley recognized and encouraged Fuller's genius, calling her "the greatest woman whom America has yet known." Still, even as he helped publicize and circulate her ideas that women could, in Fuller's words, "wield the scepter and lyre" in public intellectual life, he never quite accepted them.

Mathew Brady, the editorial staff of the *New-York Tribune*, c. 1845. *Seated, left to right*: George M. Snow, Bayard Taylor, Horace Greeley, George Ripley. *Standing, left to right*: William Henry Fry, Charles A. Dana, Henry Jarvis Raymond. Library of Congress, Prints & Photographs Division

Fuller, and the other women with whom Greeley maintained largely private intellectual relationships, always remained outside the editor's grand public visions.[68]

On a practical level, the working world of "Intelligence" belonged to men. The print shops and editorial offices in which Greeley formed his visions for journalism and shaped his editorial persona were overwhelmingly male spaces. A careful floor-by-floor, room-by-room, department-by-department description of the *Tribune* building in 1853 did not mention a single woman among the concern's 301 workers (during her time on the *Tribune* staff, Fuller rarely worked in the office itself). For his writers and subeditors, Greeley favored, with hardly any variation, self-educated young white men whom he could mentor, shape, and often vastly underpay. Those with an ornamental college education were expressly discouraged. "Of all horned cattle," Greeley said, "the most helpless in a printing office is a college graduate." In the precious few glimpses we can gain of Greeley as a private man, the bonds and relationships he formed around the work of journalism and politics appear more lively and comfortable than anything in his domestic life.[69]

Indeed, the private torments of Greeley's distant, difficult marriage to the former Mary (Molly) Cheney, a schoolteacher from Connecticut, reflected his public expressions about women. Molly had the makings of an ideal partner for Greeley in all phases of his life. Like Horace, Molly was a New Englander of curious mind and reformist bent. The two had met through their shared commitment to the Graham dietary movement, and Molly was plugged into the leading intellectual currents of the day. It was she who introduced Greeley to Margaret Fuller, having attended Fuller's "conversations" in Boston and visited the Massachusetts utopian community at Brook Farm. But shared interests did not make for a happy marriage. The couple endured the loss of a several young children, beginning in the late 1830s— horrific strains that were only exacerbated by Molly's ill health and Horace's near-constant absence. Circumstances aside, Greeley largely blamed Molly herself for their shared torments. In correspondence with Fuller and others, Greeley railed against Molly's behavior and referred to the family's ramshackle farmhouse in the still-undeveloped reaches of Manhattan as "Castle Doleful." Reflecting on the erratic ways of his favorite son "Pickie" (who also died young, at the age of five), Greeley blamed the presence of Molly's intellectual friends. "There were ladies then making part of our household," Greeley said, "whose nerves were a source of general as well as personal discomfort."[70]

Greeley's close bonds with Fuller no doubt added to the tensions of his marriage. Fuller began as Molly's friend in the early 1840s but quickly became Horace's intellectual companion. Greeley was well familiar with her work on the Transcendentalist journal the *Dial* and became her advocate and adviser through the publication of her first book, *Summer on the Lakes*, in 1844. The following year, he published Fuller's *Woman in the Nineteenth Century* under the imprint of Greeley & McElrath. By Greeley's account, the book was "the ablest, bravest, broadest assertion yet made of what are termed women's rights." At the same time he was promoting Fuller's great masterpiece, Greeley convinced his friend to come to New York City and serve as the *Tribune*'s literary editor. Against Ralph Waldo Emerson's advice that she avoid "the foaming foolishness" of newspapers, Fuller agreed and began her tenure "in care of the literary department" late in 1844.[71]

Fuller affirmed and challenged many of Greeley's articles of faith about journalism. Over roughly twenty months, Fuller's writing—some 250 critical reviews and essays, and many more unattributed translations, introductions, and synopses of new publications—occupied ample space within the pages of the *Tribune*. Fuller's signed pieces were denoted with an asterisk to distinguish the work as her own, rather than to deceive readers about her identity or sex. As Fuller wrote, "we always write under one signature, and any one who wishes may know to whom it belongs." Some, like the reader who thanked "the writer for his bold and manly independence," simply assumed a male author; others, like the one who remarked on "your philosophical (though female?) review this morning," were vexed. But none could gainsay the quality of Fuller's work. Her contributions ranged from piercing critical assessments of sacrosanct figures like Henry Wadsworth Longfellow and Thomas Carlyle; to bold advocacy for people like Frederick Douglass and the controversial French female novelist who wrote under the pseudonym George Sand; to fierce social criticism on poverty, gender inequality, and slavery. All of it helped realize Greeley's vision for an elevated form of cheap metropolitan journalism. As the *Tribune*'s prospectus for 1845 noted, "We are determined, moreover, to render this paper inferior to no other in the extent and character of its Literary matter."[72]

In many ways, Fuller's time at the *Tribune* amounted to a meeting of minds that Greeley marked as his own editorial triumph. By Greeley's account, he tempered Fuller's high-minded literary impulses and fitted them into the sensibilities of the newspaper. As he recalled, "Fortune seemed to delight in placing us two in relations of friendly antagonism." Though Fuller was drawn to the idea of the newspaper as a literary medium, she was keenly aware that she had stepped into a different space from her New England circles. Greeley, she said, was entirely a "man of the people and of the *Amern* [sic] people, but I find my way to get along with all that." She knew—and Greeley continually reminded her—that newspaper work was different. The *Tribune*, she remarked, was an "emphatically American journal," which meant squelching some of her own sensibilities and influences. Greeley claimed Fuller's work as his own success. Where her *Dial* pieces had been "more elaborate and ambitious," her *Tribune* output was "far better adapted to win the favor and sway the judgment of the great majority of our readers." Here was the kind of "Intelligence" he promised.[73]

In helping Greeley realize his vision for journalism, Fuller also helped affirm his singular sense of himself as an editor—and the peculiarly male burdens of the role. There can be little doubt that Greeley and Fuller shared a deep mutual respect and a close personal bond; both said as much in reflections on their collaboration. Yet, in his final estimate of Fuller, Greeley could only understand her—and other women writers—in light of his deeply gendered understanding of the public sphere. Greeley's close domestic intimacy with Fuller, who lived as "an inmate of [the] family" in his ramshackle farmhouse on the East River, colored his impressions of her work. Boasting of his own capacity for "incessant labor," Greeley carped that too often Fuller was slowed by her "nerves or moods" and "headaches and other infirmities." These decidedly feminine limits on her productivity, Greeley said, were unsuited to the moment-to-moment urgency of a newspaper. Greeley also took issue with Fuller's feminism, albeit sometimes gently, such as when he was teasing her on her famous dictum in *Woman in the Nineteenth Century*: "Let them be sea-captains, if they will!" But, more sharply, Greeley believed that Fuller was limited by her distance from conventional womanhood. "Noble and great as she was," Greeley wrote in his memoirs, "a husband and two or three bouncing babies would have emancipated her from a good deal of cant and nonsense."[74]

⌒

If, by the early 1850s, the image of Greeley as a towering editor was well on its way to being fixed in the public mind, it was already firmly established in his own. Early in 1851, the feminist Elizabeth Oakes Smith wrote to Greeley, seeking his support for a reformist women's newspaper. In a response Smith marked as "full of conceited assumptions by no means warranted by my communication to him," Greeley reprised and expanded on his epistolary performance for Harvey Hubbard, the hapless young supplicant who had dared beg his advice back in 1844. Smith, according to Greeley, was not singular enough to carry her own newspaper in the marketplace. There were already at least fifty women's papers and periodicals edited by the likes of Jane Swisshelm and Sarah Josepha Hale. None could succeed if they embraced the kinds of reforms Smith wished to champion. "Advocacy of Reforms that are vital," Greeley informed Smith, "cannot be made a source of personal gain to the Advocate. . . . A true Reform article must benefit the world at the expense of its proclaimer." Yes, Greeley had been a champion of reform, but only at great personal and pecuniary cost. "If the object of my life had been Wealth, Consideration, Popularity, I should have taken a very different course," he said.[75]

Great were the "Editor's" burdens. In his journalistic education, Greeley had learned not just how to shoulder them, but also how to articulate them. Few others could do the same. Smith would be better off making her name as "an intellectual Champion of Reform," writing for "widely circulated periodicals" that others (like Greeley) had sacrificed to build, and then going on to the lecture circuit. Greeley, for his part, would carry on, whatever the costs. But could the *Tribune* and the great editorial figure behind it guide the people to their destiny?

James S. Baillie, "Patent Balancing by an Amateur" (New York: James Baillie, 1848). Library of Congress, Prints & Photographs Division

CHAPTER TWO

The Nation in the Balance

The image might well have been taken from a nightmare that shook Horace Greeley in the summer of 1848. There he was, standing on a three-legged stool, which was balanced on a loaf of bran bread perched on a tightrope stretched across the Salt River, in which his hero, Henry Clay, was drowning. To steady himself, Greeley held a long pole, with the bust of Free Soil presidential candidate Martin Van Buren on one end and the bust of Whig candidate Zachary Taylor on the other. Along one bank of the river, the metaphorical stream of political ruin, a bespectacled poet intoned a verse: "On slipp'ry heights, I see them stand / While briny billows roll below." Upstream, a barker figure riding an ass displayed a sign advertising the scene: "Graund & Lofty tumbling. Mr. GREELY's [sic] first appearance in that Character." Greeley had committed himself to turning journalism and politics into something more than a circus. Now, he had become a circus act himself, his imminent ruin a spectacle for all to see.

This phantom dreamscape, conjured in an 1848 political cartoon, was a far cry from what Greeley had imagined for himself and for the United States at the beginning of the decade. After launching the *Tribune* in 1841, Greeley had built his paper into a national publication and himself into a figure of nationwide recognition. With the invention of the telegraph in 1844, the moment beckoned for Greeley to realize his grand and lofty visions of becoming an oracle on the Hudson. As a *Tribune* editorial noted, the new device would "annihilate space and run in advance of time with a net-work of nerves of iron wire, strung with lightning." Ideas and information would "ramify from the brain, New York, to the distant limbs and members" around the country. The United States, too, was on the verge of great things. Americans had long regarded their country as providentially destined to light the fires of liberty throughout the world. Now, they believed their boundless future was upon them. Promise rang out everywhere—in the millennial raptures of religious seekers, the hopeful optimism of reformers, the brash rhetoric of expansionists, even the cautious plans of conservatives. Greeley rooted his particular national vision in politics and reform. He believed that the Whig Party of Henry Clay, tinctured with a dose of reform, would nurture consensus, heal social ills, and break sectional fevers over slavery.[1]

By the summer of 1848, however, Greeley's hopes had largely come to naught. The "unity of thought and feeling" on which he had rhapsodized as a rising journalist had been lost amid a jumble of competing visions for national destiny. In politics, sectional division reigned. Expansion and war, carried out in the service of a conception of America antithetical to Greeley's, had battered the Whig Party and sent Greeley reeling. With the presidential election looming, Greeley found the tightrope stretching out before him. He would need to balance his fealty to national Whig principles with his commitment to the Free Soil Party's sectional stand against the spread of slavery (in the cartoon, the tightrope is labeled "Mason & Dickson's [sic] Line"). Greeley's reform commitments—signified in the cartoon by the loaf of bran bread, in reference to a dietary fad—raised the degree of difficulty. His blustery support for "isms" of all kinds turned "Philosopher Greeley of the Tribune" into an easy target for ridicule and jeopardized his standing among Whigs.

The nation had not fared much better than Greeley. It, too, was swaying in the balance between the divergent points of view by 1848. Victory in the Mexican War that year ushered in vast new territories and realized the promise of Manifest Destiny. That triumph, however, was what David Potter called "an ominous fulfillment for the impulses of American nationalism": it unleashed forces of sectionalism that would tear the country apart within little more than a decade. Across the Atlantic, events in Europe in 1848 underscored the threats to the American national project. Various uprisings in the Continent that year affirmed Americans' belief that liberty was destined to spread by their example, but the forces of reaction crushed liberal nationalist movements abroad, while internal divisions rent the United States in the wake of the Mexican War.[2]

Greeley was prominent among them. As the events of 1848 revealed the deep gulfs belying Americans' bold national rhetoric, Greeley kept up a quixotic fight to maintain his dreams of unity and consensus—and his own calling as a voice of the people. Faced with a choice between a fracturing national party and a dangerous sectional uprising, Greeley held out hope that he could keep the promises of both. His tortured efforts to do so reveal the nation, as much as Greeley himself, torn between competing ideas of its own meaning and haunted by the specter of slavery.

Expanding Benevolence and All-Embracing Sympathy

In the early 1840s, Greeley's schemes for improvement, harmony, and consensus were so grand and so expansive that they could be exhausting. This was the conclusion that Ralph Waldo Emerson drew when he first met Greeley in 1842. Not long into an uncomfortable evening at a Graham boardinghouse in New York City, Greeley's wide-eyed enthusiasm had Emerson pining for the solitude and retirement of Concord, Massachusetts. "What can I do with such an abettor?" Emerson asked Margaret Fuller. "I saw my fate in a moment & that I shall never content him." Greeley, teamed up with the socialist Albert Brisbane, barraged Emerson with questions, entreaties, and schemes. Would Emerson commit to mastering the works of the French socialist Charles Fourier? Was he ready for popular action in the name of reform? Could he explain how the Transcendentalists "established the immortality of the soul?"[3]

No lifelong friendships were formed that night, but Emerson captured something of the energy and optimism bursting from Greeley and the columns of the *Tribune* in the early 1840s. The promise of the age—what Greeley variously called "the Spirit" or "Genius of the Nineteenth Century"—was grand. He saw immense possibility in the universe of reform—in the "expanding Benevolence and all-embracing sympathy" that could be found in a variety of efforts.[4] The sheer number of ideas, causes, and schemes could be overwhelming, and Greeley seemed to relish the chance to call the roll of his various commitments. The same month in which he met Emerson, Greeley described a lecture he was to give in Albany as a rollicking performance "of the ultra school, transcendental, grahamite, tee-total . . . [with] a sprinkle of abolition." Three years later, he added to a conservative Whig paper's "catalogue of [the *Tribune*'s] enormities," noting that his newspaper was "Anti-Slavery, Anti-War, Anti-Rum, Anti-Tobacco, Anti-Seduction, Anti-Grogshops, Brothels, Gambling Houses, [in addition to] several other . . . heresies." The list was long, but Greeley believed that when bound together, reform efforts assured progress and improvement.[5]

Among all of Greeley's heresies, none stood out more saliently than his advocacy for "Association"—the American incarnation of Fourierist socialism. Association was largely the work of Albert Brisbane, a wealthy intellectual drifter who had bounced around European Romantic circles before studying with Charles Fourier himself. Brisbane domesticated Fourier's system of socialism for American audiences in a lengthy tract, *The Social Destiny of Man* (1840), that promised to heal the ills of the emerging industrial society. The book and the short-lived socialist newspaper that followed it would not have garnered much attention had it not been for Greeley. Seeing in this system an all-encompassing approach to social problems, Greeley threw open the *Tribune* to Brisbane's writings and his wallet to several of the Associationist "phalanx" communities that sprang up in the 1840s. The support came at some cost to the *Tribune* (and at great financial loss to Greeley himself), but he pressed for Association with the same brash enthusiasm he brought to other reform causes—perhaps even more so.[6]

Association, Greeley believed, held the key to a harmonious future amid sweeping social change. Contrary to critics who chastised him for a divisive radicalism, Greeley favored the movement as an organic solution to the social conflict wrought by industry and capitalism. By emphasizing collective needs and the value of work, Association would heal class antagonisms. No longer in competition, capital and labor could unite in a "harmony of interests."[7] To Greeley, this was just the beginning. Association would also "embosom all other reforms" and "impel the great Social movement" forward. Slavery, for instance, would be eliminated safely and gradually when Association opened Americans' eyes to the true dignity and value of labor. Other improvements would follow: "Demon Rum" would lose its charms when workers were no longer imbruted; capital punishment and flogging would be eliminated in the absence of crime; slums would disappear with the alleviation of poverty and want. "In short," Greeley said in a lecture on Association, "I see no reason why the wildest dreams of the fanatical believer in Human Progress and Perfectibility may not ultimately be realized, and each child so trained as to shun every vice, [and] aspire to every virtue."[8]

Greeley might have found reason for doubt in the daily excoriations from critics of all political stripes. But even they did not dampen his enthusiasms. He took on all comers as a happy warrior. At times, Greeley seemed to luxuriate in the recriminations, especially those from conservative Whigs seeking to write him out of the party. Answering back not only made for lively copy, it also afforded him the chance to define the Whig Party as a rightful home for reform. Greeley identified himself as a "mediator, an interpreter, a reconciler between Conservatism and Radicalism," and he hoped that the Whig Party would be much the same. To him, this was no impossible contradiction, but rather the safest and most gradual way to ameliorate social ills and realize collective destiny. Conservatives alone must not be allowed to define the party. As Greeley told fellow Whig Thurlow Weed, "You will find it impossible to resist the current within as well as around you in favor of Reforms generally. We cannot go back into the last century, and it would be alike disgraceful and disastrous to attempt it." Greeley thus gave as good as he got when it came to his conservative Whig critics, most notably taking on eventual *New-York Times* founder Henry Jarvis Raymond in a back-and-forth debate over Association in 1846 and 1847.[9]

The dawning of the telegraphic era only affirmed the grandest hopes embodied in Association and reform. A year after Morse's invention had promised to "annihilate space," a *Tribune* editorial rhapsodized on the implications. At long last, the press was poised to become a great instrument of "Progress" and "Unity." With instantaneous communications and up-to-the-minute intelligence, newspapers could be purged of their scurrilous and distracting content. A new "philosophical Press" would arise, lifting the "Public Mind" and liberating the people from "their ignorance, their lethargy." Gone would be the "'Important and Thrilling News from Bungtown!,'" the "gossip and horrible accidents," and the "unmeaning acres of disjointed incidents." In their place, the "true Synthesis of Science as a Unity will be discussed and discovered"; "the progress and destiny of Humanity . . . will form the 'leaders' and 'articles' of the Daily Press." And so "the deeper thoughts and capacities of the world will at length be aroused, and the Press, become the arena of all great ideas and discussions, upon which hinge the centuries that are to bring us Paradise and the Future."[10]

But until that bold future arrived, Greeley would continue to use the *Tribune* to advance his reformist vision for the Whig Party and national politics. To Greeley, it was no great leap from an Associationist community to the central articles of Whig faith—protective tariffs, internal improvements, and national banking. All shared the same goals of bettering individuals, rewarding labor, and fostering national unity. "Each single improvement appears but a link," Greeley wrote in 1847, "in a golden chain of benefits and blessings, calculated to bind together, indissolubly, the states composing this vast republic."[11] This was not a call to some starry-eyed reform scheme. Instead, Greeley was reflecting on the power of transportation infrastructures, working in concert with intelligence and communication, to knit the nation together. He believed the rest of the Whig national program to be equally effective in delivering the same kind of social and moral benefits that came with reform: national markets would harmonize the economic interests of antagonistic sections; growth and opportunity would ameliorate the mounting tensions between capital and labor; just rewards for work would make laborers sturdy republican citizens; markets would diversify the Southern economy and undermine the institution of slavery. Beyond economic infrastructure and mass communications, the Whigs just needed some great champion to bridge their own differences and realize the party's national vision.[12]

That Truly National Man

For Greeley, as for many young Whigs of his generation, that champion was the Kentucky statesman Henry Clay. Clay was a great political genius, capable of achieving America's national destiny by sheer force of personality. "That truly national man," as Abraham Lincoln would call him, was born during the Revolutionary period and had been a central political figure since the War of 1812. As Clay's very life had begun with that of the nation, it was only fitting that he had written himself into its annals. He had become synonymous with the Union in orchestrating the compromises over Missouri's statehood in 1820 and the Nullification Crisis in 1832. Renowned as a spellbinding orator and magnetic presence, Clay won the plaudits of even his bitterest enemies and the undying affection of his supporters, Greeley among them. "I have admired and trusted many statesmen," Greeley reflected in his memoirs; "I profoundly loved Henry Clay."[13]

Greeley loved Clay as the visionary of the Whig Party's lofty national schemes and as a healer of divisions. It had been Clay who first articulated the "American System"—the program of tariffs, internal improvements, and banking that Greeley believed held the key to national consensus. But beyond his policies, Clay also embodied the Union itself. As a border-state Kentuckian, "Harry of the West" had a sectional identity that was slippery enough to neutralize existing antagonisms between the North and the South. In particular, Clay stood out to Greeley as a "truly national man" on the issue of slavery. Though himself a slaveholder who had built a fortune on the backs of bonded laborers, Clay opposed the institution and supported its gradual dissolution. To Greeley, this did not make Clay a hypocrite, but instead a leader uniquely suited to contain and neutralize the bitter sectional disagreements over "the peculiar institution." As Greeley told a friend in 1843, "I can't say a word calculated to hurt noble Henry Clay. I consider him less of a slaveholder than many a man who never spoke to a Nigger—less at heart than almost any of our public men." According to Greeley, Clay occupied a middle ground on an issue that seemed not to have one. As a gradualist and a supporter of colonization schemes, he simultaneously recognized the moral claims of slavery's opponents and the property rights of those who practiced it.[14]

Clay embodied these Whig visions of unity, but could he gain the power to realize them? Though the White House had eluded Clay for the whole of his public career, Greeley and many Whigs were confident that his victory in 1844 was all but assured. "Nothing can prevent the election of Mr. Clay but his death," one Whig had boasted in March of that year.[15] They were wrong. With less than a year left in his presidency, John Tyler opened the door to annexing the slaveholding Republic of Texas. In an instant, what seemed a certain triumph for Clay and the Whigs' "great national objects" became instead a tense sectional balancing act. Taking on the aggressively expansionist Democrat James K. Polk, Clay wobbled. When his initial opposition to annexation cost him Southern support, Clay whispered in the Southern press that he had changed his mind. Anti-slavery Northern Whigs heard him and threatened to defect from the party altogether. It seemed that the "truly national man" was neither true nor national.[16]

As Clay teetered, Greeley strained to hold him up as a unity candidate with moderate positions on slavery. Greeley turned from battling the conservatives in his party to placating the progressives as he concentrated his efforts on assuring those anti-slavery Whigs that Clay could satisfy their consciences. It was hard work. Moderation notwithstanding, Clay remained a slaveholder, after all. Many anti-slavery Whigs remembered his 1839 speech on abolitionists, in which he had condemned those who opposed slavery even more harshly than those who practiced it. Defections to the avowedly abolitionist Liberty Party seemed imminent, and it infuriated Greeley. Seeing the threat as early as 1843, he had warned that deserting Clay on anti-slavery grounds would "unavoidably tend to transform our National into a Sectional party" and "divest us of any sympathy or support from the Slave-Holding States." Moreover, defection would be counterproductive. A radical "one idea party" like the Liberty Party would only embolden pro-slavery firebrands in the South and set back the cause of abolition. Clay's gradualism, mixed with his American System, promised a surer path to the goal of eliminating slavery. "If the Abolitionists would just all together vote for him," Greeley told a friend, "I am sure they would advance their cause more than any other way. But that would make [abolitionists like] Gerrit Smith and Alvan Stewart great men, and it will not be done." Great men, in Greeley's estimation, thought beyond single issues to the interests of the nation as a whole.[17]

Greeley appealed to national interests to avert the disaster of a Polk presidency through the summer and fall of 1844. He printed and distributed Epes Sargent's campaign biography of Clay, which portrayed its hero as a "fearless and consistent" advocate for gradual emancipation and a champion of American unity. Greeley also plumped the anti-slavery writings of planter-class apostate Cassius M. Clay, the candidate's distant relative. The pleas grew increasingly desperate and direct as the canvass drew to a close. "Be you firmly assured of this," Greeley warned in October, "if you do break down the Whig party and give the victory to Polk and Texas, your leaders shall rue it to the last days of their lives." A vote for the Liberty Party, he said over and over again, was a vote for Polk and slavery. And he was not wrong.[18]

When the votes were counted and Polk had won, Greeley's worst fears had been confirmed: the anti-slavery conscience had cost Clay the election.[19] In New York, where the state's thirty-six electoral votes decided the race, Polk had edged out Clay by a mere 2,100 popular votes, while the Liberty candidate James G. Birney had polled nearly 16,000. It was the bitterest defeat of Greeley's political life. He later described himself as "the worst beaten man on the continent . . . worn out by incessant anxiety and effort, covered with boils, and thoroughly used up." Readers of the *Tribune* would hear spirited execrations against Birney and "one-idea parties" for the next eight years: what they thought were votes for principle were really votes "in favor of Annexation, War, and eternal Slavery." The true meaning of Polk's victory quickly became clear. It was the triumph of a profoundly different national vision than the one shared by Greeley, Clay, and the Whigs.[20]

What Means This War?

Not long after James Knox Polk's inauguration in April of 1845, the *United States Magazine and Democratic Review* gave a slogan to the new president's extensive plans. The annexation of Texas and the subsequent conquest of the remaining portions of the West would represent "the fulfilment [*sic*] of our manifest destiny to overspread the continent allotted by Providence for the free development of our yearly multiplying millions." To Polk and his supporters, realizing the promise of Manifest Destiny amounted to the fullest expression of American nationhood and national character. While achieving divinely appointed continental unity and spreading the nation's institutions ever farther, white Americans would hone and develop the manly traits on which a great nation would rise. Western lands also stood as the great "safety valve" for the preservation of America's character and institutions. So long as the West beckoned, Jeffersonian ideals could breathe in wide-open spaces, never to suffocate amid the crowds, vice, and dependency of great cities.[21]

This was not, however, Greeley's vision for going west. More than just a rival national concept to Clay's American System, Manifest Destiny threatened its total repudiation. "Opposed to the instinct of boundless acquisition stands that of Internal Improvement," Greeley wrote after the Mexican War. "A nation cannot simultaneously devote its energies to the absorption of others' territories and the improvement of its own." Democratic expansionism would destroy the careful Whig plan to "unite, harmonize, and improve," as Clay put it, within bounded areas. New, far-flung settlements acquired through conquest would serve to weaken social bonds, sap the collective morality, and, above all, give vast new domains over to the institution of slavery. The West to which Greeley called young men was one of orderly development, gradual settlement, and freedom.[22]

The speed and effectiveness with which Polk turned the rhetoric of Manifest Destiny into a war of conquest with Mexico gave terrible accuracy to Greeley's dire predictions for Polk's presidency. Ralph Waldo Emerson is perhaps best known as the doomsayer of the Mexican War with his prediction that "Mexico will poison us." But he said so only in his diary. From the moment Polk called for war in May of 1846, Greeley shook the columns of the *Tribune* with his antiwar rage and became perhaps the most forceful and prescient critic of the war.

If ever Greeley earned the designation as "a sort of municipal Diogenes" —which a magazine gave him in 1849—it was during Polk's administration. Again and again through the Mexican War years of 1846–1848, Greeley harangued Americans that their country had embarked on a woefully misguided adventure. "No true Honor, no National benefit, can possibly accrue from an unjust war," he warned. There was little doubt that the United States would win—that its forces would "defeat the armies of Mexico, slaughter them by the thousands"—but, Greeley asked, What next? "So sure as the Universe has a Ruler will every acre of territory we acquire from this War prove to our Nation a curse and a source of infinite calamities." In the rush to war in the spring of 1846, Greeley implored the public to see the moral dangers lurking behind the spread-eagle rhetoric. "People of the United States," he raged, "your Rulers are precipitating you into a fathomless abyss of crime and calamity. . . . Awake and arrest the work of butchery ere it shall be too late to preserve your souls from the guilt of wholesale slaughter! Hold meetings! Speak out! Act!"[23]

Many other Whigs spoke out against the Mexican War, but the quickness and fury with which Greeley stood against it put him on the leading edge of party opinion. While some tried to maintain a principled opposition and avoid charges of disloyalty at the same time, Greeley refused to tiptoe around public sentiment. Amid an outpouring of sensational reportage of heroic deeds, steamy wartime romances, and toe-tapping war songs, Greeley responded with blistering criticism. As many New Yorkers took to the streets in boisterous pro-war demonstrations, Greeley thundered like a camp meeting Jeremiah, asking, "What means this war?" "It means," he said, "that the Commandments are to be read and obeyed by our People thus— Thou *shalt* kill Mexicans; Thou *shalt* steal from them, hate them, burn their houses, ravage their fields, and fire red-hot cannon-balls into towns swarming with their wives and children." The list went on. It meant that the US Treasury would go bust and taxes would explode; that factories would churn out "the devilish enginery of human carnage" rather than the everyday needs of life; that "Butchery, Rape, Devastation, and Horror" would become the order of the day. It meant, in short, that the progressive spirit of Greeley's nineteenth century would expire: "Improvement is to be arrested, the blessed arts of Peace, neglected, and the world recede toward the midnight of Barbarism."[24]

Such fire-and-brimstone fare made Greeley subject to threats of assassination, calls for mob action against the *Tribune*, and general reprisal for disloyalty. He did not back down. The conservative Whig *New-York Courier and Enquirer* warned that any further agitation from Greeley was "sure to lead to scenes of violence" and noted "the necessity of crushing [his] recklessness." In response, Greeley vowed that "all the powers of Land-Jobbing and Slave-Jobbing cannot drive us one inch from the ground we have assumed of determined and open hostility to this atrocious war." Such threats from "cowardly ruffians," he said in another editorial, came with the satisfaction of knowing that he was close to the truth.[25]

Greeley deplored the war in all its phases and facets—its ginned-up origins, seen as a defensive operation; its aggressive prosecution; its mindless public support; its great monetary and human costs; its threatened propagation of slavery. Overall, Greeley decried it as a destructive national endeavor. All of his objections came back to this point. The Mexican War poisoned the United States by diverting it from the great (and proper) national objects embodied in Henry Clay and the progressive Whig agenda. Instead of working for internal improvements, beneficent commerce, and moral development, Americans were choosing an empty form of nationalism, the "sort of Patriotism whereof Falsehood, Despotism, Slavery, and Murder appear to be the chief ingredients." On both a practical and a spiritual level, the war was a terrible mistake—one that could not be hidden from judgment by a "few flimsy rags called banners."[26]

What Polk and his pro-war supporters branded as a venture in the name of national destiny, Greeley savaged as a perversion of national purpose. If the United States was, to the world at large, the shining example of "Progress" that Americans believed it to be, an aggressive imperial war was a crooked way of showing it. Again and again, the *Tribune*'s lurid descriptions of wartime carnage and atrocities pointed to such gross contradictions: an adventure in the name of liberty to preserve and extend slavery, a violent war in the name of "Justice and Peace." History, Greeley warned, was not on their side. Certain doom lay waiting in such "gross infidelity to the principles which made us a Nation." The annals of Rome, Britain, and Napoleonic France were replete with cautionary tales of "the dangers and disasters sure to follow the perpetuation of a national crime."[27]

Improbably, however, Greeley retained his faith in collective progress and national purpose against all currents during the war years. Even amid splintering sectional jealousies, Greeley held out hope that the real impulses of Manifest Destiny imperialism would push the public back to less divisive national expressions. To be sure, Greeley played his part in the polarization of political discourse that began in 1846. He urged Northern resolve and unity in the face of Southern aggression, and he fought vigorously against the spread of slavery into new territories acquired in the Mexican War. Yet he was certain that the Southern, pro-slavery interests had overplayed their hand. When viewed in light of slavery, the war looked less like a glorious national endeavor than a sectional land grab cloaked in the American flag. It was, Greeley said, "purely and avowedly Southern . . . a general crusade for the propagation of Slavery . . . by cannon-shot and sabre-cut." Under the veil of patriotism, a small cabal of Southerners demanded "that the whole nation should fall down and worship its graven images." The men who were pressing the nation into war and reaching out for still more ter-

ritory (Greeley did not yet invoke "the Slave Power" by name) had no national vision at all. They were the same congressional leaders who had killed
a protective tariff, voted down internal improvements, and refused (through
the "gag rule") to hear anti-slavery petitions in Congress, all in the name of
their narrow sectional interests—and all at the cost of national progress.[28]

Now, perhaps, the nation would see the truth. The political crisis brought
on by the Mexican War offered the possibility of resolving sectional tensions over slavery and returning to great national objects through the power
of publicity. (Greeley would reprise these arguments with the outbreak of
the Civil War, fifteen years later.) With forces gathering in 1847 for a fresh
congressional fight over slavery and the new territories, Greeley welcomed
John C. Calhoun's fire-eating threats of disunion should Northern interests
press for limiting the expansion of bondage. "It is high time," he wrote,
"that this decisive battle were fought and the issue known. . . . Let the war
of Freedom against Slavery . . . now be fought out manfully." When the issue
became apparent, Greeley was certain that a long-silenced Southern majority would overthrow Calhoun and his cabal. "There are thousands of Southern consciences on which Slavery has long weighed heavily, though the
familiar pistol and bowie-knife have silenced all outward manifestations,"
Greeley wrote. When those sleeping Southern masses awoke to their bully-
ing leaders' true feelings, they would also rally to the nation: "Owning no
slaves themselves [they] will not consent to give up their interest in Bunker
Hill and Bennington, Saratoga and Monmouth . . . in the cause of the Slaveholding aristocracy." The choice was becoming clear. Americans could be
a divided slaveholding empire, or a unified nation committed to liberty and
internal development.[29]

Greeley's conviction that Americans were ready to choose nation over
empire was rooted in a broader sweep of events. As he would also do in
1861, he clung tightly to the belief that the great mass of white Southerners
were naturally opposed to slavery and were at the ready to revolt against
the planter class. The Mexican War, he thought, contained the beginnings
of the uprising. "Free Laborers in the South" were beginning to "to realize
the mark of degradation Slavery everywhere sets upon Labor." Even as the
Wilmot Proviso (which declared` that slavery should be barred from any
new territories won in the war) went down to repeated defeat, Greeley

seemed genuinely to believe that the shift was happening, and he tracked anything that suggested the merest hint of right thinking on slavery. He cheered Delaware's near passage of a gradual emancipation bill and noted the rise of anti-slavery societies in Maryland. He found "Just Views of the Wilmot Proviso" in South Carolina, caught word that the *Tribune* was increasing in popularity among Southern Whigs, and followed the movements of anti-slavery Southerner Cassius M. Clay. A year and a half into the war, Greeley was ready to proclaim "the rapid progress of Southern opinion" on slavery, confirming what he had long suspected. "When the adversaries of Slavery in Slaveholding communities are emboldened to say what they think," he claimed, "then be sure the days of Bondage are numbered."[30]

Henry Clay lurked behind Greeley's optimistic reading of the tea leaves. With the presidential election of 1848 approaching, Greeley believed that circumstances once again beckoned for Harry of the West to seize the White House. Though Greeley did flirt with the idea of other candidates—notably the blisteringly antiwar Ohio Whig Thomas Corwin—Greeley returned to the familiar themes of the 1844 election. Clay was, as he had been, a singular figure capable of embodying national vision and compromise over slavery. As an October 1847 exchange with an anti-slavery newspaper suggested, there was still much work to be done to convince at least some Northern Whigs that Clay was a safe candidate. But Greeley was more than happy to take up the cudgels. With a disastrous and divisive war drawing to a close, he was convinced again that the nation awaited Henry Clay.[31]

A National Slaughter-House

As the election year of 1848 dawned, Greeley had a prescient anticipation of the year's great historical import. On January 1, he wrote that it was "destined to be one of momentous consequences": "War and Peace, Freedom and Slavery, Debt and Payment . . . the election of a President who will shape the National Policy to promote a gigantic Iniquity or . . . the dictates of sound Morality." These, Greeley said, were "among the issues now trembling in the balance." Though he could not have known it at the dawn of the new year, Greeley himself would be trembling in the balance, as suggested by the "Patent Balancing by an Amateur" cartoon, in a matter of months. He swore to be "faithful to Duty, to Justice, and to Humanity through the trying ordeal of 1848." What was left of the national idea? What of the visions of unity and consensus? The ordeal of 1848 rested in these questions.[32]

Greeley set himself to securing the Whig nomination for Clay, but he was moving against the currents of party feeling. The Whigs, like the nation itself, had been badly fractured by the Mexican War, and few of them shared Greeley's faith that Clay was the man to put them (or the nation) back together. Clay's advanced age—he turned 71 in 1848—and his losses in three previous presidential contests already cast doubts on his viability. More immediately, Clay's unpopularity in both the North and the South belied Greeley's claims that he occupied a "broad, comprehensive, and truly National ground." For Southern Whigs, Clay had been disqualified by his antiwar stance; many Northern Whigs remained skeptical of his slaveholding background. Greeley worked closely with Clay to help him win favor with both constituencies, but to no avail.[33] A frail consensus was gathering within the party around the heroes of the late war. A victorious general with vague political belief could ease the Whigs' internal tensions and mitigate the perceptions of disloyalty that had come with the party's opposition to the war. Winfield Scott and Zachary Taylor stood out. Both had stellar war records, cloudy political identities, and, as "Old Fuss and Feathers" and "Rough and Ready," respectively, monikers ready-made for success in antebellum popular politics.[34]

To Greeley, such "Hero-candidates" were of "foreign manufacture" and represented a dangerous turn for the Whig Party—a choice of empty national symbols over substantive national policies. The party stood for real things, not the "sway of popular passion, the lust of conquest, and the intense craving of hot blood for wild adventure and lawless gratification." Greeley commenced what William Henry Seward called "a quixotic battle against generals in politics." The fight became desperate when Taylor—"the old savage"—emerged as the favorite. Taylor's views on a variety of Whig positions—the tariff, currency, public lands, the extension of slavery into new territories—were virtually unknown. "The concealment," Greeley said in January, "argues that somebody is to be cheated; and we do not choose to be classed with either the swindlers or dupes."[35]

By the time the Whig convention met in Philadelphia's Chinese Museum Hall in June of 1848, Clay's prospects for the nomination were dim—and so, too, were the prospects for national consensus. Greeley remained in contact with Clay and continued supporting him vocally, but he was also hedging his bets toward other possible candidates in a hopeless attempt to stop the Taylor movement. As Greeley had told a friend in April, "If we nominate Taylor, we may elect him, but we destroy the Whig party. . . . I wash my hands of the business." A Whig Party united around Taylor was a party that stood for nothing in particular.[36]

Greeley left the convention in disgust the night Taylor won the nomination, reportedly tramping off into the darkness to begin walking to New York City rather than wait for the morning train. He did not miss much. The Whig Party could not agree on a platform and never wrote one. Upon returning home, he called the convention a "National Slaughter-House" and penned a premature valediction of his hero.[37] "Thank God," Greeley said, "the day has at length come in which no man can hope to advance his own interests by defaming and slandering HENRY CLAY!" A brief account of Clay's achievements and the glories of "THE AMERICAN SYSTEM" followed, along with a happy vision of Clay's hard-earned retirement to the shades of Ashland, his Kentucky plantation. But the grapes were sour. "Such [was] the man rudely thrust aside that the winner of three or four brilliant but fruitless victories" might be president. A political cartoon circulating around the time of the Philadelphia convention portrayed a group of Whigs, knives drawn, reciting lines from Shakespeare's *Julius Caesar*. They were encircling Henry Clay, who was placidly reading a copy of the *New-York Tribune* by the fire. But the assassins at Philadelphia had mixed up the plot. They had killed Brutus rather than Caesar.[38]

I Could Shake Down the Whole Rotten Fabric with a Bugle Blast

The year 1848 was filled with uprisings. Abroad, the fall of the French monarchy in February touched off a wave of revolution and upheaval in places like Germany, Hungary, and Italy. As Americans watched this European "springtime of the peoples" with a mix of admiration and terror, uprisings stirred at home. News of events across the Atlantic inspired American radicals and reformers to coordinate their efforts against a variety of social ills. Abolitionists cheered the French Republic's measure to eliminate slavery from colonial holdings in the West Indies. Labor reformers hailed the cre-

W. J. C., "The Assassination of the Sage of Ashland" (New York: H. R. Robinson, 1848). Library of Congress, Prints & Photographs Division

ation of national workshops in France. Claiming that "the spirit of freedom is arousing the world," women's rights advocates met at Seneca Falls, New York, to demand equality and suffrage. Nor were mainstream party politics immune to the revolutionary bug. The nomination of Zachary Taylor suggested what Theodore Parker called "a revolution in political parties" and inspired a revolt by anti-slavery Northerners that would become the Free Soil Party.[39]

Greeley and the *Tribune* were at the center of the ferment. Even as Greeley battled his fellow Whigs to secure Henry Clay's nomination through the first half of 1848, the paper emerged as a clearinghouse of information on the revolutionary spring abroad. With regular dispatches from Margaret Fuller and *Tribune* subeditor Charles A. Dana, as well as from several radical European correspondents, the paper cheered the events as a hopeful counter to the ominous postwar state of affairs at home. "Courage, friends of Progress!" Greeley urged. "The world is *not* what it has been.... Forward! is the watchword of humanity." Such affirmations captured the optimism of American reformers but brought on renewed abuse from conservative elements of the American press and complicated Greeley's efforts on behalf of Clay. By June, with Zachary Taylor receiving the Whig nomination and events taking an even more radical turn in France, Greeley was faced with difficult questions. How far forward was he willing to go in the name of humanity? Was he prepared to lead an uprising of his own?[40]

In the confused days following the disastrous Whig convention, upheaval seemed imminent, and Greeley signaled that he would be a part of it. He faced pressure from fellow Whigs to stifle his dissent and support Taylor but showed no urgency to do so. It was, he said in the *Tribune*, "a time for reflection." He was contemplating the possibility of a radical change in his political orientation—one that would take him away from the national orientation of his Whig faith and toward the sectional politics of the moment. If "the Free States are now ripe for the uprising which must come sooner or later," Greeley said, "why then we are ready." Greeley was wary of anything that might serve to elect Democratic candidate Lewis Cass and his "all-creation-annexing administration." But he was also wary of Zachary Taylor.[41]

The uprising of the Free States was already in the works. An internal spat among New York Democrats at that party's national convention in May saw the anti-slavery "Barnburner" faction walk out of the hall. The group would reconvene in mid-June to nominate former president Martin Van Buren as their candidate for the White House. Across the North, similar revolts were brewing among Whigs after Taylor's nomination, with members of the doggedly anti-slavery Liberty Party eager to join in with them. Though of different parties, the groups were united in a common commitment to the restriction of slavery and a common conviction that the institution represented what the Barnburner platform called "a great moral, social, and political evil—a relic of barbarism which must necessarily be swept away in the progress of Christian civilization." A Free Territory convention in Columbus, Ohio, issued a call for a meeting of "all friends of Freedom, Free Territory, and Free Labor," to be held in Buffalo, New York, on August 9 and 10. There, the Free Soil Party would be built from the splinters of other fracturing political parties.[42]

This was the tightrope. Joining the Free Soil Party meant abandoning a national vision of politics in favor of a sectional one. It also meant joining in common cause with Democrats. Greeley's editorials through the summer of 1848 suggested that he was ready to make the leap. Anticipating the fledgling party's August convention, Greeley rang the bell in the *Tribune* for the Free Soilers' stands on slavery and its restriction in the new territories. If realizing the party's ends meant "shivering the Whig party to atoms," Greeley, at least, was ready. Though he did not attend the convention, he unequivocally applauded its outcomes. A "vast assemblage of discordant elements" had come together to put forward a platform that was "emphatically right" on slavery and a host of other questions. At long last, here was a political movement coalescing around vital ideas and principles rather than blind fidelity to the party. "The moral," Greeley said, "is the superiority . . . of a living, cherished principle to any decaying organism." This was nothing short of "the transformation of many thousands of mere party machines into deliberative and independent freemen." Here was precisely the kind of informed democracy that Greeley had championed from his earliest days in journalism. It just happened to be expressed through a sectional rather than a national party.[43]

Greeley's decision the following month to remain a Whig and support Zachary Taylor was thus greeted with varying degrees of surprise, relief, and disgust—feelings that Greeley himself held toward his decision. Informing a friend of his intentions, even Greeley could hardly believe what he was saying. "I am going to vote for Gen. Taylor—at least, I think I am, and I am not clear that this is right," he began. "If I could make Van Buren President tomorrow, I would. I don't like the man, but I <u>do</u> like the principles he now embodies—Free Soil and Land Reform. And, very properly, the Free Soil Party is the only live party around us. It ought to triumph, but . . . it will fail, but fail gloriously." There was even more to lament. Greeley was not only abandoning the Free Soilers, but also the towering role he might have played among them: "I could have been the oracle of the Free Soil Party, with my extent of circulation, had I chosen . . . I could shake down the whole rotten fabric with a bugle blast."[44]

Greeley kept his bugle silent for a variety of reasons. First and foremost was the prospect of another Democratic administration, this one under the pro-expansion Michigander Lewis Cass. As Greeley told Schuyler Colfax, even though "the banditti who triumphed at Philadelphia" deserved "a visitation of that fat-bellied, mutton-headed, cucumber-soled Cass," the country did not. By Greeley's self-assured calculations, if he were to swing a large bloc of Whigs into the Free Soil camp, he would succeed only in helping to elect Cass.[45]

There were also hesitations born out of the Free Soil Party's heavily Democratic origins. As much as Greeley applauded the vitality of the Free Soilers' principles and ideas, he was still the person who had defined his political journalism in opposition to Democrats for more than a decade. He doubted that this same group could have changed so much so quickly, especially after many of them had voted down black suffrage at New York's 1846 constitutional convention. As a result, Greeley never quite shook the suspicion that the original revolt was rooted more in "a quarrel for mastery and spoils" within the Democratic Party than in fidelity to professed Free Soil principles.[46]

Greeley still had a great deal invested in the Whig Party, both personally and politically. To Colfax, Greeley said that "party fidelity, or rather fidelity to men I love who still cling to the putrid corpse of the party butchered at Philadelphia" kept him from bolting. Were he to bring down the party, "good men I love would be crushed beneath its ruins." Yet the truth was that he might not have been quite so magnanimous. His old allies Thurlow Weed and William Henry Seward appear to have used a variety of means to keep Greeley in line, but most effective among them was the promise of political office. A Democratic congressman from New York City had been unseated from his first term for election fraud, leaving an open seat for the single remaining session of the Thirtieth US Congress. In the grand scheme of things, it was a bauble, but attractive enough for the office-hungry Greeley. By the end of September, Greeley and the *Tribune* were at long last in support of Zachary Taylor.[47]

Greeley toed the line for Taylor through the remainder of the canvass, but he did so while holding his nose. He told Colfax that he did not have the stomach to do much more than he did, and anyone reading the *Tribune* could see the obvious lack of enthusiasm for Taylor. Conservative Whig and former New York City mayor Philip Hone recorded Greeley's apologetic endorsement of Taylor as an act "in abominably bad taste"—the last ditch of a scoundrel trying to play both sides at once. The usual ballyhoo of songs, poems, and biographical anecdotes that filled a newspaper's columns during an election were notably absent from the *Tribune*. When Taylor had the election in hand early in November, Greeley did not cheer at the result. He expressed only relief that the charade had come to an end. The campaign ditties that were "unfit to be hummed in a stable," the "pestilent swarm of War narratives and Battle scenes, and Mexican-invasion romances," the "stimulants of the combative propensities of our lower nature—all ought now be buried out of sight. . . . Let them perish."[48]

Ultimately, though Greeley loathed to support Zachary Taylor, he could not stand with a purely sectional uprising. No matter how "ready" he professed to be for the revolt of the Free States, Greeley still had too much faith in the national principle—and probably too much faith in himself—both of which he took to Washington, DC, where he would try to restore Congress to its national standing in a mere three months.

The Embodied Scoundrelism of the Nation

If Greeley *could have been* the oracle of the Free Soil Party, as he had claimed during the fall campaigns, he did not much look the part when he came to the nation's capital for his brief turn in Congress from December 1848 to March 1849. In a lame-duck session otherwise consumed by intense sectional wrangling over the results of the Mexican War, Greeley played a perhaps surprisingly small role in that drama. True, he introduced a land reform bill designed to limit speculation in the territories, and he coauthored another to ban the slave trade in the District of Columbia. Toward the end of the session, Greeley pushed back vigorously against Texas's claims to large portions of the New Mexico Territory acquired in the war. In the process, he engaged in some spirited exchanges on the floor over the slave state's wanton attempt at "landstealing." Beyond this, however, he largely skirted the session's most controversial topics of slavery and expansion. As he wrote upon the session's end, he "shunned and deplored any needless agitation respecting slavery" and the "interminable speech-making" that came with it.[49]

But he did make his mark on the session. Few people in the whole history of Congress have ever made themselves so unwelcome in so short a time. "Philosopher Greeley of the Tribune," one newspaper announced of his arrival there, "bangs into that body [like a] sledge-hammer." He launched a quixotic crusade to fix Congress itself—to elevate it into something more than "the embodied scoundrelism" of the nation. Though he caucused as a Whig, Greeley was in many ways an independent, reforming nationalist targeting the bad habits and accumulated privileges that had slowly corroded the national legislature. He spent most of his energy on the culture of Congress: its lavish travel reimbursements and internal spending, its chronic absenteeism, its persistent do-nothingism, its speechifying to no particular end. To Greeley, these problems were not beside the point. They were intimately connected to the sectional questions dividing the nation and Congress itself. Improve Congress, make it a worthy and truly *national* institution led by dispassionately *national* leaders, and perhaps it would be capable of transcending sectional differences.[50]

Greeley failed to make much change, but for all the tense sectional feeling and fragile partisan alliances, he quickly succeeded in creating a general consensus around the idea that he was an exceptional nuisance. As the *Congressional Globe* reports noted repeatedly, Greeley was barely audible when speaking on the floor of the House, but his status as one of the nation's most visible editors assured that his voice boomed far beyond the Capitol.[51] By day he exasperated colleagues with a brazen ignorance of the rules of order and a principled opposition to all calls for adjournment. By night, he infuriated them, playing the role of protomuckraker and writing dispatches to the *Tribune* exposing the shame of the Congress. Merging the work of congressional correspondent into his official duties as a US representative, Greeley began to unravel the "doings, misdoings, un-doings, and not-doings" of the House and Senate in the name of the nation at large. It was, he said in his memoir, Congress versus the people: "a party of ten-score, confronted by twenty-odd millions," with Greeley acting on behalf of the latter.[52]

Though he knew very little of the actual workings of Congress, Greeley wasted no time in laying them before the public. In his very first letter to the *Tribune* as a congressman, penned on just the second day of the session, he was already excoriating his colleagues for inaction. Little more could be expected of such an undistinguished gathering. Of the 290 men who made up both houses of Congress, Greeley claimed that the vast majority were incompetent placeholders, "shuffled into responsible places as a reward for past compliances." (He did not acknowledge that his own presence there was largely the result of his own late compliances.) Once there, he said, these men were bent solely on winning distinction, plundering the US Treasury, and "intriguing their way into some . . . lazier and more lucrative post." Subsequent reports to the *Tribune* marked "every motion to adjourn at an unseasonably early hour," every failed quorum, and the name of every absentee US representative. Greeley's theatrics on the floor won him no favor, either. When he rose on December 23 and "moved to substitute *Tuesday* for Wednesday, and demanded the Yeas and Nays," Greeley was not grossly overestimating his own power, or that of Congress. He was protesting what he deemed an excessively long recess for Christmas, demanding that the members take a three- rather than a four-day weekend.[53]

From the perspective of Greeley's colleagues, cataloging dereliction was offensive, but quantifying it was outrageous. The December 22, 1848, issue of the *Tribune* featured a bombshell exposé of the inflated travel reimbursement claims of each member of Congress. By law, elected officials journeying to and from Washington, DC, were entitled to be paid $8 for every twenty miles along the "usually traveled route." This language—"the usually traveled route"—opened a loophole large enough for a representative to zigzag through on his way to the nation's capital and be fully reimbursed for it. As a congressman, Greeley had access to confidential records of mileage and compensation. As an editor, he had access to a reporter who could subtract the distance of the "most direct postal route" from the distance claimed along the "usually traveled route." That difference totaled roughly 78,000 extra miles traveled and "roundabout allowances" of more than $62,000 in excess disbursement.[54]

Greeley gloried in the ruckus that ensued from the article. As the House returned from the Christmas recess on *Wednesday*, December 27 (the motion to substitute Tuesday for Wednesday had failed), Greeley reported with great satisfaction that the House was at long last doing something: "Contrary to the general usage in the holiday season, we have had a breezy, stirring, spicy sitting in the House today." No, he and his colleagues were not taking on the great questions of the day, but the exposé had touched raw nerves and set in motion a furious backlash. The public at large would at long last see the corrupt inner workings of the national legislature.[55]

In a parade of denunciations, the general theme was that the honorable gentleman from New York (one speaker corrected himself after using that designation, referring instead to "the individual, perhaps the thing") was a demagogue and a slanderer, actuated by a "low, groveling, base, and malignant desire to represent the Congress . . . in a false and unenviable light." The debate was less about the substance of Greeley's charges than their propriety. Members who had been outed as "mileage elongators" contested the specifics of the charges against them, while a committee was formed to investigate the report and whether it amounted to "an allegation of fraud against most members of the House." There was strong bipartisan support in favor of such a move: a motion to table the resolution to investigate the report as a slanderous accusation of fraud fell by 128 votes to 28, and the resolution itself passed, 101 to 43. Nothing much came of either Greeley's crusade for mileage reform or the threatened recriminations against him. Still, Greeley claimed victory. As he predicted (incorrectly) to Colfax, the most egregious offenders would be cast out of Congress in favor of more-honest representatives.[56]

Greeley held to such seemingly peripheral matters right to the end of his brief turn in Congress. He kept quiet in the midst of the session's brawling final debates over the questions of territory and slavery. On his final night in the House, he watched as a group of Democrats assaulted Joshua Giddings, certain that he himself would be beaten or killed if he physically intervened. But he rose twice, once to offer his ill-starred resolution that the country's name be changed to Columbia, and again to protest a publicly funded party for the members. Of his final hours in Congress, Greeley reflected later that he then "saw things from a novel point of view, and if I came away . . . no wiser than when I went thither, the fault was not entirely my own." He had tried, but there was ultimately "no disposition among the majority of Congress to make its own crooked paths straight."[57]

Here was the final lesson of Greeley's term: violent sectionalism thrived on the weakness of national ideas and institutions. While "men of earnest conviction" operated on both sides of the divide, the majority worked from baser motives in sounding the notes of sectional discord. The "needless agitation" and "interminable speechmaking" on explosive subjects served a variety of purposes, and few of them were honest. Some used the politics of sectionalism "for its demagogic capacities" to ensure their reelection, others to interfere with the incoming administration, and still others simply to force an extra session wherein they could luxuriate on bloated per diems and mileage reimbursements. As long as Congress remained a morally corrupt and politically inept body, there was little hope of transcending sectionalism.[58]

~

It was on the final day of his session that Greeley took to the floor with a motion to change the name of "The United States of America" to "Columbia."[59] That the measure was read twice and came to nothing, and barely rated mention in the national press, carried a bitter lesson for Greeley. The country's political discord, social ills, and sectional divides would not yield easily. He could not call forth the progress and consensus he envisioned, nor could Henry Clay. Both, however, would persist in their work. With grand invocations of the Union and its Revolutionary heritage, Clay would reemerge to introduce the Compromise of 1850 and douse, for a time, sectional fires. Greeley followed Clay, keeping his faith in the Union as a vessel of progress—one that could heal its own contradictions through mere persistence. As the 1840s became the 1850s, though, that faith became increasingly untenable. Events would show Greeley that if he *"could have been* the Oracle of the Free Soil Party," he perhaps *should have been.* They would show that to save the nation, Greeley needed to rally the forces of sectionalism—he needed to rally the North.

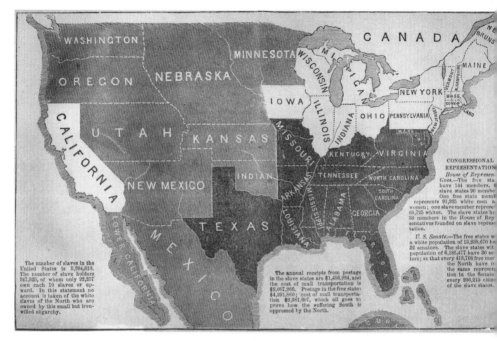

"Freedom and Slavery, and the Coveted Territories," *Life of John Charles Frémont* (New York: Greeley & McElrath, 1856), back cover. Courtesy Cornell University—PJ Mode Collection of Persuasive Cartography

CHAPTER THREE

Making the Yankee Nation

By the spring of 1854, it had become virtually impossible to visualize the nation as a unified whole. A crudely etched map of the United States above a *Tribune* editorial on "The Extension of Slavery" made this plain. The visual prop, rare for the paper's editorial page, offered "the most vivid illustration possible" of the Kansas-Nebraska Bill's grave threat to open those territories to slavery. The map depicted the country as a regional and moral patchwork—the free states in white, pinched between the South in black and the West's vast expanses in gray.[1] As a subsequent iteration would show more palpably, it was more than just a map. Published over the next few years as a broadside and in pamphlets, campaign documents, and almanacs as "Freedom and Slavery, and the Coveted Territories," it leapt off the pages as a dramatic narrative. This stark, new geography told a grim story of national politics as a form of sectional conflict between the North and the South, with the West and the country's destiny as the prize. By all appearances, the South, swollen with "the Slave Power," was winning.[2]

Americans learned to see their country anew in the 1850s. Sectional conflict extended back to the country's founding, but by the end of the decade, it would become so firmly fixed that the nation was on the brink of civil war. Horace Greeley and the *Tribune* helped draw the battle lines ever more sharply amid a protracted struggle over slavery and western expansion. Published under his imprimatur, the map on the facing page charted an important turn in Greeley's career. He, the would-be national oracle, achieved his greatest fame and influence as a voice of Northern sectionalism after 1854. Offering guidance in a shifting political landscape, Greeley and the *Tribune* narrated the drama of national life as an internal clash of civilizations.

Ironically, if sectional conflict destroyed Greeley's visions for national consensus, it helped make him the most famous and influential journalist in the United States. The *Tribune*'s growth in the second half of the 1850s was spectacular—and closely tied to the politics of slavery and expansion. Beginning with the passage of the Kansas-Nebraska Act in May of 1854, circulation numbers began marching upward, and Greeley's stature grew accordingly. His biographer James Parton may well have exaggerated when he claimed in 1854 that Greeley "addressed a larger number of persons than any other editor or man," but the figures were on Parton's side. The following year, the paper invested in the world's largest and fastest steam-driven printing press—the better to reach the nearly 200,000 subscribers for all of its editions. The editorial staff predicted growth to 250,000 by the end of 1856 (they were wrong—the number reached 280,000 by June of that year). Estimating that each subscription's paper reached five readers, an editorial crowed that the *Tribune* would be "read by a million and a quarter of intelligent, upright, and substantial people." To Parton, Greeley's importance resided not just in how many people he reached, but also in *which* people were reached. "The majority of his readers," Parton said, "live in these northern states, where the Intelligence, the Virtue, and (therefore) the wealth, of this confederacy chiefly reside." Greeley and his *Tribune* became a sectional phenomenon.[3]

The massive political realignment that gave birth to the Republican Party only magnified the importance of the editor and his paper in a moment of institutional weakness in party politics. As the Whig Party shattered and the Democratic Party crumbled at the edges, Greeley became a key figure in the search for a new political coalition that could replace the Whigs and incorporate the shards of "the Democracy." The task was difficult. Older, local party alliances proved stubborn in some places, while newer ones formed around the reactionary, nativist impulses animating the American, or Know-Nothing, Party. Greeley and other early Republicans struggled to mobilize Northern white men into a working political party and have them realize that slavery and its spread represented the greatest danger to the nation.[4]

To break through these forces holding back the Republican Party, Greeley turned to a sharply sectional rhetoric. In the absence of what he called a "real, effective North, antagonistic to the slaveholding South," he pledged to "make a North." Greeley and his staff saw the nation through the lens of "North" in the pages of the *Tribune*—a Yankee nation capable of standing up to "the Slave Power," defeating "the Democracy," and rescuing the western territories from bondage. In this vision unfolding in the pages of the *Tribune*, Northern men—sturdy, industrious, moral, and white—were the core of the nation. They were heirs to American Revolutionary ideals, battling those who would extinguish the flame of liberty in statehouses, on the plains of Kansas and the plantations of the South, on the floor of Congress, and in the streets of Washington, DC.[5]

In the process, Greeley and his staff did not just help lay the foundations of the Republican Party. They also played a critical role in a larger reimagining of the nation in explicitly sectional terms. They urged readers to see a unity among themselves as Northern stewards of the true American nation, stretching from New England to the upper Midwest.[6] So, too, did they urge readers to see a unity in events ranging from the plains of Kansas to the halls of Congress. If the dream of nineteenth-century nation builders and the power of the mass press were to transcend local identities and institutions, Greeley was a singular figure and the *Tribune* an effective instrument. But Greeley only succeeded by half. In working to imagine a Northern community hostile to the South and slavery, he would also help invalidate the national one. In integrating large constituencies of people around shared ideas and information, he would ultimately help disintegrate the nation.[7]

The Voice of the North

Greeley rose to the height of his powers in the 1850s, after being personally and politically adrift early in the decade. The elevation of Democratic nonentity Franklin Pierce to the presidency in 1852 made it plain that the Whig Party, already a zombie organization as early as 1848, was not coming back from the dead (at least in any form palatable to Greeley). As Greeley told a friend, there was only one obstacle to the realization of Whig principles, but it was an important one: the Whig Party itself. It was time to move on.[8]

At the dawn of 1853, Greeley told *Tribune* readers that he was taking his paper out of party politics for the foreseeable future. He invoked his old mantle of "public teacher" and vowed to fight for principles, not party. He would do his previous work of disseminating intelligence and preparing the public to exercise sound judgment on a variety of matters. Precedence would go to those ideas and causes that tended to build consensus, elevate individuals, and honor labor. This meant rescuing the intemperate from "Demon Rum," giving land to the landless on western homesteads, finding work for the idle, improving manufactures, modernizing agriculture, and belting the country's midsection with a railroad to the Pacific. If political parties had been standing in the way of such policies, then let the parties perish.[9]

Thomas McElrath, Greeley's more practical business partner, was somewhat less sanguine. Whig bosses in New York State had made note of the *Tribune* editor's growing disaffection from the party and were already steering business elsewhere—much of it to Henry Jarvis Raymond's upstart *New-York Times*. Though only founded in 1851, the *Times* quickly surpassed the *Tribune*'s circulation in New York City. More reliably conservative than the *Tribune*, it became the preferred advertising medium of New York's Whig business class. Soon, "the little viper," as Greeley called the diminutive Raymond, was getting lucrative state printing contracts and even advance copies of Senator William Henry Seward's speeches, a privilege that had once been Greeley's alone. By September of 1853, Thurlow Weed's paper, the *Albany Evening Journal*, officially drummed the *Tribune*—so often "carried away by its own convictions"—out of the Whig Party altogether.[10]

Greeley dug in, claiming virtue and journalistic superiority in the *Tribune*'s independence. Against the wishes of McElrath, he enlarged the paper's format, focused on improving the weekly edition, and took on Raymond directly. The *Times*, Greeley said, "lacks backbone and character. It does not speak out. It makes 'compliances.'" Free to avoid any such "compliances" himself, Greeley remarked that he would be content "to let two or three years glide smoothly away" while feeling out tremors in the shifting political landscape. Should a new "political exigency involving the necessity of a new party struggle arise," he said, then "we shall have a clearer vision for discerning our duties with the best means whereby to fulfill them."[11]

By mid-1854, the Kansas-Nebraska Act became that exigency. Put forward by Illinois senator Stephen A. Douglas to open a route for the long-debated Pacific Railroad, this law became the powder keg that exploded the American political system. Douglas proposed that the territories be organized according to the principle of "popular sovereignty," meaning that the settlers in Kansas and Nebraska would determine the status of slavery in their territories themselves. Douglas argued that this would offer the most democratic means to resolve the slavery question, but his prediction that the law would rouse "a hell of a storm" proved correct. Where Douglas claimed moral indifference to slavery and uncertainty that the institution would be suited to the distant plains, opponents of his bill saw this as mere dodge and deception. The Kansas-Nebraska Act threatened to break a longstanding provision in the 1820 Missouri Compromise that expressly barred slavery from those territories. Douglas had become a shill for the Southern "Slave Power" that was plotting to rob free laborers of their western birthright and seize power in Washington, DC. The prospect of the bill's passage amounted to nothing short of a national emergency.[12]

Greeley was well positioned to sound the alarm. Though the *Times* and the *Herald* outsold the *Tribune* in New York City, the latter's fast-growing weekly edition gave it a large audience beyond the metropolis. With a subscriber base extending from New England to the Upper Midwest, Greeley's voice boomed across the North. In the still largely local world of midcentury America, he was a rare figure who transcended boundaries through mass journalism. This stature did not escape those who shared Greeley's revulsion to the Kansas-Nebraska Bill and its enactment. Early Republican Party organizer Alvan Bovay reminded Greeley that his paper was "a power in the land" and urged him to use the *Tribune* to rally the North, lest it be "engulfed by Slavery." Eli Thayer, the founder of the New England Emigrant Aid Company, likewise pressed Greeley to use his "paper of world wide circulation & usefulness" to encourage Yankee migration to Kansas.[13]

Greeley put the full force of the *Tribune* into resisting the proposed legislation. From the moment the "Neb-Rascal Bill" came out of committee in January of 1854, he and his lieutenants limned its monstrosities in fine-grain detail. More broadly, though, the paper embraced a frankly sectional politics to rally "the North" and "Northern Freemen" to defeat the measure. In Greeley's view, the breakup of the old parties offered few alternatives.

Amid their scattering wreckage, he looked for answers not in the remains of the old Whig organization, but instead in a broader idea of the North— one that could rally together the Free Soilers, anti-slavery "conscience" Whigs, anti-slavery Democrats, and would-be nativists horrified at "the Slave Power's" latest and most brazen scheme. Never mind that it had been Douglas who had introduced the bill or that fifty-four Northerners would eventually vote to pass it. In the *Tribune*, the fight over the Kansas-Nebraska Bill would be a sectional struggle between North and South for national control.[14]

But what was the North? In many ways, the unified region that Greeley invoked through the winter of 1853 and the spring of 1854 represented an aspiration rather than a reality. In contrast to the South, which was easily imagined as a westward-marching phalanx of masters and their slaves, the North eluded definition. Six years earlier, in the throes of the debate over territories won in the Mexican War, Daniel Webster had addressed this in what was to become a famous speech. "We talk of the North," he said at Marshfield, Massachusetts. "There has for a long time been no North. I think the North Star is at last discovered. I think there will be a North."[15] As Greeley understood it in the face of the Kansas-Nebraska Bill, Webster's tentative decree had been premature. Speaking on his annual winter lecture tour, Greeley offered a grim assessment to a Boston audience in March: "The slaveholders show a united Southern feeling. Where [is] the Northern sentiment which [can] meet and withstand them?" In truth, Greeley said, "there is no real, effective North, antagonistic to the slaveholding South." The North Star had been lost, and to stop "the Slave Power," it would need to be found. The answer, then, was to *"make a North*, a nucleus in which true principles of freedom shall be held, and the rights of man practically acknowledged, then to enlarge that area of freedom."[16]

The job of "making a North" was one of intimidating dimensions. For all of the *Tribune*'s rousing coverage of the region's outrage, Greeley was even more pessimistic in his private correspondence than he had been in his Boston speech. "I have little faith in principle of the North," he told Schuyler Colfax. The people were not "ripe" for "Northern emancipation," he remarked to Alvan Bovay. To both, he suggested that Yankees' busy pursuit of gain rendered them fatally indifferent to the threats of the Kansas-Nebraska

Bill and the moral problems of slavery. "Beaten, broken-down, used-up . . . with the soreness of many defeats in my bones," he even offered a weary assessment of his own limitations: "Remember that editors can only follow where the people's heart is already prepared to go with them. They can direct and animate a healthy public indignation, but not 'create a soul beneath the ribs of Death.' "[17] It hardly helped that within the Northern press, rival editors were quick to point out just how slippery the idea of "the North" was, and how transparent the *Tribune*'s efforts were to portray it. As James Gordon Bennett's *New-York Herald* noted, Greeley and his paper were not merely "seeking to arouse a fanatical excitement against slavery." They were also "anxious to make it appear that the North was hostile to the Nebraska Bill . . . to make it appear that the North was unanimous."[18]

Bennett's *Herald* wasn't entirely wrong. Through the winter of 1853 and the spring of 1854, a steady drumbeat for Northern unity rattled from the columns of the *Tribune*. Initially, this work focused less on forming a new "Fusion Party" (though that goal would emerge eventually) and more on shaping anti–Kansas-Nebraska Bill protests into a single movement—to "direct and animate a healthy public indignation." If Greeley didn't have firm faith in "the principle of the North," *Tribune* readers would hardly have known it. Daily and weekly, claims such as "the unanimous sentiment of the North is indignant resistance" filled the paper, while each and every anti–Kansas-Nebraska Bill meeting received ample treatment. The effect was to amplify "THE VOICE OF THE NORTH," ringing from Portland (Maine) to Chicago and beyond. The strength of those rallies, the eloquence of their oratory, the sober good order of their attendees—all stood out as a powerful affirmation: here was the North. "Southern oligarchs and northern doughfaces," as one *Tribune* report declared, should take note, as "the North is not to be trifled with." "Making a North," then, was largely a media-driven endeavor—one of "Intelligence," information, and ideas. Here, on a sectional scale, were the same tactics that had once defined Greeley's visions for national consensus.[19]

In the short term, the effect of this coverage was mostly directed at Washington, DC. There, Greeley's correspondent James Pike worked between the internal machinations at the Capitol and the voice of the North emanating from the *Tribune*. If members of Congress were made aware of the extent of Northern outrage, they could ensure the delay and defeat of the Kansas-Nebraska Bill. As Pike told Maine senator William Pitt Fessenden, "the bill must be kept in the Senate as long as possible. Meanwhile, hell must be raised in the North. The ear of Congress is open. It must be deafened with a roar of condemnation."[20]

If a unified North could rally—or at least be rallied—against the Kansas-Nebraska Bill, sitting congressmen would have to obey the will of the people. The *Tribune*, it was hoped, would be a potent force in maintaining Northern loyalties in Washington. To some, it appeared to be doing just that. Elihu Washburne of Illinois told Pike that his paper was "the terror of all traitorous scoundrels here. . . . The rascals stand about the hotels, trembling when the newsboys come in with the Tribune." As the debate heated up through the spring of 1854, Pike remained in active correspondence with members working to defeat the bill. Maine congressman Israel Washburn underscored the hope that the *Tribune* would enforce sectional unity in the face of the bill: "Pray you admonish Northern members that such as show the white feather will be exposed; they are watched." Meanwhile, Lewis Campbell of Ohio testified to the power and reach of the paper when he complained to Pike that his constituents "seem quite passive" in the face of the threatened legislation. "Can't you stir them up?" he asked.[21]

Within the *Tribune*, the campaign to "make the North" operated with varying degrees of subtlety. While some of the paper's content offered cool explanation, the better part of it bellowed at high volume. Panting editorial philippics summoned "NORTHERN FREEMEN!" and subjected them to long rhetorical interrogations: "Can no measure of national legislation pass without first paying an exorbitant toll of human suffering and human life? Cannot a free people sit down to eat the fruit of their honest industry without having the foul harpies of oppression enter and pollute their banquet?" The same Northern freemen—sturdy men who did honest work—were directed to see the "brutal degradation of all Mechanical and Laboring Men, white and black, in the United States" and the "contempt which is thrown on the very nature and life of the laborer by the slave system." Southerners, one editorial claimed, would soon buy and sell Northern farmers and mechanics, if they could. The Kansas-Nebraska Bill left the fate of the country teetering in the balance, and only Northern freemen could save it.[22]

The South came in for its share of abuse as a source of negative affirmation, since its votes had already been considered lost. The *Tribune* revived the longstanding idea that the Southern states were physical and moral wastelands—their farms, fields, and people blighted by slavery. Virginia, "once the leader in our politics, once the loud trumpeter of the Rights of Man" and "the birthplace of Washington," had now been "sunk to the level of a mere negro-breeding territory." To supplement the usual editorial fare, staffers were put to work scouring the Southern exchange papers for fresh outrages. If the *Tribune*'s existing "Facts of Slavery" series was not lurid enough, additional color could be found in reprints of ads seeking runaway slaves, fire-eating editorials, reports of casual violence, and a notice that "the celebrated PACK OF NEGRO DOGS" of Marshall, Texas, was available for rent to hunt down fugitives. The methods were not subtle, the ideas were not new, but the contrasts were important, in order to make a coherent North and create sectional differences.[23]

The campaign's more measured moments added some ballast to these emotional appeals. With the Kansas-Nebraska Bill's fate still hanging in the balance, Greeley collaborated with economist Henry Carey on a series of articles examining the relative value of these sections to the nation as a whole. An 1850 pamphlet out of Charleston, South Carolina, *The Union, Past and Future*, had argued that the North was utterly dependent upon the South and had no choice but to satisfy Southern demands. Greeley certainly agreed with the proposition that "the South dictates the policy of the whole Union." But the idea—the error, as Greeley judged it—that "the prosperity of the North is due to its connection with the South" needed to be corrected.[24] Out of a thicket of population statistics, trade tables, economic data, and some sharp commentary, a comprehensive argument emerged: the North, not the South, was the nation's great engine, and Free Labor was its fuel. The North's dramatic population growth, its orderly expansion, its growing commerce and industry, came in spite of—not because of—the South and its doughfaced Northern enablers. That cabal had thwarted a protective tariff, blocked the Pacific Railroad, voted down river and harbor improvements, and killed homestead legislation. Moreover, their expansionist designs had saddled the nation with a host of expenses: a costly war, a bloated diplomatic corps, a standing army, and a lavish navy that was little more than "a floating House of Lords." That the North had grown dramatically in spite of such fetters was a testament to the power of Free Labor to develop resources and improve society. The reasons were simple: "Freedom [was] attractive and slavery [was] repulsive. Men of activity and intelligence [sought] the free states," while the South was ruled by "slave-oligarchs" and "poor white trash" who shared a common contempt for labor.[25]

It hardly mattered whether the editorials (which were sold in pamphlet form as *The North and the South*) presented a winning response to the original Southern pamphlet. The quarrel was engaged less directly with the easily vilified South than with those within the North who failed to see the great virtue of their own region. The "slave-oligarchs" were indeed a dangerous element within the nation at large, but perhaps even more so were the Northern doughfaces like Stephen A. Douglas (a lost son of Vermont), who enabled them. Southerners would continue to dominate national politics and institutions as long as a divided North allowed them to. As a "breed," those doughfaces who would "raffle off freedom" needed to be extirpated: "Break every man of them upon the wheel, and sow salt upon the ground that grows them. There is no other remedy." More broadly, however, the great mass of common Northerners—especially those workingmen who too often lent their support to doughfaced Democrats—would have to vindicate the North's honor, and the nation's, in the process. Politically, this meant speaking to "the Workingmen of the North to rouse them from their imbruted lethargy" and prying them away from their longstanding party affiliations. Ideologically, it meant inviting them into a grand vision of the North as the final bastion of Free Labor. Though the Free Soil movement suggested possibilities in this regard, the scope of the Kansas-Nebraska Bill's threat called for something much larger and more enduring. Even if the precise shape of the new political coalition was hardly clear in the spring of 1854, its outlines could already be seen in both the high and low manifestations of the *Tribune*'s campaign to "make a North."[26]

Some Simple Name like "Republican"

The North was not "made" in the spring of 1854, however. In quick succession that May, the Kansas-Nebraska Act became law and federal authorities returned the celebrated fugitive Anthony Burns to slavery in Virginia. While "the Slave Power" demonstrated its reach far into the North, a vast portion of the West had been opened up to slavery with the votes of fifty-four Northern members of Congress and the signature of a Northern president. Greeley reached a new level of indignation. Southern firebrands weren't quite calling the roll of their slaves at the foot of Bunker Hill, but they were getting closer. There was much work to be done.

Through the remainder of 1854 and up to the 1856 elections, the task turned to creating a pan-Northern anti-slavery party—one that would unite splintering political factions and bridge fierce local loyalties. Amid the ongoing resistance to the Kansas-Nebraska legislation, Greeley had expressed the need for a new Northern party of freedom, but only vaguely. He never explicitly endorsed the growing movement for a new "Republican" party beyond its local manifestations, in spite of the entreaties of some of the early organizers. Greeley had previously demurred because he believed that the Northern public was not ready. First, Northern unity needed to be rallied, and Northern minds needed to be enlightened before he could take such a step. The party could come later.

But now he could wait no longer. In June of 1854, Greeley began sounding the call for "fusion" in the *Tribune*. If allegiances to old parties and organizations were enabling the extension of slavery into the West and the consolidation of "the Slave Power" in Washington, DC, it was time to form a new party. Building on the efforts of organizers in the *Tribune* regions of the Upper Midwest, Greeley suggested "some simple name like 'Republican.'" This, he said, would "fitly designate those . . . united to restore our Union to its true mission of champion . . . of Liberty rather than propagandist of Slavery." Whatever it was called, this would be a new kind of party. It must "embody and give effect to enlightened Public Sentiment" and not be built on the compromises and contradictions that had doomed the old parties. In New York State, the process would begin with a fusion convention, to be held in Saratoga in August.[27]

The Empire State would be critical for this new, Northern anti-slavery coalition. As the most populous and politically diverse state in the Union, a Republican New York could energize the fledgling movement in the Midwest and lead neighboring New England states out of the darkness of nativism. Greeley thought he had the key to success: yoking anti-slavery to the growing movement for alcohol prohibition. A strong stand against slavery and its expansion would attract progressive Whigs and Free Soilers; temperance reform would lure conservatives flirting with nativism. Though Greeley believed that this coalition might well vault him into the governor's mansion in Albany, his vision encompassed more than bare political calculation and personal ambition. To him, anti-slavery and anti-rum stood as the foundation on which to make the North and restore the nation. In his long-held view, "the Slave Power" and "Demon Rum" were in league—merely different sectional expressions of the same vicious plot to denigrate labor, undermine industry, and extend the political power of false political leaders. When the sober and industrious freemen of the North united to oust the forces of vice at home, it was only a matter of time before they would vanquish those forces in the South and the West. They would remake the nation in their own image.[28]

The fall campaigns in New York State, though, would reveal the stubborn obstacles standing in the way of a pan-sectional Republican Party. The vision of Northern unity rising from the *Tribune* through the first half of the summer of 1854 was grand and energizing, but then it was gone. Around the middle of July, the barrage of editorials calling for a dry North, a free West, and a redeemed nation ceased. When Greeley broke the *Tribune*'s silence on the subject, he explained, without much conviction, that he saw "no indications that the great body of anti-Nebraska voters of our State are prepared for this step." He said no more about it until the eve of the meeting in Saratoga, which had been downgraded from a full fusion convention into two separate rallies, one for temperance reform, and the other against slavery and the Kansas-Nebraska Act. Responding to criticism that the *Tribune* had failed to "evince sufficient zeal in behalf of the Convention," Greeley halfheartedly claimed that fusion was a matter for those present to decide. The truth, though, was that the decision had already been made.[29]

Local and personal interests had trumped the broader vision for sectional unity. Not for the first time, and not for the last, Thurlow Weed and William Henry Seward had squelched Greeley's plans. When Greeley said that New York's anti–Kansas-Nebraska Act voters weren't ready for fusion, he meant that Weed and Seward weren't ready. Weed had too much capital invested in the old New York Whig machinery to see it liquidated. Seward was up for reelection to the US Senate and was wary of taking his chances in a legisla-ture disordered by partisan realignment. Both worried that a fusion con-vention might end with a gubernatorial nomination for Greeley. Given Greeley's colorful stint in Congress, neither had much faith in his capacities for any political office, much less the governorship. Weed traveled from Albany to Gotham to persuade his junior partner privately that his plans would do no good for the state. Publicly, Weed threw his weight behind another temperance candidate, to ensure that Greeley wouldn't be on the ticket in any capacity—not even as lieutenant governor. That Greeley acqui-esced is a measure of both his support for Seward in the Senate and his acceptance of Weed's continued power to command what was left of New York's Whig Party.[30]

Greeley braced for a season of humiliation and compromise. Carrying the water for Weed, Seward, and the Whigs began with the unenviable task of dousing the fires of the Republican movement in the state. Greeley would have to preside over the now toothless meetings in Saratoga—Weed denied his request for a reprieve from this duty—and then throw his support be-hind the Whig ticket. The indignities only mounted through the fall cam-paigns. Weed advanced Greeley's bitter rival, Henry Jarvis Raymond of the *New-York Times*, for lieutenant governor—a nomination that Greeley had coveted as a boon for the *Tribune*. Meanwhile, to stanch the flow of conser-vative Whigs into the ranks of nativism, Weed tacked the party toward the right. If the alternative was supporting Democrats, Greeley had no choice but to fall in line. "I believe Weed has secured a Seward assembly," he told a friend, but at a high cost: "Some of those he relies on are red-mouthed Know-Nothings. . . . This is just the most scoundrelly canvass that I ever was engaged in. I feel a crawling all over on account of it." New York had wasted the chance to lead the North into a new sectional political alignment capable of standing up to the South.[31]

The fall campaigns offered a cruel repeat of the lesson from the Kansas-Nebraska crisis: there was no real, effective North. Weed and the New York-ers who complied with him had shown that politically, the North was less a unified region than a patchwork of local interests and organizations. Greeley straddled two paradigms—supporting the Whig ticket in New York, while cheering the Republican movement elsewhere. It was an awkward stance that told the larger story of the North's failure. As he wrote privately, it would "tell heavily against us that we carry all the states Whig that we can and go 'fusion' where we can do no better." As the election period neared its conclusion, Greeley began venting jets of steam. "Messrs. Wire workers and nominating conventions," he announced, "your humble journalists ... do not and will not always wait to groan 'til after the election." To anyone with "discerning vision," it was clear that "old party distinctions were superseded and unmeaning." The Free States would ultimately "triumph under a banner bearing on its folds the REPUBLICAN name, and consecrated to the advancement of Temperance and Freedom." That the colors had been struck in New York had been the result of "selfishness and short-sighted expediency" and "want of courage and common sense" among those who refused to "abdicate [their] personal consequence" in the existing party machinery.[32]

When the race was over, New York's voters had duly elected a pro-Seward legislature and a Whig governor, and voters across the North had elected a tentative anti–Kansas-Nebraska Act majority in Congress, but Greeley was incensed. Stubborn adherence to local interests had had grave consequences for the North and the nation. Without a Republican Party in the contest, the election had been "the play of Hamlet, with Hamlet not only omitted but forgotten." It had also been a terrible waste of William Henry Seward's potential to be a national leader of the new party. "The man who should have impelled and guided the general uprising of the Free States lives in Auburn," Greeley raged. Instead, Seward had "adher[ed] to the vacant shell of Whiggery" and "allowed the great movement of the Free States to go forward without a word of bold and hearty encouragement or sympathy from its national leader."[33] In high dudgeon, Greeley wrote to Seward, announcing "the dissolution of the political firm of Seward, Weed, and Greeley, by the withdrawal of the junior partner." The rest of the letter was an invoice of sorts—a meticulous accounting of every slight and snub that he had endured since 1837. Greeley would pass through several more stages of grief as he fully processed the disastrous election, but when he calmed down (and Seward had been duly reelected to the US Senate by the state legislature), he announced his final political independence. "The struggle is over," Greeley told a friend. "I am no longer anybody's partisan."[34]

The political season of 1855 proved to be no more fruitful than those of 1854, as nativism and the vestiges of Whiggery again blighted expected Republican harvests in the North. With Greeley off in Europe through the spring and summer of 1855, James Pike and *Tribune* managing editor Charles Dana continued to stoke "the great smouldering volcano of northern sentiment" and commenced a merciless "war of extinction against northern doughfaces." In June, they went after nativists directly. They sent a correspondent to infiltrate the Know-Nothing convention in Philadelphia for the purpose of exposing rifts over slavery among nativists. When antislavery Know-Nothings had been cast from the convention, the *Tribune*'s correspondent crowed, "Thank God! There is a North at last." Weed and Seward, meanwhile, warmed to the idea of fusion in the summer of 1855 and began pushing New York Whigs into line with other Northern states. "That Northern Republican party which may yet give peace to the nation and redeem it from [its] cankers and shames" was taking shape.[35]

Or so it seemed. Election results in the fall of 1855 were again dispiriting. Nativist candidates triumphed in New York and across the Northeast, in spite of the *Tribune*'s continued appeals to Northern unity amid the creeping influence of slavery. Late in the canvass, Greeley lamented, "Many thousands of our thoroughly Free-Soil men are ensnared by the [nativist] lodges and [are] made to grind in the prison-house of Slavery." As had been the case in 1854, local issues and local organizations expressed through nativism had trumped broader sectional and national concerns. As a Massachusetts man wrote to Charles Sumner, the Republicans had made their appeals based on issues of national interest, "while the officers of this election were all . . . state and local[,] [y]ou cannot bring the principles of national Politics *fully* to bear on State elections."[36]

Racist attacks on "Black Republicans" also suggested the ways in which the party's anti-slavery identity limited its broader appeal. In the fall, Bennett's *Herald* led the way with charges of "negro worship," "amalgamation," and "mingling together for Uncle Tom and the public plunder."[37] In a harbinger of his Reconstruction-era conservatism, Greeley stooped low to meet the charges. To clear away the taint of radicalism and racial egalitarianism, he offered "unpalatable counsel" to white abolitionists on the limitations of their movement, and to free blacks on the proper path to equality.

Both groups would be best served by tempering their political zeal and focusing their efforts elsewhere. "Present agitation," Greeley said, had the harmful result of "exposing popular odium to the Whites engaged in it"—and, by extension, to the whites engaged in the fight against "the Slave Power" more broadly. Radical abolitionists—white and black—should leave the political work to mainstream white politicians.[38]

With the election year of 1856 looming—the first in which the Republicans would field a candidate—the glue of popular anti-slavery politics still had not set, and the North remained unmade. In the face of these challenges, Greeley urged *Tribune* readers to fix their gaze on events beyond their immediate communities. He directed them to Kansas and Washington, DC, where separate sectional struggles over slavery and the fate of the nation were unfolding. In Kansas, the practical workings of popular sovereignty were turning violent, while in Washington, the prospect of a Republican majority in Congress put the nation's capital on knife edge. At a far remove from Kansas, and at the center of events in Washington, Greeley helped frame a new perspective on national politics rooted in sectional conflict.

The News from Kansas Is Helping Us

Bleeding Kansas was a media event. It was born on the plains, but it was reared in newspapers. The remote territory and its tumults existed primarily in Americans' imaginations. As David Potter wrote, "For purposes of understanding what took place in the nation, it is possibly less important to know what happened in Kansas than to know what the American public thought was happening in Kansas."[39] No editor—and no newspaper in the country—were more important in driving popular perceptions of what was happening in Kansas than Greeley and the *Tribune*. If settlers on the ground made Kansas bleed as they battled over the future status of slavery there, Greeley and his staff helped make "Bleeding Kansas," and they did so with expediencies far removed from Kansas in mind. The narrative of western conflict they spun was rooted in the larger struggle to rally the North around popular anti-slavery politics. In Kansas, the *Tribune* found a compelling form of Northern anti-slavery politics taking place—one rooted in the heroic actions of white men.[40]

Greeley did not set foot in Kansas until 1859, but he was deeply involved in events there in the mid-1850s. From the first stirrings of the Kansas-Nebraska Bill early in 1854, Greeley understood the doctrine of popular sovereignty as a form of competitive settlement: Kansas would be won or lost with numbers.[41] Following the passage of the Kansas-Nebraska Bill, the *Tribune* quickly became a clearinghouse for practical information about the far-off territories—"the most accurate" any "emigrant thither" could find. More broadly, though, it depicted an irresistible movement. Greeley, an investor and shareholder in Eli Thayer's New England Emigrant Aid Society, tirelessly flogged the "great mission of colonizing Kansas with a free population" as one "clothed with the moral power, enjoying the confidence, and wielding the pecuniary resources of the whole body of Anti-Slavery men in the North." Within weeks of the New England Emigrant Aid Company's incorporation, Greeley predicted a tide of 20,000 emigrants or more—"let them crowd in"—flooding the Kansas plains with their "energy and native intelligence." He suggested that some enterprising soul might cash in by selling a pocket map, as sturdy Northern men were on the move.[42]

Amid the uncertain political shifts of the mid-1850s, Greeley, the *Tribune*, and its correspondents would help shape events in the far-off territories into the compelling national drama of Bleeding Kansas. Popular sovereignty in action unfolded in the paper's tiny typeface as clashing civilizations—North versus South, and freedom versus slavery—with the nation's fate as the prize. "Kansas is to-day the Crimea of liberty," *Tribune* correspondent James Pike wrote in a typical volley, referencing the war then raging in Europe. "If it falls, no man can tell when the tide of invasion will be rolled back." Yankee settlers arrived on the scene as heirs to the Pilgrims and Puritans, bringing with them industry, sober good order, churches, schools, mills, and farms managed according to the best methods. The Southerners they encountered were a violent, boozy lot, swilling whiskey, spitting tobacco, waving Bowie knives and pistols, and subverting the democratic process. The stakes could not have been higher. As one Kansas correspondent exhorted emigrants, "Go forward in your fearless manner—you are working out results that will shape the future of the Government of this Country."[43]

The story didn't always comport with the reality of events on the ground. There were far fewer New Englanders present and far more instances of cooperation among settlers of different backgrounds than the newspaper coverage suggested. Conflict was often rooted less in differences over slavery than in disputes over land claims.[44] But there was violence and drama enough, and in both direct and indirect ways, Greeley and his correspondents staged events to fit a narrative of civilizations clashing over slavery. As an investor in the New England Emigrant Aid Company and a vocal promoter of Kansas "colonization," Greeley had already helped in a small way to populate the plains with the kind of people who would become the heroes of the *Tribune*'s coverage. Moreover, Greeley helped raise funds for the purchase and shipment of weapons—the famous Sharps rifles that became key props in the conflict.[45]

Tensions erupted in Kansas amid the setbacks and broader challenges facing the Republican movement heading into the winter of 1855–1856. Reeling from the reversals in the fall elections and looking ahead to a hotly contested fight for Speaker of the House in the upcoming congressional session set to convene in Washington, DC, Greeley and his staff turned up the volume on Kansas coverage. After Free State settlers drafted an anti-slavery constitution in the fall of 1855, reports swirled of illicit weapons shipments pouring in from the East and secret militias gathering in the anti-slavery stronghold of Lawrence, Kansas. Affairs on the "Wakarusa War" neared the brink. In quick succession in late November, one Free State settler was killed and another was arrested by a pro-slavery sheriff, only to be rescued by a vigilante group. In the ensuing standoff, posses of Missouri "Border Ruffians" and Free State forces pledged their readiness for battle. Pro-slavery men vowed that Lawrence would "soon cease to be a habitable place." Free State settlers dedicated themselves to the defense of their "wives and homes . . . to the last extremity." Tense as the standoff was, it never moved beyond bluster and braggadocio, however. Pro-slavery governor William Shannon quietly brokered a deal with Free State leaders and disbanded the irregular militias ready to lay waste to Lawrence. For the time being, disaster had been averted.[46]

From the scattered reports trickling eastward, *Tribune* editors amplified the quiet drama into the "Wakarusa War"—by their account, a resounding victory for the Free State settlers. In the story that unfolded in correspondence and editorials, Northern men on the Kansas plains had accomplished what Northern voters and their representatives to the East had been unable to do up to that point. They had stood up "manfully" to the drunken, pro-slavery brutes with "bludgeons and Bowie-Knives" who threatened their settlements, the territory, and, more broadly, the nation at large. Their order, their organization, their resolve, their upright masculinity, even their weaponry—the vaunted Sharps rifles—had demonstrated to pro-slavery Kansans and their Border-Ruffian allies the full moral and technical superiority of Northern civilization. Northern men elsewhere should take note, lest they cede more power to Southerners and their doughfaced enablers. Greeley was confident they would. Writing to *Tribune* managing editor Charles Dana early in December, he noted plainly, "The news from Kansas is helping us."[47]

The timing was fortuitous. With word of the Wakarusa standoff trickling eastward, another was taking shape in Washington, DC. The Thirty-Fourth US Congress, set to convene in December, had a tentative anti–Kansas-Nebraska Act, anti-administration majority. But far from being a confident phalanx of Yankees, like the rifle-toting Kansas settlers, this was a ragtag army of old Free Soil Democrats, conservative Whigs gone nativist, and emergent Republicans. Could they unite behind a Speaker of the House, consolidating a Northern majority? Signs pointed to a protracted struggle. In the opening vote for Speaker, seventeen different names crowded the ballot. Even when Nathaniel P. Banks, a Massachusetts Republican who had wandered into the party more by calculation than conviction, emerged as a favorite, a handful of holdouts kept the Speaker's gavel out of his reach. The deadlock would persist through two months and dozens of ballots.[48]

With tales of Northern heroism in Kansas larding the columns of the *Tribune*, Greeley intended to make a show of Northern unity in Washington, DC. He had traveled there to observe and influence the fight for Speaker of the House—to "watch events as well as help to mature them," as one newspaper put it. He took rooms at the National Hotel, opened an account at the telegraph office, and went to work with the assurance that his presence would enforce loyalty to the North. "I hate this hole," he confessed to Charles Dana soon after his arrival, "but I am glad I have come. It does me good to see how those who hate the Tribune much, fear it yet more. There are a dozen here who will do better for my eye being on them." As the session sputtered forward without a Speaker, Greeley wrote daily accounts detailing the treachery of those Northern holdouts denying the prize to Banks. The contrast between the Kansas settlers and the weak-kneed Northern representatives could not have been clearer.[49]

Operating as a sectional enforcer and the human embodiment of the most pro-Northern paper in the country, Greeley could not avoid playing some role in the drama himself. From the moment he arrived, his presence in the nation's capital had excited everything from humorous comment to outright hostility. "No man in Washington attracts more attention," one paper noted. A joke that made its way into seemingly every rag in the country that winter had a trio of Irish waiters gazing at the constellation of personages before them in the National Hotel's lobby. When one pointed out Greeley, another was surprised that the editor of the *New-York Tribune* was white: "I've bin deceived in the ould fellow intirely. . . . I thought he was a *nagur* [sic]," the punch line went. More gravely, though, Greeley's status and visibility made him a target for aggression. A Virginia editor wasted no time in accosting Greeley early in the session. After demanding an introduction in the lobby of the National, the Virginian, who was said to be very drunk, began cursing and lunging at Greeley. Only the intervention of another New York correspondent stopped a general melee, though, as one account had it, "there [would] be war here yet," so long as Greeley was on hand. Indeed, Greeley would not escape the session without suffering another physical confrontation loaded with sectional meaning.[50]

With the Speaker deadlock still dragging on late in January of 1856, Albert Rust, an Arkansas Democrat, accosted Greeley in the streets between the Capitol and the National Hotel. In one of his dispatches, Greeley had condemned Rust's resolution in the House to force all existing Speaker candidates to withdraw from the race as the most "discreditable proposition . . . ever . . . submitted to a legislative body." Stinging from the insult and flanked by an entourage of Southerners, Rust sought satisfaction in a duel. Greeley's dismissive tone sent Rust into a rage. He attacked Greeley twice, first with his fists, then with his cane. In both instances, bystanders spared Greeley a more severe beating.[51]

Though shaken by the attacks, Greeley wasted no time in casting himself alongside the Kansas crusaders, standing up in the face of violence, intimidation, and boozy provocation. Newspaper reports captured him undaunted on the night of the attack, writing away at his hotel desk with his head and arm wrapped in wet cloths. Southern reports delighted in Rust's "genteel flogging of Mr. Greeley," as the *Tribune*'s "Negro Philosopher" had been served his due, and justly so.[52] "Border Ruffianism" had come to Washington, DC, Greeley said. He would surely be subject to further outrages, but he would push on. He might "judge harshly," but he would do so "in plain speech" and in good faith. "I came here with a clear understanding that it was about an even chance whether I should or should not be allowed to go home alive," he wrote. "My business here is to unmask hypocrisy, defeat treachery, and rebuke meanness, and these are not dainty employments even in [other] times than ours." Though the means were painful, Greeley had made a show of just how closely connected were the twin dramas of Kansas and of national politics in Washington, DC.[53]

The presidential election of 1856 would help make those connections even clearer. Not long after Rust's attack, the deadlock finally broke and Banks won the speakership. Banks's election was an important moment for the Republican Party, but it was a conditional victory. As attention shifted to the upcoming presidential race, the party's broader prospects remained foggy. The persistence of the Know-Nothings across the Northeast suggested that many Northern voters continued to worry more about liquor, immigrants, and Catholicism than slavery and western territories. Would they abandon the Northern approach?

The Republican Party's first presidential election presented a novel challenge: how would a movement rooted in sectional struggle compete in a national campaign? The question would provide an easy line of attack for rival Democrats. As a York, Pennsylvania, paper put it, "the Democracy" represented "the whole American people," while Republicans "look forward to the day when the country may itself be torn into fragments and sections."[54]

Greeley believed he had answers. At an organizing convention for the party in February, he articulated an emerging article of faith among Republicans: their party was not sectional, but national. All white Americans—even Southerners—could embrace their policies. "If the Southern people fairly understand us," Greeley said, "I am sure we should have a strong, if not the strongest party in every Slave State." The Republican Party remained

committed to the ostensibly anti-Southern policies of halting the west-
ward march of slavery and breaking "the Slave Power's" hold on national
government. But it would only be a matter of time before Southerners realized that Republicans just wanted to ensure their section's "delivery from a
fearful incubus, and her rapid advancement in all the arts of civilization and
peace."[55] Greeley had already communicated this message to Dana, urging
him to tamp down the sectional fires burning on the *Tribune*'s editorial page.
There should be no more articles "calculated to incite intense aversion to
us at the South," Greeley said. "Southrons" must know that "we foment
Abolition as a means of . . . regenerating and upbuilding" their section, not
to "weaken and destroy it."[56]

National appeal became central to the Republican campaign in 1856.
Well before the party's June nominating convention, Greeley joined the
movement for western explorer and Mexican War veteran John C. Frémont
over anti-slavery stalwarts like William Henry Seward and Ohio governor
Salmon Chase. Though Frémont was, in Greeley's estimation, "the merest
baby in politics,"[57] he had much to recommend him as a national figure
capable of transcending the party's sectional base. "The Pathfinder" (as
Frémont was known) carried the romance of far western adventure—a
mystique enhanced by his good looks and marriage to Jessie Benton, daughter of Missouri statesman Thomas Hart Benton. But more importantly,
together "Frémont and Jessie" embodied the notion that Republican ideas
—including opposition to slavery—were consonant with the concepts of
Union and the nation. John had been born and educated in Georgia and
South Carolina and had family ties to Virginia elites. Jessie had been raised
in a slaveholding family and had been navigating the politics of slavery in
the West her whole life.[58]

Greeley and the *Tribune* played a central role in diffusing this image of
Frémont and Jessie as models for the Republican Party's national appeal.
Frémont, Greeley told a friend, could head a ticket "that would be truly
National," garnering support in "Massachusetts and Kentucky, the East and
West; the Free and the Slave, the Old and the New."[59] Such was the message
of the *Tribune*'s coverage of the party convention and canvass, as well as the
cheap biography that went out in bulk under the Greeley & McElrath im-
print. Frémont's exploits were those of a truly national character (an idea

underscored by the honorary sword presented by the citizens of Charleston, South Carolina, to Frémont in 1846); his views were an expression not of a radical sectional movement, but one rooted in the principles of "WASHINGTON AND JEFFERSON." Greeley was pleased. He had helped choose the party's candidate and framed the moderate, national platform on which he was running. "Something in my bones," Greeley said, "tells me that Frémont is to be the next president."[60]

There were sectional wrinkles in the Republican Party's national blueprint, however. As much as Greeley and other party architects believed they were drawing plans for the entire country, they did so from the thoroughly Northern perspective that had been central to the Republican organization, going back to 1854. They were, simultaneously, committed nationalists and inveterate Northerners, bent on transplanting their values and institutions to the untamed provinces. The party was a society for the propagation of a Northern gospel. Just as many Republicans dreamed of "colonizing" Kansas and the West with industrious Yankees, so, too, did they imagine missionary efforts among the Southern yeomanry. These were Yankees-in-waiting, dormant for generations under the spell of the planter class and needing only the Republicans' clarion call to awaken them to the virtues of sustained toil, scientific agriculture, and education.

The narrative of sectional struggle was inseparable from the party's national vision. Even those attempts to cast Republicans as genuinely national could not escape sectional strife in one form or another. Greeley's campaign biography of Frémont did indeed portray the Pathfinder as a national hero— one who, in Frémont's own words in the frontispiece, would "administer the government . . . in such a way as to preserve Liberty and Union." But the book also included a copy of the map "Freedom and Slavery, and the Coveted Territories" inside the back cover. Greeley joined Abraham Lincoln and other Republicans in arguing that the country's founders had seen opposition to slavery as central to the national project, but even that story was peppered with sectional strife. Greeley's campaign pamphlet, *A History of the Struggle for Slavery Extension or Restriction in the United States*, suggested that the sectional conflict for liberty was as old as European life in North America. The "CAVALIERS" who settled Virginia had been contemptuous of liberty and honest toil, "gentlemen adventurers aspiring to live by their own wits and other men's labor." The story had been different in the North, where "the fires of liberty burned brightest and earliest," first in Massachusetts and then throughout the region.[61]

More immediately, though, one need not look far—certainly not too far into any edition of the *Tribune*—to see this same narrative of sectional struggle unfolding in real time in 1856. As the election season began and events in Kansas and Washington, DC, remained entangled, images of clashing civilizations vying for national control were everywhere. In late February, not long after Greeley had made his plea for a gentler, more national Republican Party, he was back in the nation's capital to witness New Hampshire senator John P. Hale's fiery exchange with a Southern colleague over Kansas. In what Greeley commended as "the speech of his life," Hale defended Northern honor in response to the Southerner's charges of "northern aggression" and threats of "war to the knife, and the knife to the hilt": "Sir, Puritan blood has not always shrunk, even from these encounters . . . the steel has sometimes glistened in their hands; and, when the battle was over, they were not always found second best."[62] Greeley himself claimed to be at the ready for sectional tangles in the wake of the Rust attack. Upon hearing word that "Drunken Bowie of Maryland was threatening [him] in the barrooms," Greeley told Charles Dana, "We are making up a fighting party of northern men that will ultimately do good. Several pistols will be bought to-day."[63]

Events and the rhetoric that went with them only intensified as winter became spring. Kansas had produced two different constitutions and sent two separate territorial delegates to Washington, DC. Newspapers continued to relay conflicting but equally alarming accounts of what was happening in the troubled territory. Anti-slavery papers reported ruffian forces arraying for a fresh round of outrages. The Southern and pro-slavery press conjured masses of Yankee fanatics riding swollen spring rivers to Kansas to "abolitionize" the territory. Not surprisingly, a congressional commission sent to Kansas in April seeking answers and resolution found nothing but irreconcilable narratives. The nation's capital was hardly the place to sort out the confusion. If members of Congress continued to maintain cordial private relationships with one another, their public stances and pronouncements on Kansas—all of which were generously covered by the press—broadcasted images of a governing class increasingly riven by sectional difference.[64] The *Tribune* certainly played its part. As Greeley left the area in April, James S. Pike, known for his incendiary sectional pronouncements, resumed his duties as the paper's main Washington, DC, correspondent. Grim statements of sectional strife and irrepressible conflict became regular fare in the *Tribune*'s reports from the capital: "The interests of Northern free and Southern slave labor are not identical and cannot be rendered harmonious. One conflicts with the other, and will do so till the collision ceases."[65]

In May, a shocking run of incidents firmly established the narrative of sectional conflict at the center of the 1856 presidential race. In Washington, DC, a California Democrat of Alabamian extraction shot and killed an Irish waiter in a dispute over breakfast at the Willard Hotel. Just two weeks later, South Carolina congressman Preston Brooks caned Charles Sumner in brutal retaliation for the Massachusetts senator's two-day "Crime against Kansas" philippic. In Kansas itself, pro-slavery mobs avenged the shooting of one of their own by "sacking" the Free State stronghold of Lawrence, leaving the place, according to the *Tribune*'s report, "devastated and burned to ashes." Only "a few bare and tottering chimneys, a charred and blackened waste, now mark the site hallowed to all eyes as that where the free sons of the North have for two years confronted the myrmidons of Border-Ruffianism, intent on the transformation of Kansas into a breeding ground and fortress of Human Slavery." The attack touched off a summer of violence and unrest in the territory. Bleeding Kansas had begun in earnest. The narrative Greeley had pushed was unfolding in real life.[66]

In the *Tribune*, these events pointed to a pattern of white Southern violence rooted in the institution of slavery—and to a larger argument in support of Frémont and the Republican ticket. Greeley's editorial following Brooks's attack on Sumner tied it all together. "Our truly civilized and refined communities" were living under a barbaric despotism wrought by bondage. "The youth trained to knock down his human chattels for 'insolence'—that is for any sort of resistance to his good pleasure—will thereafter knock down and beat other human beings who thwart his wishes—no matter whether they be Irish Waiters or New-England Senators."[67] Insofar as Northerners themselves engaged in violence, it was only in the spirit of self-defense.

John Brown's brutal murder of five pro-slavery settlers at Pottawatomie Creek in southeastern Kansas were portrayed in the *Tribune* as part of a larger attempt to thwart the lynching of a Free State man. Thus, even the exercise of physical force expressed the civilizational divide between North and South.[68]

Through the remainder of the campaign, the situation in Kansas and its reverberations to the East dominated the *Tribune* and its coverage of national affairs. The word itself—Kansas—could be found on virtually every page of every edition. Shocking reports relaying the latest violence from the territory led the telegraphic news on the front page. Below, the classifieds were filled with Kansas-related items for purchase: "Brewerton's WAR IN KANSAS—Third thousand now ready!"; "Six Months in Kansas, by a Lady of Boston"; "Western Border Life; or What Fanny Hunter Heard and Saw in Kansas and Missouri"; "Pocket Map of Kansas"; "The New Map of Kansas." Daily advertisements plugged the *Tribune*'s in-house campaign materials ("BUY, READ, SING, CIRCULATE BY THE MILLIONS FREEDOM'S CAMPAIGN DOCUMENTS"): "The Border Ruffian Code," "Subduing Freedom in Kansas," and Kansas speeches by Charles Sumner, William Henry Seward, and Schuyler Colfax. Inside the paper, Kansas correspondents' letters sprawled across the columns, filling in the details from earlier telegraphic dispatches. Editorial items reinforced the narrative of Southern barbarism clashing with Northern civilization.[69]

The *Tribune*'s Kansas coverage and central place in Kansas activism suggested that the conflict was both a glue for Northern unity and a catalyst for Northern action. In addition to dutifully reporting every anti-Kansas meeting and sendoff for those "freedom-loving sons of Puritans" migrating to Kansas across the North, the *Tribune* became even more active in recruiting emigrants and funding the purchase of weapons and supplies.[70] In July, the paper took the suggestion of a reader to get up a Kansas collection, soliciting dollar donations to "swell THE TRIBUNE fund to something worthy of the million and a half of readers, who now form the constituency of this journal." As money rolled in over the remainder of the summer and into the fall, the paper periodically printed the donors' names and amounts given. Gifts came in from humble individuals ("A mechanic of Utica," $1.00), anonymous groups ("Lovers of Freedom and the N.Y. Tribune," $4.00), and portions of entire communities (sixteen residents of Cassopolis, Michigan, $15.50).[71]

These were not simply expressions of Northern altruism. The connections between concerns for Kansas, the self-interest of Northern white men, and Republican votes were never hard to sniff out. One Free-State Kansan appealed to *Tribune* readers—"Men of the North"—for support, reminding them that "murder, rapine, arson, robbery are boldly perpetrated [in Kansas] by the agents of the tyrannical oligarchy that has been for years endeavoring to throttle free institutions and rob you of your birthright." A September editorial examining efforts by the "Border Ruffian Democracy" to capture the election was targeted to the bone and sinew of the white North, urging them to stand up and defeat this unholy alliance of Southern slaveholders, Northern doughfaces, and pro-slavery western settlers: "Farmers, workingmen, men who wish to leave your children free and independent," the piece concluded, "it is for you to save the country from the combination which threatens to exclude white laborers from the Territories and hand them over to the sole occupancy of slaves and slave-breeders." In practical terms, such items suggested white Northern men had the most to lose from Southern designs on western territories. Whether working a rented farm or toiling for wages in a teeming city, workingmen's livelihoods and prospects were utterly dependent on the ready availability of western land and the ability to "emigrate from the great hive." In promising workingmen a safety valve, a free Kansas would extend the blessings of propertied independence to thousands, while raising the wages and improving conditions for those left behind.[72]

These appeals to white Northern voters' economic interests were coupled with images of a strong workingmen's masculinity. This language had been in place from the earliest resistance to the Kansas-Nebraska Bill, when a *Tribune* editorial summoned "all mechanics or farmers! No Reverends, Doctors, Honorables, Generals. No titled shams—only *men*."[73] It emerged even more forcefully through the Frémont campaign and the Bleeding Kansas narrative. Frémont himself stood out as a paragon of rugged masculinity. The noted explorer and Mexican War veteran who emerged from the campaign biography promulgated by Greeley shared much with the strapping "free sons of the North" facing down the "myrmidons of Border-Ruffianism" in Kansas.[74] The contrast could not have been any more striking with the Southerners who caned senators, killed hotel waiters, and harassed upstanding communities of free men and women.[75]

All of the campaign's central elements came together in Lydia Maria Child's novella, *The Kansas Emigrants*, which Greeley ran in serial form through October and early November. As relative calm descended over the plains following a violent summer, South Carolina's *Charleston Courier* quipped that Greeley would truly become concerned, now that "Kansas is really in great danger of suffering peace and quiet."[76] Greeley resumed the drama with Child's fiction, interrupting the *Tribune*'s serialization of Charles Dickens's *Little Dorrit* midstream. In Child's account, two idealistic New England couples make their way west to save Kansas. The Bruces and Bradfords, people who are dripping with classical references and virtue, find themselves beset by barbarians who are dripping with tobacco juice and vile curses. They do their best to improve the land and save the nation. They make homes and farms, and even manage to bring one goodhearted ruffian from darkness to light. As William Bruce explains to his wife Alice, darkly, "The antagonistic principles of slavery and freedom have come to a death-grapple here in Kansas; and you, my delicate little flower, are here to be trampled in the struggle." William is right. Alice doesn't make it, and neither does he. Their efforts alone are not enough, and they are betrayed by an utterly indifferent Northern public. Ruffians kill William, and Alice dies of a broken heart soon after. In her final moments, though, Alice has a shimmering, delirious vision. Church steeples, orderly farms, schoolhouses, and beautiful homes spread out before her, and she believes she is back in New England. No, she is told, this is Free Kansas. Her gaze is directed to a shining university on top of a hill. "Little Johnny is President," she is informed. "And the Blue Mound is called 'Free Mont.'"[77]

Alice's vision was destined to remain illusory as the results of the 1856 election scuttled Greeley's premonition of a Frémont presidency. James Buchanan took all of the Southern states, plus Pennsylvania, Indiana, and Illinois—enough of the North to claim the White House. In some respects, the omens for a Republican future were bleak. Kansas, for one, was surely lost. "The good, easy people who dream of moderation or decency in the settlement of the Kansas question have not yet awakened to the character of their Southern rulers," one post-election *Tribune* editorial remarked. The same issue that reported the election's results also included a frank, detailed response to the question, "Who Are and Who May Be Slaves in the United States? Facts for the People." When taken with reports that Southerners were readying to reopen the slave trade and that "the institution was as applicable to the white man as to the negro," the election results looked disastrous.[78]

In another light, though, elements of victory could be found in the defeat. There was ample "evidence of the buoyancy of spirit, resolution, and energy infused into Republicans" across the North. The "tremendous set of the Northern current disclosed in the election" revealed a bright future for a party that was only in its infancy. Only a year or two before, much of the North—New England, especially—had been subservient to "'cotton Lords and capitalists," but now it had delivered "immense majorities for Fremont" in all but a few states. The North may not have been entirely "made," but it had been awakened.[79]

Greeley-Phobia

Late in 1855, as Greeley arrived in Washington, DC, to observe the election for Speaker of the House, a Worcester, Massachusetts, paper identified a flare-up of "Greeley-Phobia" in American public life. Defined as "the habit some people have of attributing all the evils of the land to Horace Greeley," the term was useful for the tense and uncertain political environment of the 1850s. Early strains of the syndrome could be found going back to the previous decade, but this full-fledged outbreak had been developing since 1854, when sectional conflict gave new life to the *Tribune* and its editor.[80]

The most virulent expressions of Greeleyphobia came from the South, where Greeley was regarded as even more dangerous and loathsome than radical abolitionists like William Lloyd Garrison and Wendell Phillips. In 1855, a Virginia editor described Greeley as "hurl[ing] his thunderbolts at the South with impunity," giving life to "that cowardly and cringing spirit with which abolitionism stalks into our kitchens and negro quarters at night" (this in spite of the fact that most Southern postmasters simply refused to deliver copies of the *Tribune,* and local statutes were known to make subscribing to that paper a crime). Following Preston Brooks's caning of Charles Sumner, another Virginia paper predicted that "Master Horace Greeley . . . will jump out of his boots and breaches, have about four thousand fits, and thus put up the price of asafoedita and burnt feathers [a method believed to calm the nerves] throughout the country." Later, when an unfortunate Dr. Holacher was caught distributing abolitionist literature in Georgia, he was tarred, feathered, and addressed "to Horace Greeley, Tribune office, New York city, right side up, handle with care."[81]

In the North, too, many feared, reviled, and mocked "Philosopher Greeley" in equal parts. Even as political opponents ridiculed his appearance and oddball notions, they invested his station as the *Tribune*'s editor with great power and symbolism. Already associated with radical ideas and dangerous "isms," Greeley quickly became the face of "Black Republicanism" and sectionalism among Northern Democrats after 1854.

When the deadlock in Congress broke and Nathaniel Banks finally won the speakership of the House early in 1856, a Democratic paper captured the moment with a cartoon depicting Greeley as a midwife, dressed in women's clothes and holding a half-white, half-black "fusion" baby swaddled in a copy of the *Tribune*. In May of 1856, an Albany Democratic paper published an "intercepted letter" as proof that Greeley had invented Bleeding Kansas for political purposes.[82] Pennsylvanian Jeremiah Black worked himself into a lather in a letter to a fellow Democratic operative on the subject of Greeley. "No greater service could be rendered to the cause of truth than by putting Greeley where he ought to be," Black wrote. "Shall this political turkey buzzard be permitted to vomit the filthy contents of his stomach on every decent man in the country without having his neck twisted?" Soon after, Black coauthored a campaign pamphlet, *Short Answers to Reckless Fabrications, against the Democratic Candidate for President, James Buchanan.* The document's very first sentence was about Greeley.[83]

By the eve of the Civil War, Greeley and the *Tribune* had become associated with disunion. In February of 1861, the Washington, DC, *Confederation* ran an editorial blasting Greeley as "a bad man . . . one of the worst men, if not the worst man in America. The present crisis, so full of impending evil to our common country, in a great measure has been brought about by his agency." The same sentiment could be heard widely. Commentators who identified the press and its cynical operators as villains responsible for the

"The Interesting Event," *Young America*, vol. 1, no. 2, page 87. The image's secondary caption reads, "*Horace Greeley* (to Jonathan, loq.)—Well, Jonathan, it's a boy, and his name is BANKS." Courtesy, American Antiquarian Society

nation's impending collapse looked to Greeley as the most visible and divisive editor in the United States.[84]

Such images of Greeley were rooted in the very real power and reach of the *New-York Tribune* and the mistaken notion that its editor was responsible for every word within it. After 1854, the *Tribune* had become more than a newspaper and Greeley more than an editor. They both evolved into stand-ins for a larger constituency slowly taking shape in the latter half of the 1850s—the constituency that became the Northern Republican Party. A cartoon from the 1860 presidential election (see the introductory chapter) captured this in shorthand. Captioned "The Republican Party Going to the Right House" (in this case, a lunatic asylum), it depicts Greeley carrying Abraham Lincoln on a rail, with a merry parade in tow of "free lover" proponents, Mormons, blacks, socialists, women's suffragists, criminals, and Irishmen. Less cynically, historian James Ford Rhodes wrote early in the twentieth century, "If you want to penetrate into the thoughts, feelings, and ground of decision of the 1,866,000 men who voted for Lincoln in 1860, you should study with care the New York Weekly Tribune."[85]

Greeley had achieved something of the oracular status he had long craved, but not quite in the way that he had hoped. He had become a sectional oracle, rather than a national one. Following the 1856 presidential election, he returned to the idea that the Republican Party truly was national in its reach and orientation. Through the remainder of the decade, Greeley urged his fellow Republicans to embrace candidates and platforms that could incorporate as many people as possible and repudiate their associations with Northern radicalism. Greeley's hopes of making a national Republican Party led him to some unlikely places in the late 1850s, like a brief alliance with Stephen A. Douglas in 1858, and to unthinkable places after the Civil War.

But it didn't matter. Even as fellow Republicans became infuriated with Greeley and his inconsistencies, to those outside the party he remained the evil genius behind all manner of Northern radicalism and sectionalism. As much as Greeley helped create a self-conscious political North, he was perhaps even more effective at convincing his opponents that such a North existed, which, in turn, fueled the narrative of sectional conflict. In projecting fears about Northern moralizing, radicalism, and racial egalitarianism onto Greeley, Southerners, especially, could affirm their own sectional imaginings of the nation through him. It hardly mattered that Greeley was never quite the radical that Southern editors and politicians conjured. To conceive of Greeley behind every word in the *Tribune* was to imagine something much larger—a growing constituency of Northerners hostile and antagonistic to the South and its institutions.

The formation of the Republican Party, the election of Abraham Lincoln in 1860, disunion, the coming of the Civil War—none of these were the exclusive work of Horace Greeley, whatever his contemporaries or subsequent commentators might have said. The forces and contingencies behind these momentous developments and events were too complex and too variable to ascribe that much influence to a single individual. Yet there was meaning in "Greeleyphobia," in the belief that forces of such complexity could be condensed and stuffed inside the *Tribune* editor's old white coat. The political realignments of the 1850s—around explicit sectional identities and a larger narrative of sectional conflict—represented a profound shift in national political life. Assigning responsibility to Greeley made sense of such momentous change. The nation could survive one dastardly individual. The question in the coming years was whether it could survive the transformations that he signaled.

THE

AMERICAN CONFLICT:

A HISTORY

OF

THE GREAT REBELLION

IN THE

UNITED STATES OF AMERICA,

1860—'64:

ITS

CAUSES, INCIDENTS, AND RESULTS:

INTENDED TO EXHIBIT ESPECIALLY ITS MORAL AND POLITICAL PHASES,

WITH THE

DRIFT AND PROGRESS OF AMERICAN OPINION

RESPECTING

HUMAN SLAVERY

From 1776 to the Close of the War for the Union.

By HORACE GREELEY.

ILLUSTRATED BY PORTRAITS ON STEEL OF GENERALS, STATESMEN, AND OTHER EMINENT MEN; VIEWS OF
PLACES OF HISTORIC INTEREST. MAPS, DIAGRAMS OF BATTLE-FIELDS, NAVAL
ACTIONS, ETC.; FROM OFFICIAL SOURCES.

VOL. I.

HARTFORD:
PUBLISHED BY O. D. CASE & COMPANY.
CHICAGO: GEO. & C. W. SHERWOOD.
1864.

Horace Greeley, *The American Conflict: A History of the Great Rebellion in the United States of America, 1860–'64* (Hartford: O. D. Case & Co., 1864). Courtesy, American Antiquarian Society

CHAPTER FOUR

Horace Greeley's American Conflict

Preliminary Egotism

Horace Greeley began writing a history of the Civil War on August 31, 1863, more than a year and a half before it ended. Working from a tiny, rented office on Eighth Street, he sifted through documents and wrote for eight hours a day, six days a week before repairing to the *Tribune* offices downtown in the evening. Believing himself to be in a race with a war rushing toward its inevitable conclusion, he wrote at a rate of two chapters per week. The first volume, a massive tome of 648 double-columned pages treating of the war's origins, would be published under the title *The American Conflict: A History of the Great Rebellion in the United States of America, 1860–'64*. The book, which (prematurely) marked the war's end at 1864, appeared on the market in the spring of that year, just as the fight was grinding to its most intractable stalemate.[1]

At first, Greeley rejected the offer of "liberal compensation" from publisher O. D. Case of Hartford, Connecticut. His labors were already too great, he said. But events in July of 1863 changed his mind. First came the Union triumphs at Gettysburg and Vicksburg. Not long after, the Draft Riots brought torch-bearing mobs to Printers' Row in New York City, seeking to shut down "the nigger-loving Tribune" and to kill "that God-damned black-hearted Abolitionist," Horace Greeley. Terrifying though they were, the mobs crystallized Greeley's understanding of the war as a moral struggle between slavery and freedom within the nation as a whole, not between "the

Union" and "the Confederacy." Gettysburg and Vicksburg convinced him that the correct side would win.[2]

Paying Horace Greeley handsomely for *The American Conflict* seemed a good bet for O. D. Case & Co. (indeed, the book sold more than 125,000 copies by 1867 and made the publisher more than $15,000 by 1868).[3] Few doubted Greeley's power to chronicle the war or define its meaning, whether they loved or hated him. The Draft Rioters baying for his blood outside the *Tribune* building testified to his powers as forcefully as did anti-slavery Union soldiers when they spoke of the "Editorial Philosopher" with a kind of religious awe, writing letters home to wives and families, begging to know "What is Greeley saying these days?" As *Arthur's Home Magazine* put it, no one was better qualified for the work of chronicling the American Civil War. Greeley, after all, had *"done* as much work in moulding public opinion" for the last thirty years. Who better to capture its progress over the previous three or four?[4]

Greeley had much to gain from *The American Conflict*. For starters, he could certainly use the money. Notwithstanding his newspaper's great success and his favorite refrains on the virtues of thrift, a series of bad loans and investments had left Greeley clinging to just a handful of *Tribune* shares and chronically strapped for cash. Still, the project's appeal went beyond its potential windfall. *The American Conflict*, Greeley hoped, would mark his lasting stamp on the actual American conflict. Though he rarely referenced himself or the *Tribune*, Greeley was never quite absent from a chronicle that began with an introduction that he called "Preliminary Egotism."[5]

In the book's account of the war and its origins, Greeley was necessarily at its center. According to *The American Conflict*, the Civil War, far from being a train of political and military events, encompassed something more fundamental: the great ordeal of American nationhood raging within the hearts and minds of the people, in both the North and the South. Battlefield heroics paled in comparison with the work opening the people's eyes to the glories of American nationhood and the moral fetters of slavery standing in its way. It was, in short, a war of "Intelligence"—the climax of Greeley's original editorial mission. If the war's central struggle was "the progress of Opinion toward absolute, universal justice," then its history must be, as the book's dedication put it, the "record of a Nation's struggle up from Darkness and Bondage to Light and Liberty." The war's brutal material realities—"the agonies, the sacrifices, the desolations"—were necessary, so as to "engrave those truths so deeply on the National heart that they can nevermore be effaced or forgotten."[6]

Yet in his race to narrate the nation's glorious past, Greeley showed a weak grasp for what Oliver Wendell Holmes called its "terrible present."[7] *The American Conflict*'s title page and the advertising circulars marking the war's (anticipated) end in 1864 represented but one of many wartime misapprehensions for Greeley.[8] In a conflict encompassing shocking brutality, endurance, and volatility, Greeley had ample opportunity to lose the plot. Between 1860 and 1865, he charted a wild course through the cataclysm: from neglecting secession to accepting it, and then into full-throated calls for conquest; from leading a moral crusade for emancipation into blathering pleas for peace on any terms; from faithless peacemaking efforts into exhortations for magnanimity in triumph. He "may write good history," the *Massachusetts Spy* stated in August 1864, "but his efforts to make history have not been to his credit." In some respects, Greeley was simply not cut out for the scale of the American Civil War. As the Polish émigré Adam Gurowski noted in his diary, reflecting on Greeley's book, he "is useful to the people only in the normal condition of society only in peaceful times. . . . These mighty events . . . overawe, confuse his intellectual capacities." Such traits, Gurowski stated, amounted to "poor qualifications for a historian of his own epoch."[9]

Greeley's seemingly vacillating course through the Civil War went beyond a lack of mettle. His framework for understanding the conflict—as a struggle for the realization of national destiny—could never contain its unruly contours. Greeley's most unaccountable reversals thus came when the war did not to conform to the schemes he laid out for it. The title he gave to the war chapter in his memoirs, "The Civil War—Ideal and Actual," was unintentionally apt. The real Civil War, rooted in the failure of American nationhood, could never match the ideal one, which he believed must yield deliverance and redemption. "We live in an age when the word is Nationalization, not De-Nationalization," the German American intellectual Francis

Lieber wrote in 1863.[10] Greeley agreed, and his insistence on that principle between 1860 and 1865 tortured his positions and led him into the arms of a series of unlikely bedfellows.

Greeley's clumsy efforts to shape the war's meaning and, indeed, its very course, were also rooted in a practical problem. The Civil War temporarily diminished the power of opinion-driven political journalism as battlefield reporting took precedence over all else. When Oliver Wendell Holmes wrote, in his famous "Bread and the Newspaper" essay, "we must have something to eat, and the papers to read," he wasn't describing a burning need for the latest editorial. He was capturing instead the public's reliance on newspapers to gather basic war information. In this environment, correspondents became the newspapers' most valuable commodities—and the scourge of military leaders and government officials seeking to regulate reporting. Members of this "Bohemian Brigade" risked life and limb to provide color and detail beyond the reports that came over government-controlled telegraphic networks. As Greeley would learn—painfully—following the Union debacle at Bull Run, the ground had shifted for the oracular "Editor." While newspapers were more vitally important than ever, their editors seemed less so in wartime, especially when their turns as "newsprint generals" appeared to muddy military affairs.[11]

Greeley's most important interventions in the Civil War were thus not as the editorial persona behind the *Tribune*, but as Horace Greeley himself. The notorious "Prayer of Twenty Millions," imploring Lincoln to embrace emancipation in 1862, ran as a signed public letter from Greeley, rather than a *Tribune* editorial. Greeley's most important pronouncements on the war, meanwhile, went under his byline in Theodore Tilton's weekly newspaper, the *Independent*. He made his ill-judged peace efforts through his personal agency, rather than by vigorous editorializing. He also tried to become the war's definitive chronicler, with a book rather than a periodical or newspaper.

In his memoirs, Greeley said that he "proffered" *The American Conflict* to the people as his "contribution to a fuller and more vivid realization" of the divine truths contained in the war. In practice, however, it was the war's grim, earthly truths about the people and their nation that Greeley struggled to grasp. A friend told Greeley early in 1865 that the book's two volumes would be his most lasting "monument"; that friend was not entirely wrong. Though the book is long forgotten, it remains as a monument of a sort—one to Greeley's grand and lofty hopes for the war, and his own often troubled understanding of it.[12]

The Vital Principle of Nationality

Nearly three years before the Draft Riots, another torch-bearing crowd lit up the *Tribune* building to announce an altogether more successful political uprising. On the night of October 3, 1860, in the waning days of that year's presidential canvass, legions of young Republican "Wide-Awakes" marched through the streets of New York, with their signature torches blazing their support for Abraham Lincoln. The marchers—"20,000 Lincolnites in Line," "Seventy Acres of Republicans"—took care to stop at the *Tribune* building, whose windows had been illuminated by red, white, and blue lanterns. After the marchers had assembled for their grand finale in Union Square, many doubled back to Printers' Row. Their enthusiasm "not a jot abated," they "tarried long" into the night in front of the *Tribune* building, "paying repeated Tributes and huzzas and brilliant evolutions [marching maneuvers]." The affair, the *Tribune* reported the next morning, was a testament to the "simplicity, solidity, and honesty of the Republican cause" and the "generous and vigorous Yankee character." Surely, skeptics had to have been convinced that the Republicans were actuated by peaceful rather than bellicose impulses. After all, "a reign of terror cannot follow the triumph of Freedom."[13]

Greeley read the promise of consensus in the harbingers of disunion. He understood the elections of 1860 and the secession crisis that followed not as a danger to the nation, but as an opportunity. The enthusiasm embodied in "Wide-Awake" marches and the imminent ascendancy of Republican principles promised a new era in national politics. If that enthusiasm drew out the mad secessionist ravings of the slaveholding elite, so much the better. Greeley's notorious call to allow the "erring sisters to go in peace" was rooted in an unshakeable conviction that the claims of the nation were greater than those of a tiny, fire-eating cabal. Secession represented a failing gambit that would spark a rebellion of another sort altogether: not an uprising of slaves, who hardly figured at all into Greeley's calculations, but an awakening of the white Southern masses and a deliverance for white American people.[14]

Greeley's bleary vision of the secession crisis was founded on an unshakeable faith in white Southern yeomanry. Whether they knew it or not, these non-slaveholding Southern whites were the "Republicans of the South." Greeley had long divined their presence and had been encouraging them to gather their forces in the years leading up to 1860. *Tribune* articles and editorials had been noting the harmful moral and economic impact of slavery on Southern whites for years, and they explored the subject with increasing vigor through the remainder of the decade.[15]

The publication of Hinton Rowan Helper's *The Impending Crisis of the South* in 1857 affirmed Greeley's hope that the message was getting through.[16] Helper, a white North Carolinian with little sympathy for slaves or African Americans, attacked slavery as an economic blight for poor Southern whites. Greeley quickly became an enthusiastic promoter of the book. He first called for funds for 100,000 copies, which were to be sold at a low cost, but he was soon thinking in grander terms. An abridged "compendium" edition of *The Impending Crisis*, widely distributed, might even turn the elections of 1860: "Were One million copies of Mr. Helper's work properly circulated, we do not believe another Slavery Propagandist would ever be chosen President of the United States."[17]

By 1860, letters from the South to the *Tribune* suggested that change was coming. The paper's subscription rolls in Southern states were slim, and reports suggested that postmasters there regularly destroyed or refused to deliver copies. But the letters told another story. Writing from across the South, correspondents affirmed Greeley's faith that "thousands" read and, more importantly, agreed with the *Tribune*. As he suspected, the non-slaveholding whites were intensely loyal to the Union and increasingly hostile to the slaveholding elite. As one man wrote from Alabama, attitudes had "changed of late toward the aristocracy." The "poor white man of the middle [had] no chance" so long as "the Slave Interest" ruled. A writer from Memphis assured Greeley that secession talk came only from "violent political aspirants," "an insignificant clique, utterly powerless against the people. The masses are heart and soul for the Union." A Texas farmer wished only for the removal of "a few ultra political demagogues" and the introduction of a some "practical working farmers and readers of THE N.Y. TRIBUNE." "You will see this country go ahead," he predicted. The long-dormant Southern yeomanry was awakening.[18]

Abraham Lincoln's 1860 campaign and the secessionist rumblings it elicited thus filled Greeley not with dread, but with an unbridled optimism. "The moral certainty of Republican triumph," he wrote in August of that year, "evokes no menace and excites no alarm." The "signs of the times" indicated that "the Republican president [would] be inaugurated . . . by universal consent amid an era of good feelings." Greeley predicted that "thousands" in the South would vote for Lincoln, a fraction of the number who would cast their vote for him if only they were "allowed to do so." The threats of secession were empty, baseless bluster, "as audacious a humbug as Mormonism, as preposterous a delusion as Millerism." They spoke not to the strength of the Southern aristocracy, but its weakness in the face of the yeomanry's imminent rebellion. Never mind the dark visions of a slave uprising; the South's "oligarchs" feared the election of Lincoln because it would spark a revolt "not of their black slaves, but of their white ones."[19]

Greeley's thoroughgoing faith in the yeomanry could even brighten the darkest portents of catastrophe. On the eve of Lincoln's election, the *Tribune* appeared to welcome the prospect as tantamount to the nation's great redemption and realization. Drawn into the open, the South's secessionist fringe would be exposed and swiftly stripped of its power. If secessionists did take up arms, they would be crushed swiftly and painlessly, not by federal armies, but by the awakened yeomanry. "There will be no need of sending troops to the South to put down a slave-breeders' insurrection there," the *Tribune* claimed in October. "The *real* unionists of the South will deal with the hotheads most effectually. They will neither need nor desire external aid."[20]

When threats of secession became a wave of disunion in the winter of 1860–1861, Greeley plunged confidently into the crisis. "Let them go in peace," he said, not because he accepted secession, but because he deemed it a bluff. To Greeley, the secessionists' urgency bespoke weakness, rather than strength. Only let the question of union or disunion in the South be opened up to a truly democratic process, and the yeomanry would resolve the crisis to the nation's triumph. "We dare the Fire-eaters to submit the question of Secession or No Secession . . . to the popular vote of their own people," a *Tribune* editorial declared. The debate and reflection required in such a process would flood the South with the kind of "Intelligence" that not only would speed the downfall of the secessionist plot, but expose the slaveholding aristocracy once and for all. Greeley was so certain of these convictions that he enshrined them in *The American Conflict*, even after three years of war revealed the depths of Southern separatism. Of the choices facing the Union in 1860–1861, he said, the best option would have been a "pause" to allow cooler Southern heads to prevail: "From the South inflamed by passionate appeals and frenzied accusations, to the South, enlightened, calmed, and undeceived by a few months of friendly, familiar discussion, and earnest expostulation."[21]

For the promise of the moment to be realized, Greeley urged Republicans and national leaders to exhibit firmness without aggression. Buckling or offering concessions—as generations of Northern leaders had done since the nation's founding—would only embolden the secessionists. Fire-eaters must know at long last that there was no "premium on rebellion, [or] bounty for sedition." The yeomanry, meanwhile, must see their Northern allies stand their ground. As a correspondent from Mississippi wrote to the *Tribune* in February of 1861, "the Union men of the South only wait for you to show your strength." Greeley thus opposed compromise proposals in response to secession, seeing them as a betrayal of the Republican victory. He instructed Lincoln that "another nasty compromise wherein everything is conceded and nothing secured" would destroy the nation, rather than save it.[22] Kentucky senator John J. Crittenden's measures to protect slavery in perpetuity and extend the Missouri Compromise line to the Pacific would likewise result in disaster. The rebels could not "boast that they have frightened or backed down the North," Greeley told Crittenden in an open letter. "We do not capitulate to traitors."[23]

But if Northerners could not pander or compromise, neither could they threaten force. Saber rattling would give life to the rebellion, unify white Southerners, and close off the debate that Greeley was sure would break the secession fever. "Only the sheen of Northern bayonets," he said, "can blind the South wholly to the evil of secession." Besides, if the goal was to maintain the Union, military action would be the least effective means of achieving it. As a practical matter, Greeley said that a united force of Southern men would "never be subdued while fighting around and over their own hearthstones." And if they were, what then? Could Southern states be compelled to send representatives to Congress? Would they be "equal members of the Union" or "conquered dependencies?" The implications of victory were too complex and uncertain to press the issue. "Let us be patient," Greeley wrote, "neither speaking daggers nor using them, standing to our principles, but not to our arms, and all will yet be well."[24]

Slavery rarely factored into Greeley's reading of the secession crisis. He and the *Tribune* presented the lead-up to the war and its outbreak almost entirely in light of a narrow struggle for national life among white men. Following the attack on Fort Sumter in April of 1861, he remarked that the incident "ushers in a new era for Anglo-Saxon America—an era of force, blood, and rule of the strongest."[25] Within that new era, slaves and free African Americans hardly rated mention. Greeley worried that discussions of slavery would "complicate" and "pervert" what was "in truth" only a national struggle over Union. On that head, the *Tribune* urged Republicans to "stop agitating the nigger question" and proposed a sweep of economic legislation to benefit white workingmen. One of the *Tribune*'s few references to actual slaves in this period—a brief report of a threatened rebellion in Georgia—remarked on it mostly as a possible deterrent against secession.[26]

Lurking beneath all of Greeley's hopeful misapprehensions about secession was an unbreakable faith in an organic, shared experience of American nationhood among white men. Disunion was impossible, not merely because it was unconstitutional, but because the totality of the nation itself was too great. There had been many other moments when disunion *might have* come, but, Greeley said, a crisis had always been averted by the depth of the national experience. "A Nation is a reality, an entity, a vital force," he wrote, a month after the outbreak of hostilities, "and not a mere aggregation, like a Fourth of July gathering or a sleighing or supper party." And these immutable truths of "nationality" would surely make the Confederacy a short-lived experiment. Any nation, Greeley said, founded "on a denial of the vital principle of nationality" and rooted in the spirit of slavery was "a nation based on theft," and it inevitably would collapse on itself.[27]

The Nation's War Cry!

When the Confederacy did not collapse on itself, and the yeoman uprising did not come, Greeley was nonetheless resolute in his understanding of the crisis. With secession complete and armed conflict begun, he remained certain that the moment had come to purge the nation of its tiny, treasonous cabal. Indeed, the *Tribune* did not mourn the outbreak of hostilities, but cheered it. "Fort Sumter is lost," the paper's first wartime editorial proclaimed, "but freedom is saved." There would be no more offers of compromise with men who had maintained only a veneer of national loyalty as "a disagreeable fiction for the sake of personal convenience." Now that these traitors had "dared to aim their cannon balls at the flag of the Union," all would see the need to crush the rebellion swiftly. Secession would be repudiated, and the nation could realize its destiny.[28]

Thus Greeley's attitude toward armed hostilities changed; where he had once urged caution, he and the *Tribune* now cried for action. The paper offered unstinting criticism of Abraham Lincoln and William Henry Seward for coddling the secessionists in the lead-up to the Fort Sumter attack and called on the administration to throw an army of half a million men into the field without delay. Never mind the logistical problems involved in arming, training, and deploying them; there was not a moment to lose in crushing the rebellion and all it stood for. "We mean to conquer them—not merely to defeat, but to *conquer*, to SUBJUGATE them," the *Tribune* thundered. The sooner this was done—the sooner the secessionists could "find poverty by their fire-sides, and see privation in the anxious eyes of mothers and the rags of children"—the sooner the nation would be on the path to redemption.[29]

There were other reasons for swift action, too. As important as it was to stamp out treason in the South, it was also essential to maintain the morality of the nation at large. Greeley thus reflected on the prospect of war with a rather Victorian mix of priggishness and sanguinity. Wars wrought moral as well as physical destruction; they mangled souls as well as bodies. "Moral desolation, the wreck of faith, the confusion of clear distinctions of right and wrong"—these were the costs of war. Camp life, with its vices and intemperance, was as dangerous to a soldier as battle. It had taken "thirty years of peace" to clear the "moral waste" of the War of 1812. Now, Greeley said, "we have put back by more than fifteen degrees the hand on the dial which marks the progress of mankind toward a wholly Christian Civilization and Social Order." The sooner it was all over, the sooner the work of moral reconstruction could begin.[30]

Greeley and the *Tribune*'s early wartime pronouncements might not have garnered much attention had they not appeared to shape the early course of the war. The subeditors and correspondents to whom Greeley left the details of military commentary took his vision of national redemption to hawkish heights in the months between the attack on Fort Sumter and Bull Run. First, in late May, Fitz Henry Warren, a *Tribune* correspondent in Washington, DC, filed a panting dispatch in which he demanded that Lincoln advance his armies "on to Richmond." Speaking as a "Tribune of the People," Warren described "a burning martial ardor which almost consumes to the core" rising from coast to coast. He promised that the sight of the American flag flying above the rebel capital on the Fourth of July would "stir the blood" of the Nation. Then, in late June, managing editor Charles A. Dana turned Warren's "Forward to Richmond" refrain into "THE NATION'S WAR-CRY," demanding daily that the city be taken no later than July 20. Greeley, who was absent from the paper's operations from an axe wound sustained chopping wood, did nothing to soften the rhetoric.[31]

When the first Union incursion into Virginia became the debacle at Bull Run on July 21—roughly on the schedule prescribed by the *Tribune*—many concluded that Greeley was responsible for hurrying an unready army into action. "General Greeley" was quickly promoted up the ranks of public derision as accounts of the battle identified the rout as his singular blunder. With his boss still convalescing from his injury, managing editor Dana only worsened matters when he called for the resignation of the administration's entire cabinet, broadly claiming that "a decimated and indignant people will demand it."[32]

Greeley's response to the affair, an editorial that was by turns evasive, haughty, and self-pitying, had less the effect of oil on troubled waters than of gasoline on a fire. He sidestepped responsibility for "Forward to Richmond" and the offending editorial calling for the Lincoln cabinet's resignation, while also promising to abstain from any future military commentary. At the same time, he argued that the war really *should* be pushed to a swift conclusion, so that changes "might be made [in the cabinet] with advantage to the public service," and that the advance at Bull Run was poorly planned and executed. Greeley's claim that his "sole vocation" would be to "rouse and animate the American people for the terrible ordeal which has befallen them" failed to generate much sympathy. As Bennett's *Herald* noted with bitter sarcasm, "the repentant male Magdalen of New York journalism" perhaps should be pitied. He had, after all, been "accused of writing for the newspaper which he has been supposed to control."[33]

The general vituperation plunged Greeley into a temporary bout with madness. In a July 29 letter, ominously stamped "Midnight," he unburdened his soul to no less than Abraham Lincoln himself. "This is my seventh sleepless night—yours, too, doubtless," he began. "You are not considered a great man," he informed the president, "and I am a hopelessly broken one." Yet the two must transcend their limitations to do what was best for the country. Could the rebels be beaten? Greeley feared not, and in a fit of "sullen, scorching, black despair," he urged Lincoln to seek peace before the Union was "irrevocably gone." "If it is best for the country and for mankind that we make peace with the Rebels at once and on their terms, do not shrink even from that," Greeley told the president. Lincoln did not reply. Instead, he sealed the letter and showed it to no one for three years. When the president did share the missive with his private secretaries, John Nicolay and John Hay, Hay called it "the most insane specimen of pusillanimity that I have ever read."[34]

When Greeley came to after a fortnight of sleeplessness and near madness, his vision of a quick strike for national redemption had been all but destroyed. As the nation mobilized for a longer war, he struggled to come to grips with what that would mean—and what his role should be in it. He and the *Tribune* had been diminished—both of them "broken down," as he told a friend, by the debacle—and affairs would worsen over the coming months. Between July and October, his flagship weekly lost 12 percent of its subscribers, while his daily newspaper lost ground in New York City to the *Times* and *Herald*. Now, more than ever, it seemed that it was the editor's job to create consensus, perform public service, and lead public opinion to enlightened places. But the war's outbreak and indefinite timeline scrambled Greeley's sense of purpose. Events had shown that his confident mea-

sure of national sentiment and the hollowness of the Confederate commitment had been terribly wrong. What, now, would it mean to "rouse and
animate the American people"? As the clouds cleared from Greeley's vision,
he looked to the problem of slavery.[35]

The Magic Word of Freedom

In August of 1862, a little more than a year after he had unburdened his
soul to Abraham Lincoln in the wake of Bull Run, Greeley again addressed
the president. This time, he wrote not in groveling confidence, but with
peremptory authority—and not at midnight in a shaky hand, but in print, in
the *Tribune*, in an open letter before the nation at large. Presuming to voice
"THE PRAYER OF TWENTY MILLIONS," Greeley offered a dense, nine-point
indictment, detailing the president's derelictions with respect to slavery
and the conduct of the war. In tones that Lincoln described as "impatient
and dictatorial," Greeley denounced the president specifically for failing to
enforce the Confiscation Acts, which granted the military broad powers
to seize the rebel states' slaves. The charges, however, went even deeper.
The president's abundance of caution and overweening fealty to "fossil politicians of the Border States" amounted to a broader "mistaken deference"
to slavery over liberty. As slaves were being turned away—or worse—from
Union lines in the South, and "anti-negro riots" raged in the North, Lincoln's
timid approach to slavery was extending the life of the rebellion.[36]

Greeley's "Prayer" is justly overshadowed by Lincoln's concise, cannily
vague response, delivered in the *National Intelligencer* four days later. There,
Lincoln brushed off a gadfly and laid rhetorical groundwork for the preliminary Emancipation Proclamation he would issue in the following month.
Greeley's "Prayer" and his rejoinder to Lincoln, however, express Greeley's
understanding of the war, emancipation, and his own role in both during the
period between the summer of 1861 and the beginning of 1863. Those eigh-
teen months constituted the most radical season of Greeley's Civil War—a
season in which he earned the Draft Rioters' ire. As he goaded Lincoln to
embrace confiscation and emancipation, Greeley engaged in a mass public-
intelligence campaign—"a war of Opinion"—against slavery and the moral
and cultural climate that sustained it outside of the Confederacy. Along the
way, he recognized the agency of slaves as actors in the conflict, pled for

their rights as fugitives, and took on Northern racism as an element of the rebellion. Fired with his faith in a war for national redemption and the assurance that he had a singular role to play in it, he threw himself into the crusade for emancipation. Yet in the end, Greeley's dogged commitment to a national principle narrowed the broad horizons he briefly glimpsed.[37]

Greeley's assurance as a voice of multitudes reached back to his earliest days in journalism, but his conviction that slavery must die that the nation might live began germinating in his post–Bull Run brain fevers. Upon regaining his faculties in August of 1861, he was reborn as a Radical Republican. With the zeal of the converted, he abandoned his earlier caution on matters relating to slavery and emerged as a champion of the recently passed Confiscation Act. "The skies are <u>very</u> dark," he wrote to abolitionist Gerrit Smith soon after returning to work, but "I must work while strength lasts. And God yet will make my weakness humbly instrumental in the overthrow of American slavery."[38]

Greeley took up the cause with the same squint-eyed optimism that he had brought to the secession crisis and the early stages of the war. Once again, he believed American nationhood was on the verge of its fulfillment. The vigorous execution of the Confiscation Act was all that was required for the rebellion to crumble in a mere sixty to ninety days. With "a general stampede of slaves" into its lines, the Union Army would become a "resistless and triumphant" force in the South. Victorious in the field, the men in blue would be greeted as liberators, not just by slaves, but "by a large share even of the whites." The "independent and intelligent yeomanry" of the South would understand that Union forces were there not to conquer the region, but to "rescue large portions thereof from present subjugation." Routed in the field and at last toppled from power, the slaveholding aristocracy would lose its grip not just on the South, but on the nation at large. "By the light burning in Charleston," Greeley wrote in December of 1861, even "the dullest may read the handwriting on the wall. Slavery has conspired to divide and destroy the Republic. . . . Let us bury Treason and Slavery in a common grave, and thus get rid of Abolition, 'sectionalism,' and other incitements to domestic strife."[39]

Beyond Confederate forces, there were just two things standing in the way of the full realization of Greeley's vision: Northern public sentiment and the

Lincoln administration. Early in 1860, Greeley had lamented to his friend Rebecca Whipple that "the country is not Anti-Slavery. It will only swallow a little Anti-Slavery in a great deal of sweetening."[40] Wartime opinion and hysterical responses to the prospect of emancipation had underscored the truth of his observation. Well beyond the borders of the Confederacy, "Slavery" had infused "monstrous prejudice," "disgusting hypocrisies," and "blind and brutal negro-hate" into the spirit of the nation. Though slavery itself was no longer practiced in the North, its moral rot and accompanying racism remained staples of Northern culture. The rhetoric of politicians and the daily fare of Democratic newspapers—"the colloquial small-change of the pro-slavery debaters and gladiators"—limited the extent to which Northern leaders could strike at the lifeblood of the Confederacy. "Should Slavery thus be enabled to survive this convulsion," he said in the spring of 1862, "it will owe far less to Southern chivalry than to Northern sympathy."[41]

The ends of war would thus need to encompass more than just victory in the field. As the conflict was a "war of Opinion, preeminently so," Greeley made it his work to lay siege to the moral and intellectual foundations of slavery in the North. He would "dispel the clouds of misrepresentation . . . which . . . have surrounded the relation of Slavery to our great struggle for National existence." The public must be given clear arguments and correct information; they must learn "essential truths so clearly that they cannot hereafter be perverted without conscious or conspicuous falsehood." The task was great. Convincing the people to understand the connection between destroying slavery and saving the nation was one thing; convincing them to relinquish the racial ideas associated with slavery was another. "There is scarcely a besotted, vice-degraded, worthless white in the Union who does not instinctively and vigorously oppose Emancipation as 'reducing the White man to the level of the Negro,'" he wrote in March of 1862. Though Greeley did not use the word "racism," he recognized that so long as it existed in concert with slavery, the rebellion would continue, and the nation's redemption would be delayed.[42]

If Greeley recognized the extent to which Abraham Lincoln was constrained by this national culture of slavery, he expressed little sympathy for the president. Tensions between the two reached back to the 1858 Illinois senate race and had only escalated as Greeley accorded Lincoln little respect, even after the latter's victory in 1860. Early in the war, earnest efforts were made to forge a productive partnership between the White House and the *Tribune*. Through back channels, Lincoln promised Greeley exclusive access to information in exchange for editorial influence in the *Tribune* to move "public opinion on important subjects." Greeley, Lincoln said, "is a great power. Having him firmly behind me will be as helpful . . . as an army of a hundred thousand men."[43]

But as a general in the broader war of opinion, Greeley proved more of a McClellan in relation to Lincoln than a Grant or a Sherman. With emancipation as his singular goal, it didn't take long for Greeley to disregard his pact with the president. By the final weeks of 1861, he had abandoned his post–Bull Run pledge to only "rouse and animate the American people" and keep silent on military affairs. First, the *Tribune* was sharply critical of Lincoln's annual message to Congress, delivered at the beginning of September. Had the president simply proclaimed that *"Slaveholding by rebels is not recognized and sustained by the Government and arms of the United States,"* the war could be "triumphantly ended" within a matter of months.[44] Then, in case the message didn't get through to Lincoln, Greeley insisted that the president attend a lecture he was to deliver on the subject of "The Nation" at the Smithsonian, to take place early in January of 1862. "The Grumbler," as Lincoln's private secretary John Hay called him, "has come down here [to Washington, DC] to marshal the hosts of grumblers."[45] Speaking before an admiring crowd of John C. Frémont supporters (Lincoln had removed Frémont from his post as a Union Army general that fall, citing insubordination for Frémont's edict freeing slaves in his Missouri district), Greeley returned to familiar themes. Slavery was the great animating cause of the rebellion and the one great obstacle to national unity. Turning directly to Lincoln, sitting beside him on the rostrum, Greeley said, "If the Union is to be restored, it is only on the basis of Freedom. . . . It is time to look the enemy in the eye."[46]

Greeley grew increasingly restive over the first half of 1862. Campaigns were stalled in the field, Union commanders were openly flouting the law on confiscation, while those who did take action against slavery, like David Hunter, saw their orders revoked. The military delays were bad enough— they "paralyze the energies and stifle the enthusiasm of a people"—but the administration's inconsistent approach to slavery was devastating. What was needed, the *Tribune* argued, was "a definite, lucid, settled line of conduct on the part of the Government with respect to slaves and Slavery." Again and again, Greeley said the war could be over quickly if only Lincoln would take action and abandon his "faithless, insincere, higgling, grudging execution" of policy. "Who does not realize," he asked, "that were Slavery abolished tomorrow, there would be no reason for conflict among us, and no desire to protract the existing struggle?"[47]

Beyond specific matters of policy, however, Greeley also disparaged Lincoln's broader leadership. As the presumptions of the "Prayer of Twenty Millions" suggested, Greeley had a low estimate of Lincoln's qualities in this department. In Greeley's mind, the hour demanded a kind of Carlylean, great-man-of-history heroism that the president simply did not possess. Lincoln, Greeley wrote in 1864, was "less than great" and decidedly "not a genius"; he was "not one of those rare, great men who mold their age into the similitude of their own high character, massive abilities, and lofty aims." Worse yet, Lincoln's actual aims often struck Greeley as less than lofty. In his rejoinder to Lincoln after the "Prayer," Greeley suggested that the president didn't grasp the "vital truths" of the conflict as a larger moral struggle between "Slavery" and "Liberty."[48]

If winning the war and transforming the nation meant defeating slavery on a moral level, the president could not defer to public opinion; he must shape the nation to his views, rather than shape his views to the nation. A rare instance in which Greeley *praised* Lincoln during this period was instructive. Lincoln's message to Congress in March of 1862, calling for compensated emancipation in the Border States, sent Greeley into raptures. It was, Greeley said, "the Nation's expression, through her Chief Magistrate . . . one of those few great scriptures that live in history and mark an epoch in the lives of nations and races. The first era of the supremacy of the Rights of Man in this country dates from the Declaration of Independence; the second began on the 6th of March, 1862." If Greeley's reflections suggested the limitations of his own historical judgments, they also betrayed certain of his expectations for Lincoln.[49]

His reflections also suggested something of his understanding of emancipation itself—as a measure that had more symbolic, national meaning than as a human reality for those in bondage. To be sure, Greeley joined other Radical Republicans and abolitionists in condemning the Emancipation Proclamation as a "cautious, limited, temporizing procedure." He also came to argue against colonization as a policy, but his vision was anything but expansive. These "black step-children" of the republic were "humble, ignorant, timid, distrustful. . . . They are not, let us frankly admit, the equals in prowess, capacity, or opportunity, of four millions of Whites; but they are, nevertheless, human beings."[50]

Reflecting on the final version of the proclamation on January 1, 1863, Greeley focused first and foremost on the "national hopes which it [was] calculated to inspire," rather than the freedom it promised. Indeed, in a series of essays months earlier, he had enlarged on the idea of slavery's end as a national rebirth. American nationalism had been and remained a vital reality, even through the war. That nationalism had been so strong that it had rendered the people "tolerant, if not complaisant to Slavery and the Slave Power." Now, however, it was being elevated and transformed, as the prospect of emancipation sundered the "partnership of Slavery and Union." Already, Greeley said in September, "a nobler idea, a truer conception of National Unity" was taking hold in the "American Mind." Soon, when emancipation was an accomplished fact, "National unity is to be no roseate fiction, but a living reality," he said. "The United States future will be no constrained alliance of discordant and mutually repellant commonwealths. . . . Our Union will be one of bodies not merely, but of souls."[51]

Greeley was short on specifics for how these sections would be alchemized into a union of souls. It was clear, though, that information and intelligence should figure heavily in the process. "Southern hate of the North" was merely a function of misinformation and falsehood. Once the war had defeated the "man-owning aristocracy," the misunderstanding would vanish. Voices of fellowship, voices of honest labor and industry, would transform the long-wasted South, opening "new avenues to wealth, new incitements to activity and energy." Peace would "speedily re-link the golden chain of mutual interests, and all [would be] kindly again." The nation's rebirth was nigh.[52]

January 1, 1863, thus beckoned as a triumph for the nation, and for Horace Greeley. With emancipation imminent, the Civil War was following the

storyline Greeley had laid out for it: the great moral struggle between freedom and slavery was drawing to a close, with freedom triumphant and the
nation redeemed. For all of Greeley's prodding and criticism, Lincoln had
risen to the moment. With his Emancipation Proclamation due in a month,
the President defined the war's agenda and meaning in his annual message
to Congress, precisely as Greeley had hoped. "In giving freedom to the slave,"
Lincoln said, "we assure freedom to the free." All that was needed was "concert," a unity of effort to "disenthrall ourselves" from worn-out dogmas, "and
then we shall save our country."[53]

Greeley's optimism was boundless. Though the results of the November
elections had marked a rebuke to Republican leadership and the cause of
emancipation across the North, Greeley appeared unfazed. "We are at all
events morally certain to have peace in spring," he said, three days after
Lincoln's address to Congress, adding that "it may be within four weeks."
Confederates, rendered "indolent" and "self-indulgent in temper and habits" by generations of slavery, were on the verge of surrendering to armies
of men nurtured by Free Labor. As Greeley told Lincoln, they were "deathly
sick of their job, and anxious to get out of it."[54]

When emancipation came at the turn of 1863, Greeley stood out as one
of its great champions. The celebration at New York City's black Abyssinian
Church closed with "cheers for Horace Greeley, Wm Lloyd Garrison, Dr.
Cheever, and others." Nearby, at the Cooper Union, the black abolitionist
minister Henry Highland Garnet summoned huzzahs for "the President,
the nation, the flag, the Abolitionists, and for Horace Greeley." Yet Greeley remained more measured than those saluting him. Though he reveled
in "the national hopes" the Emancipation Proclamation inspired, he noted
that the moment of its issue had become "inauspicious." The late military
debacle at Fredericksburg, disruptions in Union trade with Britain, and
rumblings of French recognition of the Confederacy put "the National cause
at its lowest ebb."[55]

This caution was telling. Greeley's expansive visions for war and emancipation were giving way to narrower hopes for peace and reconciliation.
He was embarking on what a friend called a "suicidal course on the subject
of the war." Within a matter of weeks after Emancipation Day, Greeley
would declare it "impossible to make a good war and a bad peace," signal his

flexibility on emancipation as a condition for victory, enter into admiring correspondence with the notorious "Copperhead" Democrat Clement Vallandigham, and nearly land in the brig at Fort Lafayette for violations of the Logan Act (which criminalized private negotiations with foreign governments against the interests of the United States). "Believe me," Greeley's friend James White warned in February, "that your career as a man of the People is about closing in shame and ignominy if you persist in the opinions and inclinations you are now trying to force of the public mind." "Be the Horace Greeley you always were," he implored, "working for your Country and for Freedom and Humanity."[56]

Our Bleeding, Bankrupt, Almost Dying Country Longs for Peace

Reflecting on the nation's "Dark and Bright Hours" in May of 1863, Greeley remarked, "Never before were the mutations of a contest . . . so frequent and so great. . . . The signal and often sudden fluctuations of fortune and of feeling form a striking peculiarity." Though he was speaking of the Civil War, he ostensibly offered a concise account of his own course through its final two years. Between Emancipation Day in 1863 and Appomattox in 1865, Greeley's own mutations and fluctuations of feeling—what the *North American Review* would call his "criminal vagaries"—went from wild optimism to blackest despair and then back again. One month he was predicting Union triumph within ninety days; the next he was lamenting the impossibility of ever crushing the rebellion. Amid deep uncertainty, Greeley debuted his next wartime role: as peacemaker. In his advocacy, scheming, and machination for peace, Greeley baffled his allies, delighted his enemies, and confused his later chroniclers.[57]

There was consistency to Greeley's inconsistency, however. Through the course of the entire war, and no less so during its final two years, Greeley was unwavering on two points: his insistence that the Civil War was an "American Conflict"—an ordeal of American nationhood—and his conviction that *he* had a central role in defining its outcome and meaning. Greeley's grand designs for national redemption in 1861 and 1862 were not all that different from his peacemaking schemes in 1863 and 1864, which became his postwar formula for reconciliation. The former were born in an optimism for victory, the latter in fear of defeat. Both were rooted in the same belief—the war must define the very soul of the nation.

Greeley's yearnings for peace began in an abiding hatred of war's horrors and its terrible human costs; they grew when the war's stubborn realities failed to match the plans Greeley had made for it. How, he wondered, could a generation of young men, morally ruined and politically embittered, participate in a national revival after so many grueling months of war? How much good will for peace and reconciliation could be left?[58]

Indications late in 1862 and early in 1863 were that the people were running out of patience, and the nation was running out of time. Republican setbacks in Congress and Northern legislatures in November of 1862 portended a harsh reckoning. Though Greeley largely ignored the warnings and continued to trumpet emancipation, events doused his enthusiasm. In the wake of the crushing Union defeat at Fredericksburg in December, the fortunes of the Democrats' peace movement surged. Ohio congressman Clement Vallandigham's intensely racist anti-emancipation speech in January of 1863 suggested the chilling force of what became known as the Copperhead movement. Greeley was chastened. As he told Salmon Chase, "I believe we are on the brink of a financial collapse and a Copperhead revolution, and that we must have crushing victories or a ruinous peace very soon." In the face of these cold realities, Greeley felt that Republicans could neither appear to be uncompromising on questions of peace nor allow Democrats alone to define what peace might mean. "A Copperhead Peace," he said in March of 1863, was a "disunion peace" that would preserve slavery. In the face of such circumstances, Republicans could not be a "War Party" exclusively; they must show their commitment to peace.[59]

Greeley's own peace efforts, which were already quietly underway late in 1862, began with Lincoln and moved on to forge an unlikely collection of alliances—all in the name of retaining the war's national promise. Writing directly to Lincoln in December of 1862, Greeley laid out the peace vision that would carry him for the remainder of his life. The president should offer universal amnesty to Confederates and universal emancipation to slaves. The Union should assume Confederate debts and enact compensated emancipation in the Border States. Though these latter measures might monetarily rise to the tune of $140,000,000, their costs would be inconsequential, compared with the lives spared and the good will generated. Pursue this plan, and peace would be a reality in a matter of months. "I feel sure," he told the president, that it would come as soon as March of 1863, "if the right man could do it." Nonetheless, Lincoln did not follow Greeley's dictation.[60]

Convinced that *he* was the right man to do it, Greeley set to work on his own. Late in 1862, he began musing on the possibility of peace mediated by a European power. The idea caught the attention of William Cornell Jewett, a "Peace" Democrat from Maine. Jewett's western mining adventures had earned him the moniker "Colorado," and his movements abroad had given him an audience with Queen Victoria and apparent entrée with shadowy French diplomats. In correspondence, Greeley had told Jewett that he would only consider mediation by a neutral party (he'd suggested Switzerland in the *Tribune*), provided it was one that did not "desire the failure of the Republican principle of Government"—namely, France and Britain. Jewett's connections, however, didn't quite reach into the Swiss cantons, and Greeley instead would have to settle for Henri Mercier, Emperor Napoleon III's man in Washington, DC.[61]

A bad business ensued. Impressed with Mercier, Greeley took the French mediation scheme to Massachusetts's Republican stalwart, Charles Sumner, as well as to no less a figure than Lincoln himself. Meanwhile, per Jewett's promise to Mercier that Greeley would "use his journal to put France right," the *Tribune* was soon filled with bon mots detailing the French Empire. These efforts came to nothing, but they coaxed warm words from Vallandigham and astonishment from Greeley's Republican allies. Sumner indefinitely tabled Jewett's petition to Congress for mediation, while the *Times* and Secretary of State Seward mused that Greeley's efforts might well have amounted to illegal acts.[62]

Mediation was dead, but Greeley continued to support it as a way to circumvent months and years of further death and destruction, as well as the division and rancor that would surely follow. Moreover, it spoke to the broader, international context in which the American national struggle was unfolding. The coming of emancipation, Greeley argued, gave whichever European power would broker the peace no choice but to side with the

Union and against the Confederacy on the only thing that mattered: slavery. "Europe," he wrote, "comprehends that ours is a struggle between Freedom and Slavery, and consequently gravitates to the side of the former." The forces of "Progress and Reform" abroad, led by "Victor Hugo, [Giuseppe] Garibaldi, Louis Kossuth, John Bright &c." are "with us, heart and soul." Such men understood that the American war was the central front in a larger conflict "against all the powers of darkness and despotism." Even if Europe's still powerful "despots and aristocrats" did tend to support the Confederacy, they would have to support the Union, lest they stir up popular unrest at home. "Louis Napoleon," Greeley said, "has quite enough on his hands without provoking the democracy of Paris to rebuild the barricades of 1848." In the United States, the forces of despotism and aristocracy that were fomenting disunion would be defeated, never to rise again, with emancipation an accomplished fact.[63]

Mediation was also appealing on another level: it could force an end to slavery and allow the enlightenment of the people to proceed under peaceful conditions, sheltered by the umbrella of the nation itself. Yet, amid the protracted armed conflict, it could not be said that the "war of opinion" was going forward. Indeed, by Greeley's calculations at the lowest points of 1863 and 1864, the war itself could never be won amid the intense opposition to emancipation across the Northern public and within the military. Many in the North, Greeley wrote in April of 1863, were "so surcharged with the virus of negro-hate, that they are in no sense hostile to those now seeking the destruction of the Union." The average conversations in the seaports and cities of the loyal states would be "better adapted to the latitude of Richmond or Mobile than ours." New York City, Greeley said in 1864, sat atop a "Rebel volcano which rumbles ominously and does not sleep. A draft, a defeat, anything unusual, may see us in flames and drowned in blood."[64]

The effects on the war had become devastating. Resistance to the draft, misrepresentations of emancipation, exaltation of George McClellan and other foot-dragging Democratic generals—all mingled together to the detriment of Union military progress for the nation at large. Copperhead speeches, Democratic editorials, and the acts of violence and disorder they incited had chilling effects. Greeley noted that, following events like the Draft Riots or the casual killing of a black man in Detroit, slaves still in bondage would be less likely to rise up against the rebellion and fight for the Union. Non-slaveholding whites, meanwhile, would remain lost in a fog of racial animus. Collectively, the persistence of ideas "invented by slaveholders to uphold their craft" made the nation as a whole unworthy of peace or resolution. Leaving aside the willful sabotage of racist generals and soldiers (which Greeley and other Republicans were constantly detecting), victory would elude Union armies and the nation so long as hateful ideas were broadcast and accepted. "If we are beaten," Greeley wrote, "it will be because we as a people *ought* to be beaten."[65]

When defeats did come, he duly applied this same logic. After promising peace by March of 1863, and, failing that, by July 4 of that year, he reached new levels of anguish when the rout at Chancellorsville ended yet another ill-starred Union campaign in Virginia. "To think of it," a friend remembered Greeley saying, "130,000 magnificent soldiers, cut to pieces by 60,000 half-starved ragamuffins." So great was Union numerical and technical superiority that the only explanation for the disaster was a moral one. Confederate armies would continue to defy the odds so long as the nation tolerated slavery and its racist underpinnings. To some, it appeared that Greeley even welcomed the news that Robert E. Lee was turning his army northward after Chancellorsville. "Let the invading host of man-stealers come on," he crowed as the Army of Northern Virginia moved into Pennsylvania, a hotbed of Copperhead sentiment. The incursion would either force those in the North to "acknowledge the corn" and give up the fight, or steel themselves with the realization "that we are involved in a gigantic, terrible war" between freedom and slavery, a "life-or-death struggle of our Republic."[66]

Amid such grim calculations, Greeley's efforts to maintain the sanctity of the nation above all else bewildered his Republican and abolitionist allies. In his seasons of peacemaking, Greeley displayed an unsettling flexibility on emancipation as a condition for victory. When a *Tribune* editorial suggested that Lincoln could interpret the terms of his own Emancipation Proclamation as needed in the name of peace, Greeley's friend Theodore Tilton groused that "the editorial opinions of THE TRIBUNE, like Newtown Pippins, are sounder in the Fall than in the Spring."[67]

Greeley's explanations in response to his critics seemed too clever by half to quiet the noise. As he told Tilton, he never believed that Lincoln should recall or disregard the Emancipation Proclamation. He argued, however, that signaling flexibility in interpreting its precise meaning served two purposes. First, in a precursor to his "root, hog, or die" Reconstruction doctrines, he said the slaves themselves should not be given to understand that emancipation would come to them irrespective of their actions. Greeley had argued that a general slave uprising, coupled with black military service, would do much to bring down the rebellion. That scheme would work more swiftly, however, if slaves were uncertain of the extent of Union commitment to emancipation. Citing Lord Dunmore's Proclamation of 1775, Greeley suggested that the Lincoln administration go so far as to make it clear that those slaves who explicitly served the national cause would be granted freedom. Second, Greeley argued that Republican inflexibility on peace and emancipation fanned opposition to the war that was holding Union victory back. "Loyal people," he said "should realize that Emancipation policy *is* conducive to an early Peace, and does not commit us to interminable War."[68]

Though Union victories like Gettysburg and Vicksburg had a way of altering Greeley's morale, his peace fevers spiked when the war looked interminable. As Ulysses S. Grant's Richmond offensive in the spring and summer of 1864 turned the city's hinterlands into a vast charnel house, Greeley's mania deepened. With the war all but lost in his mind, he urged Lincoln and his fellow Republicans to rescue what they could from the doomed effort to redefine nationhood on their terms. As he told a British friend, "The whole country is to be surrendered to the Slave Power. . . . The Rebellion is simply Slavery letting go to get a better hold. And it will get that hold. . . . The effort to free our Country from Slavery was gallantly made, but is destined to fail." Greeley, it seemed, had given up on his once-bold vision of a nation remade in the image of "Freedom" writ large. Gone were the radical calls for emancipation and sharp critiques of the republic's racist underpinnings. The nation must live, on whatever terms available.[69]

In July of 1864, Greeley turned again to the work of peacemaking and saving the nation. "Colorado" Jewett materialized with fresh schemes for peace, and Greeley, horrified by the relentless stream of casualties, was eager to help. According to Jewett, high-level Confederate "peace commissioners" were waiting in Canada, ready to discuss terms. Greeley took up the cause directly with the president. "Our bleeding, bankrupt, almost dying country longs for peace," he told Lincoln. The administration should put forward a comprehensive peace platform: (1) Restore and "declare perpetual" the Union; (2) "utterly and forever abolish" slavery; (3) offer "a complete Amnesty" to all former Confederates; (4) pay $400,000,000 to "the late Slave states," compensating them "for the loss of their loyal citizens by the Abolition of Slavery"; (5) restore full congressional representation to all seceded states; and (6) call a national convention to "make such changes in the Constitution as shall be deemed advisable."[70]

With some forbearance—and not a little mischief—Lincoln consented to the plan and suggested just the man to carry it out. "I not only intend a sincere effort for peace," he told Greeley, "but I intend that *you* shall be a personal witness that it is made." Should Greeley find "any person anywhere professing to have any proposition of Jefferson Davis in writing, for peace, embracing the restoration of the Union and the abandonment of Slavery," Lincoln instructed him to convey those persons back to Washington at once. Greeley demurred. He had preferred to initiate rather than conduct the talks and hoped that they would proceed without Lincoln's demands. Clearly outmaneuvered, he nevertheless made a grudging trip to Niagara Falls. There, he met the shadowy Confederates, who were less accredited peace commissioners than spies running subterfuge. They, too, were ready to spring a trap on Greeley. When the editor handed the men a disingenuous letter from Lincoln laying out peace terms and inviting them to Washington for talks, the Confederates took their chance. In an open letter addressed to Greeley (who had left immediately after delivering Lincoln's message), they warmly thanked him for his "solicitude" in initiating the meetings and blasted Lincoln for tendering rude and unrealistic terms.[71]

Once again, a peacemaking venture had come out badly for Greeley. The Confederates' letter, which circulated widely in the press, included such warm words for Greeley and his efforts that it was hard not to infer treacherous intent.[72] The details that emerged in the ensuing media scrum made matters worse. While Lincoln's dispatch to the Confederates had included an unequivocal commitment to emancipation, Greeley looked somewhat less resolute on that point, as well as being openly critical of the president. "Nine-tenths of the whole American people, North and South, are sick of slaughter and anxious for peace on almost any terms," he was said to have

told the Confederates. "This is not the end of the affair," he allegedly remarked in parting with the rebels. "You must not think that all Republicans
are blackguards."[73]

Many concluded instead that *Greeley* was a faithless blackguard, at worst,
and a "nincompoop without genius," at best. One Republican remembered
Lincoln remarking that Greeley was working to "influence the peace sentiment of the North, to embarrass the administration, and to demoralize the
army."[74] Even after the debacle, Greeley continued to advocate for peace,
both publicly and privately. To add to the general confusion, he allied himself with a group of Radical Republicans seeking to replace the president in
the rapidly approaching election. Greeley would later reverse this position,
following William Tecumseh Sherman's capture of Atlanta early in September, but it had provoked Lincoln's ire. What, if anything, Greeley stood
for was open to conjecture. Lincoln perhaps captured it best when he told
his cabinet in late August, "Greeley is an old shoe—good for nothing now,
whatever he has been. . . . He is so rotten that nothing can be done with
him. He is not truthful, the stitches all tear out."[75]

༄

Through all of Greeley's contortions, his commitment to the nation as an
ideal, living entity remained. His remark to the Confederate negotiators,
that "nine-tenths of the whole American people, North and South" desired
peace, suggests that even three years of relentless fighting had not shaken
his faith in the existence of a shared idea of American nationhood among
white men. Before he had entirely recovered from his bout of peace fever
in the summer of 1864, Greeley expressed the war's stakes in stark terms:
"Are we, in truth, or are we not a Nation?" Was there anything more to the
"national existence" than a "Fourth of July gathering, a mass meeting, collected by some orator's fame, some raree-show's attractions?" The war,
Greeley said, needed to deliver "an AMERICAN answer to these questions—
specific, unambiguous, decisive."[76]

Warming to the prospects of victory in the late months of 1864 and early
1865, Greeley advanced familiar answers of his own. Above all, he called for
a deeper meaning and experience of American nationhood—something
altogether more organic and whole than what had come before. With peace
in sight, Greeley spoke as if this newer expression of nationhood was ready

to burst forth from its chrysalis. Less than two weeks after Lincoln's assassination at the hands of an unrepentant Southern nationalist, Greeley pronounced "sectionalism" dead. It was "high time to dismiss that wretched coinage of falsehood and calumny"—to cast it aside to "the limbo of worn-out impostures, of detected shams." By the Fourth of July in 1865, Americans would look as one on a cloudless "National sky," the people ready to be "harmonized." All would see, as Greeley told Orestes Brownson the following year, that there was "no interest of either section which is also not the true interest of the other."[77]

What the nation was, what it would be, to whom it belonged—these would be the great questions of Reconstruction. For answers, Greeley would revert back to his great hopes for the war, his schemes for peace, his dreams of unity, and his faith in himself.

The American Conflict, Volume 2

Capturing Richmond in war had been hard. Horace Greeley went there in May of 1867 to demonstrate just how easily it could be taken in peace. Accompanied by Cornelius Vanderbilt and abolitionist Gerrit Smith, Greeley advanced on the former Confederate capital to secure the release of Jefferson Davis on a bond of $100,000. Davis had been confined to Fortress Monroe since his capture at the close of the war, and Greeley's positions on what precisely to do with him had been evolving ever since. His support for Davis's prosecution on charges of treason and other forms of malice softened through 1865 into calls for a quick trial on a narrower charge of provoking Lincoln's assassination. By 1866, when Greeley had entered into a warm correspondence with Davis's wife, Varina, he was arguing that the Confederate president be released on bond if the government had no intent of ever prosecuting him.[78]

Less concerned with the case's legal and constitutional niceties, Greeley was keen to make Davis the object of a grand gesture. Davis, after all, was "the representative of six millions of people." Magnanimity toward him would inspire "a juster appreciation of the North at the South, which is the first step toward a beneficent and perfect reconciliation." Indeed, Greeley held that such a powerful, symbolic instance of "Universal Amnesty" from the North would inspire white Southerners to hold up their end of Greeley's Reconstruction bargain and grant "Impartial Suffrage" to freed slaves.[79]

In a speech to a mixed-race audience at the African Church in Richmond following the bond hearing, Greeley used the occasion to enlarge on the vision of Reconstruction embedded in his symbolic act. "By ordinary calculations," he said, a "perfect peace" should have taken hold within a year of the surrender at Appomattox. Horrible missteps by all parties had delayed the issue, however. John Wilkes Booth's assassination of Lincoln had quashed whatever spirit of magnanimity and reconciliation had existed in the North in the spring of 1865; the establishment of black codes, race riots, and other atrocities toward the freed people had only extended bitter feelings toward the South over the next two years. Northerners, however, were not guiltless. Military tribunals and loose talk of "confiscation" from Thad Stevens and his Radical crowd hardly amounted to olive branches proffered to the South.[80]

African Americans, meanwhile, also had work to do. Both white Northerners and Southerners owed a great debt to African Americans "for their conduct in the war," but Greeley urged them not to sit idly by, counting on confiscation or land grants. Never mind his previous support for western homestead legislation for white men, and never mind the details; Greeley exhorted the black members of his audience to obtain land for themselves. "Own something which you can call a home," he said. "It will give you a deeper feeling of independence and of self-respect." All parties, in short, must forgive and forget, compromise and contribute. They must "forget the years of slavery, and secession, and civil war, now happily past. . . . Forget that some of you have been masters, others slaves—some for disunion, others against it." The time had come to "bury the dead past in mutual and hearty good-will" and to form a "united effort" to redeem the country.[81]

Few took delight in Greeley's plans. Angry letters poured in from all quarters. *Tribune* subscribers cancelled in droves. Union veterans registered their disgust. The New York City chapter of the Union League convened a special meeting to discuss ejecting Greeley from its ranks. The abolitionist Wendell Phillips called Greeley a "fawning spaniel" who had rendered "treason . . . easy and respectable." Such responses were perhaps to be expected. As Greeley told the leadership of the Union League, he'd previously been assailed by "narrow-minded blockheads" and "impudent puppies" for taking principled and unpopular stands.[82]

Yet the Davis affair dealt an unexpected blow to *The American Conflict*, Greeley's history of the war. Though Greeley predicted that future historians and biographers would deem his gesture in Richmond "the wisest act" in a life devoted to "humanity and freedom," his contemporaries now questioned his own work as a historian. With the second volume still new to the market, sales sputtered. Subscribers who had already paid for both volumes cancelled and asked for refunds. Sales agents seeking new subscribers found precious few takers. By the beginning of 1870, the project had become a financial albatross for the publishing house of O. D. Case, which lost $12,000 in 1869. Writing to Greeley, Case suggested that the publishing arm of the *Tribune* buy out the remaining stock of *The American Conflict* for a "reasonably low price." "It has taken a great deal longer for the storm to blow over, caused by the Davis Bail Bond, than I anticipated," Case said, "and the fruitless efforts we made the first year to recover it cost us a good deal of money." In an effort to persuade Greeley to agree to the deal, Case suggested that the *Tribune* could sell 50,000 to 100,000 more copies of his book, with some added improvements, and flattered him that *The American Conflict* would "always be called for as the history of the Great Rebellion."[83]

Greeley certainly intended such a status for his work. When volume 2 appeared, he promised a different kind of Civil War history. Where others might have emphasized military heroics, Greeley's would be an altogether broader story of moral and spiritual struggle. His was a history not only of "the noise of captains, and the shouting," but also of "the silent influence . . . involved in gradually molding and refining Public Opinion to accept, and ultimately demand, the overthrow and extinction of Human Slavery, as the one vital, implacable enemy of our Nationality and our Peace." The project as a whole was to stand as a great monument to Greeley's long career, his "almost exclusive devotion to National affairs," and the singular role *he* played in "molding and refining public opinion."[84]

Not long after volume 1 had appeared, Greeley underscored such connections in a meeting with painter Francis Bicknell Carpenter at the White House in June of 1864. Inspecting Carpenter's portrait of the Lincoln cabinet, "The First Reading of the Emancipation Proclamation," Greeley told the artist that the "steel likenesses in his book 'The American Conflict' were much better." When Carpenter parried the insult by directing Greeley's eye to the newspaper on the table, modeled after the *Tribune* and representing "the agency of the 'Press' in bringing about <u>Emancipation</u>," Greeley suggested a refinement. "I would not object," he told the painter, "to your putting in my letter to the President on that subject." In volume 2 of *The American Conflict*, Greeley referred to "The Prayer of Twenty Millions" vaguely—as "a letter addressed to the President" in August of 1862—but he enshrined the sentiment within it in what he expressed to Carpenter. Lincoln, he wrote, was "habitually cautious, dilatory, reticent" and needed more urging "in the spirit of Mr. Greeley's letter."[85]

Paying Jefferson Davis's bail in 1867 both clashed with the narrative frame of *The American Conflict* and fit perfectly with Greeley's own actual, troubled course through the Civil War. As the *North American Review* noted just two months prior to Greeley's trip to Richmond, the incongruity between the grand vision of his book and the "want of faith" that marked his conduct during the war undermined the credibility of *The American Conflict* as a historical production. In the book, he had captured the war as a struggle for resolution in "the great contest between the principles of slavery and the principles of liberty." "Few men," the *Review* claimed, "[were] more competent" to do so. At the same time, however, did not the record of Greeley's "vagaries" throughout the war ultimately rob him of the credibility to tell that story? That, anyway, appeared to be the judgment of *The American Conflict*'s readers who cancelled their subscriptions and demanded refunds, as it was for those who didn't buy the book's unsold copies.

The *North American Review* had a simple explanation for the problem. Greeley operated with "an unfortunate habit of mistaking his opinions and sentiments for those of the nation."[86] That habit, the oldest of his public career, would propel him forward into his fight with an altogether more consistent and formidable wartime figure, Ulysses S. Grant.

THE CARD OF INVITATION.

(For description of the Invitation, see page 19.)

Mr. and Mrs. A. J. Johnson

Request the pleasure of the company of

on the evening of Saturday, 3d February, 1872, *between the hours of Nine and Eleven,*

TO MEET THE

> In the center of the Invitation was
> **A LIFE-LIKE PORTRAIT**
> OF
> **MR. GREELEY,**
> (on steel),
> By Geo. E. Perine, and following
> it was a *fac-simile* of Mr. G.'s
> well-known Signature.

Hon. Horace Greeley

on the occasion of his

SIXTY-FIRST BIRTHDAY.

The favor of an answer is requested.

323 *West 57th Street, New York.*

Invitation to Horace Greeley's sixty-first birthday, in Charles F. Wingate, *Sketch of the Celebration of the Sixty-First Birthday of the Hon. Horace Greeley, LL.D.* (New York: 1872). Courtesy, American Antiquarian Society

CHAPTER FIVE

The Most American of Americans

Horace Greeley ran for president in 1872 as an independent national celebrity. The party labels attached to him—Liberal Republican and Democrat—were beside the point. Greeley was a figure who transcended party and section, who could contain the nation's great multitudes and would lead them back to unity. This was the message of his sixty-first birthday celebration, held on February 3, 1872. Invitations had summoned dignitaries from every corner of the land to celebrate the great editor. In the sumptuous rooms of Alvan Johnson's Fifty-Seventh Street mansion in New York City, no differences were too great to be reconciled in the presence of "Our Second Franklin." As abolitionists and Democrats, Union men and former Confederates, dreamy reformers and stern conservatives toasted him with their glasses of cold water and lemonade (for who would dare tipple in Greeley's presence?), they testified to his singular powers.

So, at least, went the argument in Charles Wingate's pamphlet detailing the occasion, which was effectively the first piece of official campaign literature in Greeley's bid for the White House. In Wingate's telling and in the testimonials he gathered, Greeley merited favorable comparison with members of a pantheon that included Abraham Lincoln, Benjamin Franklin, Ralph Waldo Emerson, Henry Ward Beecher, Theodore Parker, William Cobbett, William Lloyd Garrison, John Brown, Martin Luther, John Knox, Thomas Carlyle, John Ruskin, Goethe, Ulysses S. Grant, and Napoleon. "Mr. Greeley," Edward Eggleston said, "is the most American of Americans. . . .

In [him] the average American sees himself magnified." Greeley, the self-made man who had wrested his fame and influence out from early poverty and obscurity, was already a giant of the nation's past; the great harmonization in his presence testified to his claims as a visionary of its future. To be sure, Greeley had his "crotchets," "vagaries," "notions," and "eccentricities," but these only added to his singularity. Perhaps they were precisely what the nation needed. What other "bold assailer of slavery" could yet have his name "respected throughout the South?" Who else could unite "New Englanders, Knickerbockers, Westerners, and Southerners?" Who else had "stood by the Union as a representative of free principles—stood by it when uncomprehended by the masses; stood by it when traitorous hands sought to render it asunder—stood by it when it assumed the proportions of its restored comeliness?" Who else could realize its great consensus?[1]

The vision of the Greeley campaign—national reconciliation at no great cost or hard compromise—was bold, optimistic, and wildly unsuccessful. From the Civil War's beginnings, Greeley had read the conflict as a great ordeal of American nationhood that would then yield its truest expression. When the guns were silenced, Greeley embraced the hope of national rebirth that so many had expressed—not as an aspiration, but as a fixed reality, waiting only to be universally recognized. All that was needed was magnanimity from the North, contrition from Southern whites, patience from African Americans, and, above all, a voice to lead the people to their destinies. Though the persistence of sectional bitterness following the Civil War would have been plain to any reader of the *New-York Tribune*, much less its editor, Greeley plunged into Reconstruction with a boundless faith that all wounds could be healed with his formula of "universal amnesty and impartial suffrage."[2]

But Greeley's celebrity, and the national coherence it was meant to embody, were both less than the sum of their parts. The celebrity was tempting to some, like the Liberal Republicans who courted Greeley's support and wound up with a nominee instead; it was intoxicating to others, above all to Greeley, who was undone by the people's failure to recognize their redemption in his leadership. If Greeley's celebrity formed the central argument for his campaign, it was also the source of the campaign's failure. Thomas Nast's famous cartoons and the thousand other calumnies that added a comic streak to this chapter of American political history were so effective because they cut to the quick of Greeley's claims to be a transformational and representative figure. Greeley was indeed famous, as the cartoons suggested, but he was famous for being a hokey relic rather than a great visionary.

Moreover, the nation that Greeley promised was neither defined nor unified. The bitter experience of war was too present, too alive for the people to accept Greeley's repeated invitations to "forget" their differences. The people would "clasp hands across the bloody chasm which has too long divided them," he promised in accepting the Liberal Republicans' nomination for president in 1872, "forgetting that they have been enemies in the joyful consciousness that they are and must henceforth remain brethren." The election was one of remembering divisions rather than forgetting them, however. To follow in Greeley's plans, the *New-York Times* suggested, would be to ignore "what was fought for in the war—to confess that the blood of tens of thousands of Union soldiers was poured forth in vain." Some Southerners and Northern Democrats did overlook who Greeley had been prior to the War, but most did not. He would win just six states.[3]

Visions of Reconciliation

If Greeley's wild inconsistencies during the Civil War had been startling, his unwavering consistency during Reconstruction was perhaps even more so. Bailing out Jefferson Davis was merely the most visible and public expression of his broad vision for national reconciliation that remained fixed from the last days of the war until the election of 1872. Greeley's starry-eyed plans for Reconstruction were rooted in an unrealistic faith in the power of a regenerated American nationalism and a simple formula of "universal amnesty and impartial suffrage."

Not merely reconstructing the nation, but redeeming it, was a matter of rhetoric, attitude, and understanding as much as one of policy. Indeed, Greeley was short on specifics for Reconstruction plans. He had been vamping on the note of what he called "Magnanimity in Triumph" as soon as the Union victory appeared imminent, late in 1864. Harsh, unreasoned retribution, hasty military trials on the drumhead, and reckless executions would have little effect beyond perpetuating the enmity that had led to the war in the first place. "We plead for restoration of the Union, against a policy which would afford momentary gratification at the cost of years of perilous hate and bitterness," he said.[4]

Insofar as Greeley did take on peace as a matter of policy, he did so in broad terms. He was generally supportive of Abraham Lincoln's generous "ten-percent plan," and he was usually hostile to the more punitive schemes of Radical Republicans. As he had remarked in response to Thaddeus Stevens, the Pennsylvania Radical, in 1864, Greeley had "no taste for either vengeance or spoliation." With the end of the war closer in sight by the turn of 1865, he savored the thought even less. Congress, marked by the Radicals' "pungent, bitter" rhetoric, should pass the Thirteenth Amendment and go home. Matters of Reconstruction and peace should be left to the president—as instructed by Greeley himself.[5]

Yet if Greeley wasn't a Radical, he was a reluctant Lincolnite. The president's turn as a latter-day Old Testament prophet in his second inaugural address didn't suit Greeley's reflections on the war or his hopes for the ensuing peace. It was altogether too harsh and insufficiently conciliatory for the *Tribune* editor. "Now is the fittest time for putting forth manifestations of generosity, clemency, magnanimity," Greeley wrote, annoyed that Lincoln hadn't heeded the speech notes the editor had provided in an earlier *Tribune* column. Even if those manifestations were certain to be rejected by the disgraced planter elite, they would do much good in emboldening "their duped, disgusted, despairing followers." Greeley had more advice for the president in the war's final weeks. Lincoln should issue a proclamation—"a direct, specific appeal and overture to the Southern People, urging them to return to loyalty and peace, and giving them substantial reasons for so doing."[6]

Fixed notions of "the Southern People"—white and black—informed Greeley's optimism for peace and reconciliation. Four years of stubborn warfare had not shaken Greeley's longstanding faith in the South's white yeomanry as the bedrock of the region's true American nationalism. Through much of the conflict, Greeley had predicted that their dormant love of the nation and Free Labor would be awakened when the rebellion's leaders were toppled. With the war finally at an end, the moment had come for these sturdy Americans to be "undeceived." All the Southern masses needed was "due assurance that they [would] be treated with magnanimity." "The Southern mind," Greeley said in the early raptures of peace, "is now open to kindness, and may be magnetically affected by generosity." Kindness, generosity, and amnesty, not confiscation and subjugation—these would bring the masses back "in thousands to the National standard" and make the nation whole.[7]

Free Labor would nurture the white yeomanry's latent "Nationality." "The time is coming when manual labor will be as respectable in South Carolina as in New-England," the *Tribune* noted in 1866. "The artificial degradation of production will pass away." With the scourge of slavery removed, the South would become a laboratory in which to validate the supremacy of free over bonded labor. Restored to "the quiet ways of industry and thrift," the region would bloom with the awakening of its yeomanry and the migration of millions from the North, the West, and Europe who would be drawn to its "cheap lands and genial climate." "Only Liberty was needed to make this the garden of the earth, and Liberty will be no more wanting." Political consensus would follow from this moral and material revival. With "the Slave Power" crushed, the old "Democracy" of cynical elites and their labor-loathing dupes would crumble.[8]

Greeley ostensibly was sincere in the commitment to black citizenship implied in the marriage he sought to arrange between "Universal Freedom" and "Universal Amnesty." In his eyes, the freed people would form the foundation of Southern Republicanism, loyal to the party of emancipation and Union. They would begin as another class of Southerners ready to be liberated and enlightened by the virtues of Free Labor. Southern whites could and should unite with them in reinvigorating their region and reintegrating it into the Nation at large. There was no other choice. "Slavery being dead," a *Tribune* editorial asked, "why should its accessories and buttresses be preserved?" The "collisions" and "contentions" of the war and the generations preceding it could only be forgotten when the South "promptly and cordially unite[d] in proclaiming Freedom for All," and when equal rights under the law—including suffrage—were fully established.[9]

Vague as the concept of "Universal Amnesty, Impartial Suffrage" was in policy terms, Greeley's commitment to the principle made him an enthusiastic supporter of the Republican program for Reconstruction when voting and equality were at stake. Early in 1866, he mobilized the *Tribune* and went to Washington in support of that year's Civil Rights Bill and a followup Freedmen's Bureau Bill seeking equal rights and opportunity for blacks. His advocacy was strong enough that *Independent* editor Theodore Tilton hailed him as the Civil Rights Bill's de facto author—a claim later enshrined by Greeley's presence on the murals commemorating the bill inside the Capitol. He likewise stood out as an enthusiastic supporter of the two Reconstruction amendments, both of which he said were necessary corollaries to the principles of "Universal Amnesty, Impartial Suffrage."[10]

In practice, however, "Universal Amnesty, Impartial Suffrage" was hardly an expansive vision of racial equality. On the question of suffrage, Greeley made it clear that "impartial" was a conditional term. There were bars that needed to be cleared before this right could be granted to all. As his suffrage committee at the 1867 New York State constitutional convention noted in its recommendations, "the right of suffrage does not belong to men whose voting will not contribute to popular intelligence and comfort." That proviso was consistent with other Greeley pronouncements on the subject. Immediately following the war, a *Tribune* editorial had made it clear that "equal rights under the law" should be extended to all, but that voting rights should be granted only to those who exhibited "intelligence, industry, thrift, and an exemplary life." When it came to codifying and enforcing voting rights (as well as addressing the safety of Southern blacks), Greeley remained equivocal. As Ku Klux Klan outrages mounted across the South, Greeley tempered his support for the Fifteenth Amendment with renewed calls for "universal amnesty" for Confederates. White terror in the South would stop—and black voting could begin, on whatever limited terms it was accorded—only when whites were re-enfranchised.[11]

An unmistakable racism rested beneath Greeley's conditional notions of "Impartial" and "Universal." In 1870, when he called blacks "an easy, worthless race, taking no thought for to-morrow," he stated directly what had been lingering beneath his policies since the end of the war.[12] While the best efforts must be put forth for equality and civil rights, Greeley made it plain elsewhere that blacks weren't to expect much more—nor would they be a critical constituency in the nation's future. As he said in his 1867 Richmond address, blacks "are and must remain, to some extent, a separate and pecu-

liar people in the land" whose "numerical importance" would "steadily decline" over the coming years.[13] Moreover, those blacks living in the South
would necessarily be limited by their status as a poor, landless, uneducated
people and should not be a source of any discord. They were, Greeley noted
repeatedly through the postwar years, "just about the most docile, valuable
peasantry on the face of the earth." The great mass of former slaves who
were not yet "intelligent" and "industrious" might well rise to full status as
"Men" and citizens, but it would take time and patience. As Greeley urged
his black audience in Richmond, they must be nurtured by Free Labor and
educated in free schools, all the while laying up the capital with which to
purchase land.[14]

Greeley's sense of blacks as a "separate and peculiar people" led him to
a harsher variant of liberalism than anything he had previously espoused.
For decades, he had been seeking ways to temper what he called "the rough
rivalry of the mart" and had been telling Northern whites to "Go West" to
seek livelihoods on land set aside by the government for homesteads. Now,
Greeley's directive to freed slaves was the far less forgiving "root, hog, or
die." "The Colored People of this country are called to evince eminent Self-
Reliance," Greeley wrote in 1869. "They must trust God and help each other,
asking of the Whites naked justice, and that only." "If negroes will not work,
they must starve or steal," a *Tribune* editorial explained not long after the
war's end. "And, if they steal, they must be shut up, like other thieves. If there
be any among them who fancy that they, being free, can live in comfort
without work, they have now entered a school in which they will certainly
and speedily be taught better." In practical terms, the freed people should
expect nothing in the way of government largesse. Southern blacks should
indeed own land, Greeley said, but they must earn it first through their own
efforts, not through land distribution or other "pernicious" schemes that
were "certain to injure those [they are] intended to benefit." Likewise, the
Freedmen's Bureau and "all manner of coddling devices" should be eliminated. The "negroes [should] take care of themselves."[15]

Greeley's tough-love paternalism for the freed people had a performative
quality to it. His pronouncements on the postwar racial order were more
tuned to those whites, in both the North and the South, whom he believed
responsible for the real work of reconciliation and national regeneration.

Neither group need fear the revolution promised by Thad Stevens and his Radical ilk. To Northern whites fretting over a mass migration of blacks out of the South, Greeley offered the pseudoscientific claim that they would remain where they were, due to a racial affinity for warmer latitudes and a latent desire to humiliate their former masters. Those Yankees reluctant to bring their capital and industry into the South could likewise cast aside their concerns. As Greeley noted in his *Letters from Texas,* "I must adjudge the question 'Will free niggers work' satisfactorily answered. The Four and a Quarter Million bales of Cotton grown in the United States in 1870 are not to be gainsayed." Those seeking to "Go South" could do so with the assurance that a reliable, obedient workforce awaited them.[16]

Greeley's emphasis on national regeneration through white reconciliation limited his consideration of black interests and experiences to abstract notions. As a "separate and peculiar people" and a "peasantry," blacks figured into Greeley's calculations only insofar as they touched upon the broader problems of national reunion. A public confrontation with the black South Carolina congressman Robert Brown Elliott in 1871 exposed the extent of Greeley's myopia. Though only recently seated, Elliott wasted little time in rising to the floor in the House of Representatives to condemn the idea of amnesty for former Confederates, even as Klan violence continued to terrorize blacks across the South. A *Tribune* editorial blasted Elliott, claiming he'd "done his race lasting harm by his first demonstration in the House." By registering such a protest against amnesty, Elliott and other blacks would only "confirm [the] malevolent and mischievous impression [that] 'These niggers around us . . . profess all manner of good will and kindly feeling toward their White neighbors; but that fellow in Congress betrays their real *animus.* Only give them power, and they would disfranchise all who are not Black.'" Moreover, the piece claimed, Klan violence was perpetrated by "wild youngsters" who were moved to act only because of the proscription from public life by their social betters.[17]

Elliott's carefully measured response captured the distance between Greeley and his *Tribune* lieutenants' ideas about the postwar South. With an air of betrayal based on the paper's reputation, Elliott noted that the editorial might "better befit the lips of an advocate . . . in a defense of these masked murderers before a petit jury than the pages of THE NEW-YORK TRI-

BUNE." "You reason, Mr. Editor," Elliott continued, "upon the Ku-Klux in the abstract, while I view them as living realities, who show no mercy, and, therefore, deserve none.... Your graciousness to the recalcitrant Confederates, would be somewhat modified if you lived, as I do, within the theater of their operations."[18]

Elliott was right. "Recalcitrant Confederates" were more important to Greeley's schemes for Reconstruction than the freed people. Beyond the yeomanry, Greeley appealed to the South's old Whigs, who, he believed, had grasped the evils of slavery, remained loyal to the Union, and were prepared to become benevolent custodians of the freed people. The postwar years need not be troubled by convulsions and racial conflict, Greeley said repeatedly. There could be a relationship of "mutual kindness and trust" between the "Capital and Labor of the South." The region's natural leaders needed only to "call the ablest, most intelligent Blacks around [them], ... inspire the negro to work, and plan, and save, by proffering the Right of Suffrage to all who shall prove worthy of it and capable of exercising it intelligently, safely, and usefully." Order and harmony would reinvigorate the region and unite the nation. Confident in peace and order, Northerners could bring their capital and Free Labor virtues southward.[19]

The Séance of Political Economy

In 1869, Greeley published a love letter to tariffs. His collection, *Essays Designed to Elucidate the Science of Political Economy*, gathered together *Tribune* and other writings to argue anew for trade protection as a sure path to national unity. Though these essays were engaged in the problems of the present, they were firmly rooted in the past. Greeley dedicated the book to Henry Clay, the great progenitor of Whig nationalism. As Greeley noted in the introduction, "My positions are substantially those held by Henry Clay, Rollin C. Mallary, Walter Forward, and their compeers; in opposition to those of John Randolph, John C. Calhoun, George McDuffie, and Churchill C. Cambreleng." Of these friends and opponents Greeley listed, only Cambreleng lived to see the Civil War, and he died in 1862. Greeley had briefly flirted with spiritualism and séances in the 1850s; now, as he campaigned for Whig nationalist economics, he was communing with the dead all over again.[20]

Greeley's postwar schemes were not limited to the South; the South was merely a laboratory in a greater national project. His plans for the region fell within a larger vision for consensus that would dissolve all sectional designations among white men. Greeley hoped to realize the dictum etched into Clay's headstone, taken from an 1850 speech: "I know no North—no South—no East—no West." In seeking to realize Clay's dream and spark a national rebirth, Greeley reverted back to a broader collection of old Whig economic policies and moral impulses. Strong tariffs, sound money, internal improvements, scientific farming, temperance, and a cooperative settlement within the nation as a whole would key this great harmonization. As capital and labor would cease to be in conflict, so, too, would sectional differences fall away. The "Great Pacificator's" plans from the 1830s and '40s had been thwarted by sectional conflict; now, at long last, they would knit the nation together in the 1860s and '70s.

Greeley's larger plans for consensus began with tariffs. With high wartime duties threatened by the ensuing peace, he vowed to instruct the masses —"the intelligent, observant, reflecting farmers and mechanics"—that their liberation and the nation's deliverance would come only through a protective trade policy.[21] Proponents of free trade had long noted the tendency of tariffs to stoke conflict between the industrial Northeast and the agrarian South and West, and they had railed against protectionism as a driver of class conflict between manufacturers, on the one hand, and laborers and farmers, on the other.[22]

For Greeley, however, tariffs were nationalist engines of unity, rather than division. They would keep cheap foreign goods from undercutting American production, allowing a truly national market to blossom. Greeley admitted that industrial and commercial centers in the Northeast *were* too powerful, but he argued that tariffs should be seen as the solution to the problem, rather than its source. Properly applied, trade protection would support the development of industrial enterprise beyond the Northeast, reducing its dominance and the regional tensions that came with it. As manufacturing became established across the land, all would benefit. Farmers, so long held up as victims of the higher prices created by tariffs, would find cheaper goods from local sources of production and fetch higher prices for their crops among the nearby industrial workforces.[23]

The social benefits of this protectionism would be no less felicitous than the sectional ones. As the full title of Greeley's book held, "protection to home industry" was substantially "a system of national coöperation for the elevation of labor." Recalling Whig economist Henry C. Carey's *Harmony of Interests*, Greeley envisioned the longstanding strife between capital and labor melting away amid the "natural and mutual interdependence of diverse pursuits and industries" that came with a secure national market. During a Pennsylvania coal miners' strike in 1869, Greeley lamented, "The antagonism between Capital and Labor—the most painful and embarrassing of social antagonisms—continues in various parts of the country to excite ill-feeling between two classes, which, for the interest of both, should act together harmoniously." Under a proper protective system for trade, they would. In a flourishing national market, laborers would command higher wages and have fewer grievances against their bosses. The strikes at present troubling more and more industries would be things of the past.[24]

Perhaps most importantly, though, labor, at long last, would be redeemed spiritually. With slavery dead, the nation could rededicate itself to work and to building up the individuals that came with it. Summoning another ghost—that of William Ellery Channing—Greeley argued that the "chief end of a true political economy" was to "fully develop and employ the entire industrial capacity of our people." He did not mean this in material terms, however. "Industrial capacity" implied turning "idlers," "profligates," and "useless exchangers or traffickers" into people who loved and valued work as an end in itself. "Infinite are the uses of Labor," Greeley said, "but its highest and noblest fruition is MAN!"[25]

Moral measures would also help. Greeley once again took up the banner of temperance and prohibition, arguing that these were every bit as important as tariffs in protecting workers' interests. Indeed, Greeley claimed repeatedly that sobriety and "habits of industry" were more effective tools for labor than even unions and strikes. A *Tribune* editorial savaged an 1866 laborers' congress, referring to the workers' fiery language of class struggle as little more than "bosh." "It is not capital," the editorial held, "it is the grog-shop, the beer-saloon, the billiard-room, the cigar-store, the gambling-den, the sink of pollution, whence the encroachment on the 'rights of the industrial classes' is most to be apprehended." Though the cause of temperance and prohibition had been set back by the Civil War, Greeley argued that people should at least be required to vote on prohibition every year, in order to be reminded that drinking and "the Liquor Traffic" represented stern moral choices for individuals, communities, and the nation at large.[26]

Elevating industrial labor was necessary, but to Greeley, no other type of work was more noble—or more important to the nation's welfare—than farming. As he told a crowd in Houston, Texas, in 1871, "The civilization of our race is evinced and measured by the growth and progress of its Agriculture."[27] Greeley had long lamented that he "should have been a farmer," and he worked to convince a "conceited generation," tempted by the glittering promises of business and trade, to avoid his mistakes. In a much-mocked collection of "brief and plain expositions" on *What I Know of Farming*, Greeley envisioned a latter-day Jeffersonian cultivator: independent and virtuous, but aided by the finest machinery and rooted in the latest science on crop rotation, plowing methods, soil quality, drainage, irrigation, and fertilizers.[28]

Between chapters with titles like "Thorough Tillage" and "Muck—How to Utilize It," Greeley rhapsodized on the farmer's calling. Working the land was hard, but it was honest: a "broad, straight highway of integrity and righteousness," most conducive to "manliness of character." The younger generation needed to be convinced that farming was an intellectual pursuit that united hand work and head work, and they must learn that their toils would be rewarded in their own spiritual renewal—and in that of the nation. A farmer's "enterprise and devotion," Greeley predicted, "will at length be crowned a signal and inspiring success . . . [and] thousands will be awakened to it by a larger and nobler conception of the mission of Industry, and the possibilities of achievement which stud the path of simple, honest, faithful persistent Work."[29]

Though Greeley held up white farmers as models of independence and virtue, he also said that they should not be left entirely on their own. Those young men looking to escape the blight and moral rot of cities in the expanses of the West and the wastelands of the South should do so cooperatively. As a *Tribune* editorial claimed in 1871, "The Daniel Boone business is played out." Settlers need not go through the hardships of establishing new lives alone; they should migrate in groups of a thousand, create "five or six embryo townships," and speed the growth of civil society. Though remaining individual property owners, they could work collectively to build the roads, bridges, mills, schools, and churches whose absence made life so difficult for lonely homesteaders.[30]

While advocating cooperative settlement plans in his writings on farming, Greeley also lent his capital—and eventually his name—to the Union Colony, located in what became the town of Greeley, Colorado. Led by former *Tribune* agricultural editor (and former Fourierite) Nathaniel Cook Meeker, the Union Colony was to be a model for "the remainder of the vast territory of our country." Advertised as a destination for "temperance men . . . ambitious to establish a good society," this colony would bring the New England town model of the seventeenth century to the West. Family groups forming the "intelligent, educated, and thrifty community" would migrate en masse. They would be granted building plots within the town and acreage for farming in the surrounding lands. Farmers would work individually, but the work of community building would be collective. "Schools, refined society, and all the advantages of an old country" would be set in place almost immediately. Rail links, telegraph lines, and newspapers would ensure that the community was connected to the nation at large through commerce and information.[31]

Greeley's enthusiasm for what became his namesake—Greeley, Colorado —was not merely a matter of egotism. He reveled in the possibilities presented by it and like communities as a bold vision for the future, rooted in the practices and virtues of the past. The town of Greeley and its model of a "temperate, moral, industrious, intelligent" society was precisely what the nation needed to slough off the divisions of war and the legacies of slavery. The community—the nation—would be a harmonious whole in which people venerated and rewarded labor, educated their children, and advanced as a collection of individuals toward a common destiny.[32]

Horace Greeley's Golden Age

What did any of this mean politically? Greeley's national visions were hard to place in any particular movement or party. His rhetoric of reconciliation, amnesty, and local control, combined with grand gestures like paying Jefferson Davis's bail, marked him as a turncoat in Republican circles. Yet none would mistake him for a Democrat. The *Tribune* remained a force in Republican politics at the state and national levels, and so long as Greeley was identified with his paper, he kept his place in the political firmament with a healthy measure of gravitational pull. His grand plans for the nation comingled with his irrepressible ambitions for political glory and placed him on a collision course with Ulysses S. Grant.

By any measure, Greeley's political star had all but winked out by the end of 1870. The elections that fall had seen him vanquished in not one, but two separate contests. First, at the New York State Republican convention in September, a Greeley-for-governor wave had briefly risen, with the backing of no less than President Grant himself. The wave broke quickly, however. After a candidate from Roscoe Conkling's rival faction was nominated on the third ballot, the enthusiasm for Greeley was revealed to be a scheme hatched by party leaders to mollify the malcontent editor. He'd never stood a chance. The nomination that did come to Greeley—for a congressional seat representing the heavily Democratic Sixth District in New York City— offered scant consolation. Amid a bloodbath for New York Republicans, Greeley's defeat by a Tammany Democrat punctuated a succession of failures in politics. Since the war's end, offices great and small—from the US Senate to the New York State Comptrollership—had eluded him. Plagued by ill health, ongoing financial troubles, and an unhappy family life, Greeley could perhaps find relief in abandoning his political ambitions; at the very least, he could tell his close associates that this was the case.[33]

Yet even as his disappointments had Greeley contemplating retirement, political chatter tilted toward bigger prizes than senate seats and governors' mansions. With the Republican Party fracturing over local struggles for patronage and broad ideological differences, the notion that *Greeley* might bridge party divides began to drip from newspapers. Though some suggested the possibility of the *Tribune* editor joining Grant on the 1872 ticket, others, like Murat Halstead of the *Cincinnati Commercial*, began to champion the notion of Greeley for president. "Think of GREELEY playing second fiddle to GRANT," Halstead fumed in November of 1870. "GREELEY, the fertile father of ideas, the intellectual revolutionist, the political iconoclast, the old party dictator, the workingman's friend and advocate of humanity." Just before the turn of 1871, Halstead officially endorsed Greeley. True, the liberal Halstead said, Greeley's "tariff tomfoolery" raised concerns, but he was honest and principled, not to mention his stance as the greatest champion of reconciliation. Could he not reconcile all political factions, as well as the nation itself?[34]

The talk of a Greeley run for the presidency aggravated existing tensions between the White House and the *Tribune* offices. Grant's support of the Conkling faction in New York State already had the *Tribune* and the White House at odds, and Greeley's tepid backing of Grant had long rankled the president. As Grant told one of Greeley's former editorial lieutenants in the fall of 1870, the "Old White Coat" was "an honest, firm, untiring supporter of the republican party," but too much of a "free thinker" and one for whom it was too easy to leap to conclusions. Still, Greeley's popularity and the *Tribune*'s influence made both a threat to Grant. As the *Albany Argus* put it, Grant was "bound to keep faith with the philosopher, for he dreads the Tribune more than he ever did Lee." Offers for dinners, casual chats, and visits to the White House—not to mention high-level offices and ambassadorships—were tendered to Greeley, and all were politely declined. Privately, Greeley expressed his wish for Grant to "only let me alone" and to "see that there is no more trouble for two years at least."[35]

Neither Grant nor the newspapers would let Greeley alone, however, and Greeley gave scant indication that he wished them to do so. Events escalated through the first half of 1871 toward a bid for the White House. Greeley's election as chairman of the New York City Republican Committee early in the year put him at the center of the party's internal conflicts, as well as at the heart of the ongoing coverage of the discord between him and Grant.[36] Though Greeley called for unity and claimed to endorse the president, indications suggested that his sympathies and ambitions rested elsewhere. A *Tribune* editorial had already made the coy prediction that in 1872, "public opinion" would "ultimately settle on the conviction that the one-term principle is, as a general rule, well grounded."[37] Within the New York City Republican Committee, he stayed on as head of the anti-Grant faction. By February of 1871, when Greeley accepted an invitation to give the keynote speech at the Texas State Fair and began laying plans for a larger Southern tour, there could be little doubt of his intentions.[38]

The very notion of Greeley as a presidential candidate "called forth a good deal of mere badinage and laughter," Halstead's *Cincinnati Commercial* noted. But why not Greeley? The case went beyond his very evident availability. Early endorsements portrayed the "Old White Coat" as a beloved man of the people whose singular popularity could heal the divides left by the Civil War and widened by Reconstruction; here was an independent, homespun hero whose virtue could purge the corrupt politics of the Grant era. Halstead's *Cincinnati Commercial* had described a singular personage who was, above all, a voice and symbol of national reconciliation. Greeley was the "author of the phrase that best expresses the only sound, everlasting basis of reconstruction—'Impartial Suffrage, Universal Amnesty.'" Here was "the simple and complete platform on which the next president should be elected. Who better to stand upon it [than] the author of it?" Greeley, moreover, was a "thoroughly honest man. There is not a bone in him that has not the true grit of incorruptible manhood." Perhaps most importantly, though, Greeley possessed something that other rivals to Grant did not: popularity. As Logan Reavis wrote in April in the *St. Louis Democrat*, Greeley was "the best known of living Americans," a man of "universal popularity, the embodiment of ability, character, moral worth . . . a representative of American nationality and civilization." Greeley, Reavis said, picking up on Grant's 1868 campaign pledge, would "let us have peace in good earnest."[39]

Greeley's Southern speaking tour in the spring of 1871 added ballast to arguments for his candidacy. The editor's "popularity," one paper remarked not long after his return, "so far from being the myth which some have tried to make it out . . . [was] a very matter-of-fact reality, not to be safely disregarded."[40] Indeed, few of the Southerners along his path from New Orleans, into Texas, and back up the Mississippi River disregarded Greeley. The *Tribune* editor was trailed by special newspaper correspondents and attended by delegations of governors, senators, and generals. On wharves and at depots along the route of the special train he took on the Texas Central Railroad, throngs of people "without distinction of party or creed" crowded to get a look at "the great national philosopher." As many correspondents noted, Greeley wore a black alpaca coat and brown straw hat, rather than the signature white with which he was identified, but he was nonetheless "instantly recognized" everywhere. Lesser dignitaries from smaller towns and cities begged him to add stops in their communities, hoping, as one report noted, "to hear words of wisdom from Mr. Greeley as a representative national man."[41]

Greeley had words aplenty for his audiences. Though the nominal purpose of the trip was to reflect on agriculture—to impart "what he knew of farming"—he returned to his familiar themes of reconciliation and national revival, universal amnesty, and impartial suffrage. Notably soft-pedaling his commitment to tariffs and trade protection, he assured white Southerners that his own good will toward the South was taking hold across the North. True, he told an audience in Galveston, he had been criticized sharply for his role in paying Jeff Davis's bail, but "the better sense of the North justified me. . . . The general sentiment of the North is [to] let bygones be bygones." White Southerners, for their part, had been treated harshly by Reconstruction policies. Ku Klux Klan violence was to be deplored and must be stopped, Greeley said, but there never would have been a Klan— and never a need for violence—had a general amnesty been proclaimed immediately after Appomattox.[42]

Greeley's editorial lieutenants back in New York City dutifully tuned the *Tribune*'s content to their chief's Southern walkabout. Reflecting on "The South—Its Sins and Sufferings," an editorial appeared just before Greeley delivered his address at the Texas State Fair, lamenting that "the most intelligent, the influential, the educated, the really useful men of the South" had been driven from the corridors of power. While those men sat prostrate, Southern people were "taxed and swindled by a horde of rascally foreign adventurers and by the ignorant class, which only yesterday hoed the fields and served in the kitchen." Greeley proved willing to travel further south in spirit than his previous pronouncements on Reconstruction would have suggested. When he stopped at a sugar plantation in Louisiana to tout the virtues of Free Labor and enlightened former slaveholders, one former slave called him "[the] whitest man in [North] America."[43]

Within the South, the Greeley tour aroused comment across all constituencies. Opinions varied across the spectrum, but moderates found consensus around the idea that the editor had come as a genuine friend, and thus that his visit represented a great opportunity for the region. As the *Houston Union* noted, he "desires to see our people truly prosperous, and advocates measures calculated to make them truly so." Moreover, the attentions of such a prominent Republican (and the warm reception he received) might serve to redeem the South in the eyes of the nation at large—a notion Greeley was happy to confirm. As he told an audience in Texas, he would be "just" in all his "representations" of the state and region and testify to its good order, safety, and vast economic potential.[44]

Blacks along the trail were no less interested, though perhaps more divided, than Southern whites. In New Orleans, where large numbers of blacks rushed to see Greeley, some questioned whether such participation in the fanfare was appropriate. Greeley's message on reconciliation and "local control" hardly needed any translation, and a reception in his honor was held at the American Union Club, which generally proscribed blacks from even entering the building. Yet the black *Weekly Louisianian* championed the visit. Noting the broad enthusiasm among black New Orleanians, editor P. B. S. Pinchback proclaimed the visit a great success, for Greeley as well as for blacks. "Mr. Greeley, the apostle of peace, 'came' and saw, and, with his peculiar weapons, 'conquered,'" Pinchback wrote. His reception marked an opportunity for blacks to claim their place in public life and the upper tiers of New Orleans society: "Native white gentlemen joined in harmonious and admiring attentions with native colored gentlemen, to the distinguished guest." The very presence of "accomplished gentlemen of our race, lent consistency and dignity to the occasion."[45]

Even fire-eating whites accorded Greeley some respect. Recording the shock that no less a Northern Republican than Horace Greeley—a man "whose name has been a byword and reproach"—was the object of such adulation, a Galveston paper remarked, "It is perhaps the first time in the history of the nation that the people of a State have stepped from their daily round of duty to do honor to a public enemy." And yet, the editor owned, the visit was "a remarkable event." Greeley was a "private citizen, holding no office, with a voice more potential than any public man in the nation." Though he had long represented the views of a party altogether hostile to the South, Greeley "was and is honest." His visit offered hope of rehabilitating the image of Texas and the South in the eyes of the nation at large.[46]

Horace Greeley as the lion of Southern society was a story indeed, "one of the most extraordinary and noteworthy events of the day." The news rippled across the country. The "southern exchanges contain nothing but gossip of Greeley—Greeley—Greeley," the *New-York Herald* carped. Greeley's "conquest" of his Southern audiences filled columns from California to Maine, often with flattering commentary. "The influence of Mr. Greeley's visit will be most wholesome," a Providence, Rhode Island, paper noted. It showed that the nation's deliverance was nigh, and that "deep ploughed furrows caused by slavery and the war are rapidly filling up." Even papers like the *Cleveland Plain Dealer*, which had long made a sport of mocking Greeley's positions and pretensions, couldn't avoid favorable comment on his "triumphal progress" through the South.[47]

Greeley's dispatches back to the *Tribune*, later published as his *Letters from Texas and the Lower Mississippi*, described a region ready to embrace the nation anew. Habits of industry needed only to mingle with scientific farming methods and a robust newspaper press, and the long benighted land would flow with milk and honey. Whites imbruted by generations of slavery and the denigration of labor were at long last learning the glories of honest toil. The freed people, as Greeley gleaned from their former masters, were still given to "idleness and improvidence" but wanted only benevolent guidance to become a reliable peasantry. The South was open for business and eager to share in national glories. Yankee migration ("if ten thousand Northern farmers would settle just below Houston") and a wave of *Tribune* subscriptions ("if every farmer would devote two hours a day to reading and reflection") would speed the process along.[48]

In case there was any doubt, Greeley expressed his availability to lead the imminent reconciliation and revival. Upon his return to New York, he spoke to the "spontaneous gathering" in his honor in the tortured language of a man running for something. "I shall never decline any nomination that has not been offered me," he said, amid an oil painting, a bust, and numerous lithographs and photographs of himself adorning the rooms of the Lincoln Club. He told this audience that he had gone south merely to "vindicate the right of this nation" and to "promote clearer understanding" across sectional boundaries. It was a pity he hadn't gotten there sooner. If a "representative Northern man could have traversed the South, and there boldly and openly asserted the convictions of the North," Greeley said, the "terrible Civil War might have been averted." Now, though, the time was coming when the war might become a touchstone of national unity, rather than division. The "sentiment of nationality and patriotism" was awakening, and soon Americans would honor Robert E. Lee and Stonewall Jackson along-side Ulysses S. Grant and William Tecumseh Sherman. The formula was dizzyingly simple: crush out the Klan, restore the South's "leading men" to office, eradicate corruption from government, and bury the past.[49]

The speech answered a wider enthusiasm. Greeley Clubs were already forming across the country. "Friends in Kansas" implored their man to answer their call. With no disrespect to Grant, they said, "we believe that no living American statesman has the claims of yourself to be President." Home in New York, Theodore Tilton used the pages of his new paper, the *Golden Age*, to announce the dawn of Greeley's golden age: "Our first and early choice . . . is the large-minded and humane statesman—the Benjamin Franklin of his time. . . . The kind-hearted Northern farmer who has gone South to plant with his own hand an olive of peace in that fire-scattered land."[50]

A Crooked Stick

If the purpose of Greeley's tour had been to demonstrate his own popularity and the possibility of a transpartisan, transsectional politics, he still could not escape the basic organizational structures at the heart of the American system. He needed a vehicle for his popularity and appeal. From the early stirrings of his campaign, Greeley was gunning for the Republican nomination. His dedication to the "one-term" principle and his scrapes within the New York State organization spoke to his desire to take hold of and transform the broader party into one of national consensus. The trouble was that few Republicans seemed to share his particular vision or the idea that he should lead them. Admiring crowds at Southern train depots meant nothing to Republican wire-pullers in Washington, New York City, and Albany. That hard truth left only one option: the Liberal Republicans.

Emerging from the ranks of Yankee moral reformers and western Republicans, these Liberals were a heterogeneous coalition of those disaffected from Grant and Reconstruction. Shared views and grievances gave them a mounting political clout and coherence through the early 1870s. Liberals were appalled at the corruption of the state and local party machines that so often left them on the outside looking in, and they believed the rot began

at the top, with Grant's boorish unfitness and his scandal-plagued administration. They shuddered at the ease with which the untutored masses might
be manipulated by demagogues and thereby pollute public life. They were
sharply critical of Republican-led Reconstruction in the South as an unnecessary perpetuation of sectional animosity and an invitation to naked graft
and corruption. But, most significantly for Greeley, they held a commitment
to laissez-faire and free trade, and an opposition to tariffs and other forms
of state intervention.[51]

Greeley and the Liberals thus made for an unlikely pairing. Beyond their
shared commitment to amnesty and reconciliation and a belief that leaders
should direct the masses, common ground was scarce. The *Tribune*'s early
recognition of the movement as a "conspiracy to destroy the Republican
party" suggested how ill-suited their marriage would be in 1872. Above all,
differences on protective tariffs, what the *Independent* called "Mr. Greeley's
. . . first and last love," seemed irreconcilable. When the Liberal movement
began to coalesce in 1870, Greeley was still plumping his 400-page billet-
doux to protectionism. To Greeley, the Liberal commitment to "revenue reform" appeared as nothing more than Democratic policy by another name,
which was wholly against the interests of the nation. Greeley was unlikely
to relent on economic principles he likened to the laws of gravity or to "the
perfection of the Golden Rule." Indeed, already critical of creeping free-
trade doctrine within the Grant administration and the Republican Party, it
made little sense for him to bolt toward a movement that was even more
hostile to tariffs.[52]

Many Liberals were no more enthusiastic about claiming Greeley for
their cause. Though he possessed an enviable popularity and influence that
some Liberal editors would champion, they feared a compromise of their
principles. "If we must swallow Greeley for the sakes of carrying a political
end," one Liberal wrote, "I think it will be dearly bought." Such suspicions
went beyond what one editor called Greeley's "tariff tomfoolery." Former
Free Soilers within the Liberal Republican movement still felt the sting
of Greeley's betrayal and "the bad faith of the Whigs" in the 1848 election.
Greeley had once been a Whig, and he would always remain one at heart.
Those who were keen about civil service reform, meanwhile, noted the
weakness of his commitment to that cause. Indeed, Greeley got religion on

the issue only after the Conkling machine in New York had cleared out a crew of Reuben Fenton's cronies—"a ring of ward politicians" whose crooked mediocrity hardly put a wrinkle in the *Tribune* editor's white coat up to that point.[53]

Greeley was now a hermit crab looking for a new shell, and Liberal Republicanism looked like the best one available. With the 1872 presidential contest approaching, he began to fit himself to its contours, even as he held out hope of stealing the Republican nomination from Grant. Early in 1872, just a few days before Greeley's birthday celebration, the *Tribune* reiterated its dedication to the one-term principle when it came to Grant, but it also signaled a broader approbation of the Liberal movement. Greeley, in other words, was very much available, should the Liberals agree to leave a free-trade plank out of their platform. When asked if he would compromise his own tariff orthodoxy, he told a friend, "<u>that</u> I can't go, even though it would make me president." All the while, civil service reform and public corruption became ever more urgent matters in the pages of the *Tribune*. Greeley and his paper redoubled efforts to explain the failings of Reconstruction as the result of a corrupt administration and an insufficiently magnanimous Republican Party.[54]

As the Liberals' convention approached, Greeley signaled that he was ready to cast his lot with their party. In late March of 1872, the *Tribune* officially came out "For Cincinnati" and the paper suggested that the tariff question was less a national issue than a local one, to be worked out in individual congressional districts. All Greeley asked was that the matter of trade protection be open to reasoned discussion at the convention. Such astonishing compromises on tariffs suggested Greeley was in dead earnest about winning the nomination for president at the party's convention in early May.[55]

Greeley would win the nomination not merely because he wanted it, however; he would win it because of the perception of popularity that had been attached to him since the first whisperings that he should run, late in 1870. As deeply and as quickly as Liberal Republicans would come to regret their choice, it had been Liberal newspaper editors like Murat Halstead and Samuel Bowles who first plumped Greeley's status as a "representative" national figure worthy of the office.[56] And, for all the Liberal Republicans' enthusiasm and intellectual vigor, none of its leaders and representatives possessed the kind of broad recognition that Greeley did. Carl Schurz, the German émigré who served as chairman of the convention, understood this as the central tension of the gathering. "Cheap popularity," he told the crowd, should not win the day. Instead, it was imperative that "superior intelligence, coupled with superior virtue, should guide our affairs; not that merely an honest and popular man, but that a statesman" should lead.[57]

The warning was well founded. As Bowles's *Springfield (MA) Republican* reported on the convention's first day, "There is a greater and wider personal feeling for Greeley . . . than for any other man." The leading contender, Charles Francis Adams, perhaps possessed the intelligence and virtue Schurz had referenced, but, as one who had been aptly described as "the greatest Iceberg in the Northern hemisphere," he had limited appeal. Others, like Justice David Davis and Senator Lyman Trumbull, simply could not best Greeley, who gained support throughout each of the convention's six ballots. As the votes swung Greeley's way, reports confirmed what had been the argument for his candidacy from the beginning—he was an independent, national figure whose appeal was "confined to no state or section, but coming from all quarters of the Union." "The majority of the convention," Bowles's *Republican* declared, "sincerely believed that he would prove the most popular candidate." The idea of Greeley's popularity endured in support of his candidacy. Greeley's old friend, poet John Greenleaf Whittier, defended the nomination to a skeptical friend, not merely on Greeley's morality and intelligence, but also on his status as "one of the most popular men in the United States. . . . He is a man on whom his countrymen, irrespective of politics, can be proud."[58]

Die-hard Liberal Republicans recognized the triumph of Greeley's popularity as the eclipse of their movement. Carl Schurz, by one account, walked into a postconvention party, sat down at a piano, and played the first strains of Chopin's *Funeral March*. Not long afterward, he sat at a desk and penned an eleven-page letter to Greeley, begging him to decline the nomination altogether. William Cullen Bryant, a longstanding Greeley rival in New York journalism, fumed that a nominee for president ought, at the very least, be a gentleman. E. L. Godkin of the *Nation*, who had been one of the early leading lights of liberalism, washed his hands of Greeley and the movement altogether. Citing another Greeley-related debacle, Godkin called the nomination the greatest national disaster since Bull Run and offered a bare assessment of Greeley's contributions through the years as little more than "the glorification in all human concerns of the Rule of Thumb."[59] Many Liberal Republicans who did support Greeley, meanwhile, did so only grudgingly. The best that could be said of the candidate was that he was not Grant. As former Secretary of the Navy Gideon Welles put it, "a crooked stick may be made to beat a mad dog." Another Liberal, writing to Gerrit Smith, captured the wide gap in enthusiasm: "I have always regarded Greeley as an awkward, ill-bred boor, and though a sort of inspired idiot, neither a scholar, statesman, or gentleman. I wouldn't give Grant's little finger for a Congressional district full of him. Yet, I want him elected."[60]

The denunciations slashed to the bone of Greeley's well-honed persona and challenged his stability throughout the campaign. Following the Cincinnati convention, the calumny was so intense that he considered turning down the nomination altogether. In June, after he had accepted it, Greeley struggled with the "brain fever" that so often visited him in times of strain. Mostly, he rode it out at his farm, tending to his ill wife and daughter, receiving visitors and supplicants for office, and responding as best he could to the torrent of correspondence streaming in.[61]

He was buoyed, however, by what he believed to be the strength of his own case and the extant enthusiasm for his campaign that could be discerned in any number of expressions. As he renounced his editorship of the *Tribune* and made his official acceptance of the Liberal Republicans' nomination, Greeley returned to his familiar postwar themes. The "long-estranged people," he asserted, "shall reunite and fraternize upon the broad basis of Universal Amnesty and Impartial Suffrage." Speaking to the Democrats he hoped would endorse a cross-partisan candidacy, he promised that failed efforts in the South would give way to "local self-government." A "true, beneficent National Reconstruction" was coming, and he was the man who had been called forth by "these masses of our countrymen" to bring it about.[62]

Responses from those close to him, as well as among "the masses of our countrymen," gave him further hope. Theodore Tilton, Greeley's longtime friend and supporter, was ebullient: "It is Glorious! I shall take the stump! I shall wear a white hat! We shall redeem the land." Greeley Clubs mushroomed up in every corner of the land. Speakers fanned out to preach the message of fighting Grantism and the corruption, disfranchisement, and sectional hostility that came with it. They hammered on the topics of amnesty, civil service, good government, and reconciliation. Pro-Greeley publications, like *Frank Leslie's Illustrated Newspaper*, depicted the choice starkly: "Peace & Plenty" versus "War & Devastation," and a tranquil, quill-wielding Greeley versus a frenzied, Napoleonic Grant with a limp sword. Greeley, always pictured at his sylvan retreat in Chappaqua, New York, was a humble Cincinnatus, separate from postwar conflicts and corruptions. Popular zeal flashed in reports of shortages of white hats and the swelling popularity of wood chopping, Greeley's favorite pastime. A Texas newspaper noted that Greeley's signature headpiece had been elevated to "an emblem of political power," every bit "as historic as the Log Cabin of Gen. Harrison and the old hickory of Andrew Jackson." And others could belt out the chorus of "The Old White Hat" from the *Farmer of Chappaqua Songster*:[63]

> Then hurrah, my boys, for the old white hat
> that covers a mighty head.
> May he wear it long
> And be hale and strong
> When his radical foes are dead.

Or Vote for Horace Greeley

Greeley's hopes reached their apogee in July, when he could squint and see the postpartisan national consensus he imagined. On July 9, the Democratic convention in Baltimore accepted the Liberal Republicans' platform and candidate. Fighting their own internal divisions and combating the sweltering heat with their Horace Greeley paper fans, they took as their standard bearer a man who had dedicated very nearly his entire career in journalism to extirpating their political party. The news was shocking to some, rich to others. A joke circulated that Dr. David Livingstone, whom Henry Morton Stanley had found that summer, decided, upon hearing the news that Greeley was running for president as a Democrat, that he would just as soon remain in Africa.[64] Greeley disregarded the jokes, grumbles, and outrage and marveled at the fact that *Democrats* had accepted him as their candidate, as well as a platform that included the Reconstruction amendments. "I hail this as a genuine New Departure from outworn feuds and meaningless contentions in the direction of Progress and Reform," he wrote in his letter accepting the nomination. A new era was dawning; the promise of 1776 would be fulfilled just in time for the nation's centennial.[65]

The critical endorsement came on July 29, when the Radical Republican Charles Sumner of Massachusetts wrote his letter about it being the "interest and duty of colored citizens" to vote for Greeley. Sumner, too, hailed the Democratic acceptance of the Liberal candidate and platform as a moment of mass "conversion," a sea change in the life of the nation. Greeley's election would mark "the inauguration of Republican principles, under the safeguard of a Republican president . . . with Democrats as avowed supporters." Not only was Greeley a better and longer-standing friend to blacks than Grant, but his status and respect among Southern whites would also bring about a fuller acceptance of emancipation and equality. The alchemy of Republican principles and Democratic support would forge a golden consensus.[66]

Any enthusiasm for Greeley, however, was equaled and superseded by the outpouring of abuse and mockery that marked the 1872 campaign. Never had a target been richer. If Rutherford B. Hayes's greatest virtue in 1876 would be that he was "offensive to no one," a case could be made that Greeley was offensive to all in 1872. His tenuous connections to Liberal Republicanism notwithstanding, many obstacles stood in the way of Greeley's hope to operate as an independent national candidate. His record throughout forty years of journalism and politics amounted to a gold mine for even the most casual oppositional researcher. Republicans seeking to sway Democrats away from Greeley could merely remind them that the *Tribune* and its editor had been equating their political allegiances to forms of criminality and vice since 1841. Indeed, during the previous presidential cycle, the paper had casually suggested, in a typical volley, that "every one who chooses to live by pugilism, or gambling or harlotry, along with nearly every keeper of a tippling house is politically a Democrat." Now, Greeley asked those whom he'd called "lewd, ruffianly, criminal and dangerous" to vote for him. The sheer hypocrisy, along with the decades Greeley had spent as the radical face of anti-slavery fanaticism and other dangerous "isms," made him an unmissable target.[67]

Persuading Republicans to remain with Grant was perhaps even easier. After all, while Greeley claimed to offer the deliverance of the nation, it had been Grant who had saved the Union. Thus party chieftains needed only to remind the rank and file of Greeley's unforgivable apostasy to the Republican Party's principles and his careless dismissal of the war's trials and accomplishments. In scarcely more than a decade since the outbreak of the Civil War, he had racked up a collection of monstrosities that could well have supplied three elections' worth of content to Republican editors, pamphleteers, and stump speakers. Some of Greeley's real actions—counseling the nation to let the Southern states leave the Union, entering into secret negotiations with Copperheads and Confederates, paying Jeff Davis's bail—were so outlandish that fake ones seemed plausible, such as having been a slaveholder who enjoyed whipping his chattel, planning to pay Confederate soldiers' pensions, and assuming Confederate debts. There was also the matter of the apparent indifference with which Greeley dismissed Reconstruction violence against the freed people. "Go vote to burn school houses, desecrate churches and violate women," Benjamin Butler said, "or vote for Horace Greeley, which means the same thing."[68]

The most substantive attacks came from former abolitionists and Radical Republicans. By their lights, a vote for Greeley amounted not to a vote for the nation, but one against the most hard-won results of the Civil War. Frederick Douglass captured the situation most concisely. "My friends say, Why, Mr. Douglass, are you going to desert Horace Greeley?" he told a New York crowd. "I answer, No, but Horace Greeley has deserted us." Greeley's pleas for reconciliation, along with his naïve assurances that white Southerners had accepted the lessons of the conflict, were "little better than mockery." Southern whites supported Greeley only because "they can see with Horace Greeley in power, the old master is again brought back into power." Wendell Phillips, William Lloyd Garrison, and other former champions of abolition echoed Douglass. Greeley was a "turncoat & traitor" to the very causes he had once championed, and his cozy calls for reconciliation were tantamount to a full capitulation to the worst white Southern outrages.

That such attacks were effective spoke to a critical point: black rights in the South and the violence that challenged them remained potent issues to many Northern Republicans.[69]

The attacks on Greeley came from many angles, but a common theme emerged from all of them: Greeley was not the honest, "representative man" he and others claimed. The pamphlets, broadsides, cartoons, songbooks, joke books, newspapers, and other ephemera that flooded the marketplace revealed Greeley as a mendacious hypocrite and an inauthentic sham. As Thomas Nast's "Red Hot!" *Harper's Weekly* cartoon framed it, Greeley's "own words and deeds" supplied the best possible argument against his candidacy. Indeed, many campaign documents were merely compendia of Greeley's past statements that contradicted his 1872 stance. Nast proved devilishly effective at turning oft-used Greeley phrases, like "clasp hands across the bloody chasm," into savage attacks. Greeley, always rendered as a fat halfwit, could be seen clasping hands with a series of villains, from Confederate soldiers to John Wilkes Booth.[70]

Greeley's claims to rustic, self-made authenticity were just as easily mocked. Satirical takes on his 1867 memoir, such as J. Bowker's *Wreck-Elections of a Busy Life*, had already laid the groundwork. Far from a model for "American boys, born in poverty, cradled in obscurity," Greeley was a clumsy prig who wouldn't know a hoe from a hatchet and mistook his own delusions for "philosophy." A paper fan, inspired by those distributed at the Democratic nominating convention, showed a dopey Greeley face on one side and scenes from his worn-out life story on the other. There, he appeared to be tipping backward while swinging an axe ("WHAT I KNOW OF FARMING") and contemplating his own ass ("EARLY IMPRESSIONS OF STERN REALITIES"). "It is believed," *The Comic Life of Horace Greeley* deadpanned, "that however good his intentions may have been, that he has ruined more young men, and old ones too, who have followed his advice than any other Agricultural Sage that ever lived."[71]

By the beginning of August, Greeley's electoral odds were already long. North Carolina, an early-voting state, went for Grant, and more bad news was to come in September, with Republican wins in Maine and in Greeley's boyhood home state of Vermont. Desperate, Greeley lit out for the territories, barnstorming through New Jersey, Pennsylvania, Ohio, Kentucky, and

Indiana. Along the way, he preached himself nearly to death's door, giving some fifty speeches in just ten days. He spoke on the familiar themes: reconciliation, forgetting old divisions, and a "common platform of American Nationality." His victory, he promised, would leave none vanquished. "Our triumph is not the triumph of a section; it is not the triumph of a race; it is not the triumph of a class," he told one crowd. "It is the triumph of the American people, making us all, in life, in heart, and purpose, the people, the one people of the great American Republic."[72]

The nation had other visions of triumph, however—visions that began with Greeley's defeat. If the canvass produced any consensus at all, it was that Greeley was a used-up old fool with no business in the White House. Angry veterans heckled him in Pittsburgh. Someone smashed the window of his train car in Ohio. A Thomas Nast cartoon likened the tour to Andrew Johnson's ill-fated "Swing around the Circle." "Who is the traitor now?" its caption asked. The limited enthusiasm for Greeley was rooted in the illusory vestiges of his popularity, according to William Cullen Bryant's *Evening Post*. "His notoriety has been mistaken for fame," the paper claimed, "and the good-natured amusement with which the public has regarded his eccentricities and follies, has been unwittingly supposed to prove him popular."[73]

Election returns in October and November delivered a hard truth to Greeley: he may well have been a representative man, just not one who represented the nation's reconciliation. When all the votes were tallied, he had carried just 43.8 percent of the popular vote and only six states—Georgia, Kentucky, Maryland, Missouri, Texas, and Tennessee. It was the most comprehensive popular-vote defeat suffered by any presidential candidate between 1836 and 1892. The great harmonization and new political future he imagined simply had not happened. Republicans didn't believe Greeley's claims of white Southern contrition. If the latter were ready to embrace reunion, it would not be on Greeley's terms. The chasm remained too wide, too bloody. If Democrats voted at all—300,000 fewer turned out than in 1868—they did so with persistent memories of Greeley's decades-long campaign against them. In Pennsylvania, 100,000 Democrats cast ballots for their party's gubernatorial candidate but abstained from a presidential vote altogether.[74]

In the end, it is hard to overstate the depth of Greeley's failure in 1872, which went beyond mere electoral defeat. The campaign had accomplished almost precisely the opposite of what he had set out to achieve. Above all, Greeley's celebrity worked not to bridge divides, but to entrench them. Politically, the party organizations he promised to transcend saw revival rather than ruin. Democrats, whose halfhearted embrace of Greeley had all but guaranteed their defeat, came away with a new hold on Reconstruction and national politics. Endorsing Greeley had freed them of their associations with violence, disloyalty, and racism and offered a comfortably vague language with which to resist Reconstruction. In victory, Republicans commenced their own shifts. While Greeley was never a serious challenge to the party, he sparked a sorting of the compound coalition that had formed in the 1850s. Those old reformers and Radicals who bolted toward Greeley and the Liberals never came back, and they took their zeal and idealism out of politics altogether. Old Free Traders, whose economic commitments had always made them sit uncomfortably in the coalition, began a migration back to "the Democracy." Those left behind were the strict organizers whose pro-business ethos would carry the party confidently into the Gilded Age of the future.[75]

With the hardening of these partisan battle lines, the "bloody chasm" between the sections remained as wide as ever; it had just become less important politically. Greeley had given both camps a hollow but useful rhetoric of reconciliation and nationhood that allowed them to ignore the chasm when expedient. Democrats could continue with vague commitments to a "New Departure" while resisting Reconstruction with cries against corruption and calls for "local control." Grant's tepid pleas for "peace and prosperity" and "the restoration of good feeling" presaged the increasingly tepid Republican commitment to Reconstruction in its waning years. Greeley would never fully realize the depth of his failure, but what he did grasp of it was enough. Within weeks of his defeat, Greeley would be committed to a sanatorium in Pleasantville, New York, and would die there on November 29, 1872. In his final days, the once-towering editor, who had spoken to multitudes over three decades, was unable to speak.

A Union Printer

The nation's failure to recognize its unified destiny in Horace Greeley made for an impossible reckoning. With his electoral fate sealed, and his once-grand prospects gone, what was Greeley to do? George Templeton Strong, among many others, suggested that Greeley—and the sham mythology surrounding him—be unceremoniously consigned to obscurity. "I see nothing left for him," Strong wrote in his diary, "but to spend the rest of his days chopping with his little hatchet at the cherry trees of Chappaqua." Return to Chappaqua he did—although it was to attend to his wife Molly on her deathbed. There, at her side, Greeley prayed for his own hasty demise. He was "used up," he told a friend, "the worst beaten man who ever ran for high office." When Molly died on October 30, he buried her with "hard, dry eyes," unable to shed tears after weeks of sleeplessness.[1]

Scarcely more than a week later, Greeley returned to the *Tribune* offices, to the astonishment of the paper's staff. On November 7, a small notice announced that after "embarking on another line of business some six months ago," the paper's founder and editor was taking up his old job. Greeley would remain "heartily" committed to uniting "the whole American People on the platform of Universal Amnesty and Impartial Suffrage." He had learned, though, that his "silence and forbearance" on the subject would best advance the cause. Now, he promised, the *Tribune* would be an independent organ, merely seeking the general advance of "Human Freedom."[2]

But the light had gone out. Some of the ensuing calumny was to be expected; the *New-York Times* wondered if "nothing [would] shake his faith in that most delusive of all the shams he has publicly supported—himself." But even in the eyes of longstanding allies, he was a sadly diminished figure. On the very day—indeed, on the very page where the vaunted editor announced his return—a young staffer's insubordinate squib announced that Greeley "has not influence enough at Washington or Albany to get a sweeper appointed under the Sergeant-at-arms, or a deputy-sub-assistant temporary clerk into the paste-pot section of the folding room." Whitelaw Reid, the paper's managing editor, refused to publish a retraction, even over Greeley's demands. Meanwhile, Theodore Tilton's *Independent*, once the loudest organ in support of Greeley's candidacy, moralized that it was only proper for Greeley to be subjected to such reproach. "Those who offend the moral sense of the public," that paper declared, "must suffer the consequences."[3]

In his victory lap, Thomas Nast completed the indignity for Greeley. His final cartoon, "Our Artist's Occupation Gone," depicted Nast himself standing forlorn before a crowd, with placards announcing "SHAM REFORM EXPOSED," "THE GREELEY TRIUMPH POSTPONED," "H. G. GONE WEST." In truth, Nast had scant reason for dejection. Approbation rained down, and speculation slated him for all manner of high-level appointments and diplomatic sinecures. "You more than any other man have won a prodigious victory for Grant—I mean, rather, for Civilization and Progress," Mark Twain told Nast. Even James Parton, whose biography had enshrined the Greeley legend, told the cartoonist, in a similar vein, "No one has contributed to this glorious and astounding victory of Honesty over Humbug as much as Thomas Nast."[4]

The opprobrium, on top of the death of his wife and the shambolic state of his finances, was too much to bear for Greeley. If his "enemies" would only kill him at last, Greeley said, he would thank them "lovingly." In their way, they were doing his bidding. Within days of his departure from the *Tribune*, Greeley slipped into what was called "a nervous prostration." In one final flurry, Greeley liquidated what remained of his estate, most of which he'd squandered in bad investments and ill-judged loans. He had just six shares of stock left of the newspaper he'd founded. In between settling what he could of his disordered affairs, Greeley laid bare his tortured soul in a final testament. Only months before, he'd dreamed of national deliverance; now, "having done wrong to millions," he took on the burden of its ruin. "I stand naked before my God," he said, "the most utterly, hopelessly wretched and undone of all who ever lived. I have done more harm and wrong than any man who saw the light of day." Just a week later, Greeley was committed to a sanatorium in Pleasantville, New York. Reports of his worsening mental condition had him announcing, "The country is gone, the *Tribune* is gone, and I am gone."[5]

When Greeley *was* gone, on November 29, the misdeeds of 1872 were forgiven, almost immediately. Jokes and jibes may have hounded Greeley to his grave, but they did not follow him into it. Merciless humor gave way to merciful solemnity. Late to the news, the far-flung *Yankton Press*, in the Dakota Territory, captured this pivot. The paper's issue for December 4 contained both an admiring profile of Nast's "terrible aggressiveness" over the campaign and an admiring memorial to Horace Greeley, the great champion of the American people.[6]

In the ensuing testimonials and grand public obsequies, the argument that had failed Greeley in the final year of his life supplied the script for his death. Here had been the essential American—a man, Henry Ward Beecher said in his eulogy, whose character was "commensurate . . . with the genius of this great Republic." Charles Sumner, whose endorsement had been a source of hope that summer, restated the 1872 campaign's argument one last time. "Standing at the open grave of Horace Greeley," he said, "we are admonished to forget the strife of party, and to remember only truth, country, and mankind, to which his honest life was devoted. In other days . . . may we bury animosities, if not the badge of the past. Then, indeed, will there be a victory for the dead which all will share." In New York, Greeley's body lay in state in City Hall beneath a crest bearing an ox and an eagle's plume, "the one indicative of Mr. Greeley's love for agricultural pursuits, the other his power as a writer." On December 3, an estimated 100,000 mourners paid their respects, waiting hours in the cold to pass by their "old friend." The following day, the president and vice president, senators, Supreme Court justices, and generals all attended the funeral. Another 100,000 turned out to observe the cortege. By one paper's estimate, it was "the greatest demonstration of grief since the funeral of Mr. Lincoln."[7]

Foes and antagonists from the 1872 campaign and beyond joined the chorus. Thurlow Weed, who had so adeptly conducted that year's symphonic calumnies, praised his former ally's "vigorous manliness, rugged strength, and great works." James Gordon Bennett's *New-York Herald*, which had assailed Greeley for decades as a fraud and a sham, now gushed about "the love entwining itself about the hearts of men" and Greeley's "holy enshrinement" in the nation's annals. Southern editors, white and black, reflected on Greeley's magnanimity, his consummate service to "our national life," and his great service to the enslaved, "though we may lament the tangent at which he recently flew off." Exhausted and under censure for his final twists of the knife, Thomas Nast all but disappeared from public view.[8]

The whole outpouring savored of mawkishness and insincerity, though; "a more rancorous mood," Constance Rourke wrote, "might have been a greater tribute." George Templeton Strong saw through it all. The "general wail of the newspaper press over the great newspaper man" represented a "preposterous" reversal, since it had been the same papers denouncing him "as the basest of mankind" only weeks before. The crowds standing in the rain and mud did so out of a vague and misplaced guilt at contributing to the demise of the "miserable old rooster." In Strong's eyes, Greeley, "the miserable old charlatan and traitor," had deserved his fate. It would have been better for the nation, and for Greeley, if he had died a year earlier. "Had God granted him a little plain practical sense," Strong concluded, "Horace Greeley would have been a great man."[9]

The speed with which the world moved on from its attention to Greeley bore out Strong's observations. The process was already underway in the *Tribune* offices, where Greeley's ignominy had degraded the paper's standing and sparked a crisis of succession. Staff, shareholders, and potential investors jockeyed for control of the sagging enterprise. At the center of the scrum were publisher Samuel Sinclair and managing editor Whitelaw Reid, the latter backed by crooked financier Jay Gould. Just before the turn of 1873, Reid purchased a controlling stake in the corporation with some $500,000 of Gould's capital. When Reid succeeded Greeley as owner and editor, he assured the public that he had resisted "intrigues and outside efforts to gain control of the paper." The *Tribune*, he promised, was safely "in the hands of Mr. Greeley's chosen editorial associates—men whom he trained for this particular duty." Reid never admitted to—and later expunged all traces of—his own intrigues that gave him control over the paper.[10]

Reid wasted little time in retuning Greeley's organ of antebellum idealism into a fit instrument for the Gilded Age. He began with the building. The *Tribune*'s "Old Rookery" building, an artifact of Greeley's bygone age, was razed in May of 1873. In its place, Reid commissioned a skyscraper that crossed a French chateau with a Florentine villa. With a grand campanile rising from its mansard roof, the new *Tribune* edifice would become the second-highest structure in New York—just a shade shorter than the steeple of Trinity Church. Opening the "Tall Tower" on April 10, 1875, the thirty-fourth anniversary of the *Tribune*'s first issue, Reid leaned heavily on Greeley's memory and legacy. The paper remained committed to its founder's mission. The "growth of intelligence throughout the country" was the "hope and constant effort of Mr. Greeley's life. He drew steadily nearer to his ideal every year that he lived." Now, his successors "reverently took up his work."[11]

In many ways, though, the new building marked a "New Tribune," a fact that quaint memories of Greeley's "astonishing industry and courageous enthusiasm" served to mystify. Whispered about as being Gould's "stool pigeon" and "hireling," Reid was hardly the independent operator that Greeley had been. In addition, where Greeley had once worked in a shared office among the paper's section editors, Reid commanded from a "nexus of push-buttons and pneumatic tubes" in a private suite. Meanwhile, the new building's basement saloon, where pressmen, reporters, and editors could retire for lunchtime and after-work beers, stood as a cruel rebuke to Greeley. Soon the tower itself would come to overshadow Greeley's memory; it would replace the "Philosopher in the Old White Coat" as the symbol and metonym of the *New-York Tribune*.[12]

On the national stage, Greeley was quickly forgotten amid the ongoing tumults of Reconstruction and the Gilded Age. His defeat and death in 1872 had marked an abrupt end to his visions of a great national harmonization. The year 1876 became a kind of bitter coda to his story. Grand centennial celebrations notwithstanding, 1876 was a year of fracture, not consensus. The fraud and violence of the presidential election revealed a nation still riven by unreconciled sectional identities; labor strife revealed a society increasingly divided by class and economic interests. And yet, even as Greeley's "union of souls" and the "harmony of interests" slipped away, his rhetoric endured. It survived as hollow aspiration, such as when a South Carolina centennial orator exhorted his listeners, "Let us clasp hands / to work as one / for all the Nation's good / And stand together as one man / as once our fathers stood."[13]

More directly, though, it endured as a rhetoric of capitulation to division and disharmony. The blandly inoffensive Republican presidential candidate Rutherford B. Hayes campaigned on warmed-over Greeleyan promises of a "fraternal spirit of harmony" and an ending to "the distinction between North and South." When Hayes took office under a cloud of illegitimacy, bound by a shady backroom deal, he returned to the same rhetoric to announce the end of Reconstruction. Southern whites would be left to enjoy "the blessing of wise, honest, and peaceful self-government." "Harmonious efforts of both races, activated by mutual sympathy and regard" would bring peace to the region; "the loving devotion of a free people" would unite the nation as a whole. Greeley had made such promises under the delusion that they were true; Hayes made them under the certainty that they were not. Hayes used Greeley's language of collective national destiny to announce, in effect, the abandonment of Greeley's vision.[14]

Amid sweeping changes at the *Tribune* and in the nation at large, printers became the principal keepers of Greeley's memory. Upon his passing, members of New York's Typographical Union No. 6—"The Big Six," as it was known—laid plans for a monument to their fallen "fellow craftsman" and the organization's inaugural president. They quickly settled on an idea. The memorial to Greeley should not be cast in bronze or set in stone, but composed of type. "Type-metal," the group's committee resolved, "is specially adapted to reproduce sharp and definite outlines, and peculiarly fitted to speak in mute form." They asked printing shops across the nation to contribute at least a pound of "type-metal, which has been cast into type and worn out in the service of teaching the people." The spent types would then be melted down and recast into a "life-size" statue of Horace Greeley. By the beginning of 1876, the printers had gathered "a sufficiency" of old type to make the statue, only to realize that the alloy of lead, tin, and antimony would not withstand the elements "for any length of time." They commissioned instead a bronze bust on a stone pedestal, to be placed in Brooklyn's Greenwood Cemetery, and dedicated it on December 4, 1876.[15]

The printers were animated by more than affection for Horace Greeley. Tensions between the editorial offices and the pressroom at the *Tribune* had been mounting since Whitelaw Reid took over as managing editor in 1868. With Greeley no longer a presence, the printers felt marginalized from the intellectual life of the newspaper. The self-made Greeley, who always had contempt for the formally educated, had been one of them; Reid was not. "As a rule," chief compositor Amos Cummings remarked in 1869, "thoroughly competent printers have better judgment and newspaper tact than editors manufactured out of college graduates" (Reid had been educated at Miami University in Ohio). At the dedication ceremony for Greeley's memorial, *Tribune* writer and ex-printer Bayard Taylor remarked that "the only university at which Horace Greeley graduated" was "the composing room of a printing office."[16]

Greeley's death and Reid's accession only widened the divide. As improved technology—in particular, the introduction of larger types—made presswork more efficient, Reid forced the printers to take a series of pay cuts. By the end of 1876, when the printers dedicated the Greeley monument, affairs were drifting to the brink. In June of 1877, members of the Big Six went on strike. The dispute dragged on for nearly two decades, and the printers continued to invoke the memory of the great "typo-journalist." In addition to establishing a Horace Greeley post for the Grand Army of the Republic, the printers' union commissioned a second Greeley monument—this one to anchor "Greeley Square" at Thirty-Third Street. At its dedication in 1894, Amos Cummings, then a Democratic congressman, said that Horace Greeley was "more than a printer; he was a union printer."[17]

Cummings nearly wrote the perfect tribute; he got the words right, but their sense wrong. Greeley, who didn't believe in strikes and was a waffling friend to labor, had never wanted to be a "union printer," serving as a symbol in a labor conflict. He had wanted instead to be a "Union printer," who would use newspapers and the "Intelligence" they transmitted to bind the nation together into a single, harmonious whole.

Abbreviations

LOC	Library of Congress, Washington, DC
NYDT	*New-York Daily Tribune*
NYHS	New-York Historical Society, New York City
NYPL	New York Public Library, New York City
NYSL	New York State Library, Albany, New York

Introduction • Print and Legends

1. *Congressional Globe*, 30th Congress, 2nd Session, vol. 20, 694 (1849); [untitled] *(Washington, DC) Daily Globe*, March 21, 1849, 4; "A Name for Our Country," *New-York Weekly Tribune*, January 3, 1846. On Alleghania and earlier ideas, see *Proceedings of the New-York Historical Society for the Year 1845* (New York: Press of the New-York Historical Society, 1846), 115–124; "Alleghan or Alleghanian America," *United States Magazine and Democratic Review*, May 1845, 492–494; [Washington Irving], "National Nomenclature," *Knickerbocker*, August 1839, 158–162; Gordon Wood, *Empire of Liberty: A History of the Early Republic, 1789–1815* (New York: Oxford University Press, 2009), 41–42.

2. On the problems of American nationalism and nationhood, see Benjamin E. Park, *American Nationalisms: Imagining Union in the Age of Revolutions, 1783–1833* (Cambridge: Cambridge University Press, 2018); Peter S. Onuf, "Federalism, Republicanism, and the Origins of American Sectionalism," in Edward L. Ayers et al., eds., *All over the Map: Rethinking American Regions* (Baltimore: Johns Hopkins University Press, 1996), 11–37; John M. Murrin, "A Roof without Walls: The Dilemma of American National Identity," in Richard R. Beeman et al., eds., *Beyond Confederation: Origins of the Constitution and American National Identity* (Chapel Hill: University of North Carolina Press, 1987), 333–348; Susan-Mary Grant, "When Is a Nation Not a Nation? The Crisis of American Nationality in the Mid-Nineteenth Century," *Nations and Nationalism* 2:1 (1996), 105–129.

3. James Parton to Horace Greeley, May 15, 23, 1854, Horace Greeley Papers, NYPL; Horace Greeley to Moses A. Cortland, April 14, 1845, Horace Greeley Papers, LOC.

4. James Parton, *The Life of Horace Greeley, Editor of the New-York Tribune* (New York: Mason Bros., 1854), iii–vi; Milton E. Flower, *James Parton: The Father of Modern*

Biography (Durham, NC: Duke University Press, 1951), 25–33; Scott E. Casper, *Constructing American Lives: Biography and Culture in Nineteenth-Century America* (Chapel Hill: University of North Carolina Press, 1999), 220–227.

5. On the culture of biography in nineteenth-century America, see Casper, *Constructing American Lives*, 3–15. François Furstenberg, *In the Name of the Father: Washington's Legacy, Slavery, and the Making of a Nation* (New York: Penguin, 2006), 123–130.

6. In taking this approach to Greeley, I have been influenced by critic and pioneering scholar of American studies Constance Mayfield Rourke, in her *Trumpets of Jubilee: Henry Ward Beecher, Harriet Beecher Stowe, Lyman Beecher, Horace Greeley, P. T. Barnum* (New York: Harcourt Brace, 1927) and her *American Humor: A Study of American Character* (New York: Anchor Books, 1953), 91–93. As Rourke wrote, "But popularity is a large gauge and a lively symbol; the popular leader is nothing less than a vicarious crowd, registering much that is essential and otherwise obscure in social history, hopes and joys and conflicts and aspirations which may be crude and transitory, but nonetheless are the stuff out of which the foundations of social life are made" (*Trumpets of Jubilee*, 3). Also see Parton, *Life of Horace Greeley*, 412.

7. Glyndon G. Van Deusen, *Horace Greeley: Nineteenth Century Crusader* (Philadelphia: University of Pennsylvania Press, 1953). On Greeley as propagandist, see Jeter Allen Isely, *Horace Greeley and the Republican Party, 1853–1861* (Princeton, NJ: Princeton University Press, 1947). On Greeley and Whig politics, see Daniel Walker Howe, *The Political Culture of the American Whigs* (Chicago: University of Chicago Press, 1979), 181–209; Mitchell Snay, *Horace Greeley and the Politics of Reform in Nineteenth-Century America* (Lanham, MD: Rowman & Littlefield, 2011); Robert C. Williams, *Horace Greeley: Champion of American Freedom* (New York: New York University Press, 2006); Adam Tuchinsky, *Horace Greeley's* New-York Tribune: *Civil War–Era Socialism and the Crisis of Free Labor* (Ithaca, NY: Cornell University Press, 2011). On Greeley and the American West, see Coy F. Cross, *Go West Young Man! Horace Greeley's Vision for America* (Albuquerque: University of New Mexico Press, 1995).

8. "The Literature of the Age," *New-Yorker*, August 1, 1835, vol. 2, no. 20, 1; Howe, *Political Culture*. On the national Republican antecedents to the Whigs, see Daniel Walker Howe, *What Hath God Wrought? The Transformation of America, 1815–1845* (New York: Oxford University Press, 2007), 203–285; Horace Greeley, *Why I Am a Whig: Reply to an Inquiring Friend* (New York: Tribune Office, 1851). On Greeley's nationalism, see Glyndon G. Van Deusen, "The Nationalism of Horace Greeley," in Edward Mead Earle, ed., *Nationalism and Internationalism: Essays Inscribed to Carlton J. H. Hayes* (New York: Columbia University Press, 1950), 431–454.

9. The literature on print, nationalism, and education is vast. The following texts have been useful in forming my ideas: Robert Parkinson, *The Common Cause: Creating Race and Nation in the American Revolution* (Chapel Hill: University of North Carolina Press, 2016); Furstenberg, *In the Name of the Father*; David Waldstreicher, *In the Midst of Perpetual Fetes: The Making of American Nationalism* (Chapel Hill: University of North Carolina Press, 1997); Michael Warner, *The Letters of the Republic: Publication and the Public Sphere in Eighteenth-Century America* (Cambridge, MA: Harvard University Press, 1992); Carolyn Eastman, *A Nation of Speechifiers: Making an American*

Public after the Revolution (Chicago: University of Chicago Press, 2009); William Gillmore, *Reading Becomes a Necessity of Life: Material and Cultural Life in Rural New England* (Knoxville: University of Tennessee Press, 1989); Tim Cassedy, "A Dictionary Which We Do Not Want: Defining America against Noah Webster, 1783–1810," *William and Mary Quarterly* 71:2 (April 2014), 229–254.

10. Parton, *Life of Horace Greeley*, 96–97.

11. On Greeley's reading and education, see Horace Greeley, *Recollections of a Busy Life* (New York: J. B. Ford, 1868), 40–47; Parton, *Life of Horace Greeley*, 36–47; Horace Greeley, "Counsels to the Young," *Every Youth's Gazette*, October 22, 1842, 316–317; Horace Greeley, *Hints toward Reforms in Lectures, Addresses, and Other Writings* (New York: Harper & Bros., 1850), 160 (on the importance of Benjamin Franklin's and George Washington's biographies). On the broader uses of Bingham (the first book Greeley owned), Morse, Webster, and Murray, see Furstenberg, *In the Name of the Father*, 147–186. Though these practices and assumptions were thoroughly Anglo-Protestant, Frederick Douglass presents another case of a figure who was a "creature of print," both in his self-education as a reader (including his name, assumed from Sir Walter Scott) and his emergence as public figure after the publication of his *Narrative* in 1845. See David W. Blight, "The Peculiar Dialogue between Caleb Bingham and Frederick Douglass," introduction, in Caleb Bingham, *The Columbian Orator*, reprint ed. (New York: New York University Press, 1997), xiii–xxix.

12. Thomas Carlyle, *Sartor, Resartus: The Life and Opinions of Herr Teufelsdrokh* (London: Chapman & Hall, 1831), 30. On Greeley and Carlyle, see chapter 1. Also see Alexis de Tocqueville, *Democracy in America*, Gerald Bevan, trans. (New York: Penguin, 2003), 600. Greeley's *New-Yorker* followed the publication of the first American translations of *Democracy in America* and included a long review in 1840: "The Social Influence of Democracy," *New-Yorker*, May 23, 1840, 145–146. On editors and newspapers in 1830s New York City, see Edward L. Widmer, *Young America: The Flowering of Democracy in New York City* (New York: Oxford University Press, 1999), 9.

13. Parton, *Life of Horace Greeley*, 412, 138–139.

14. The R. Hoe & Co. Lightning Steam Press was capable of making 8,000 impressions in an hour and cost some $25,000. See Frank Luther Mott, *American Journalism: A History of Newspapers in the United States through 260 Years, 1690–1950* (New York: Macmillan 1950), 316. On the *Tribune*'s circulation, see "A Few Figures," *NYDT*, December 22, 1855, 4; Parton, *Life of Horace Greeley*, 54, 119–120, 412. On the *Tribune*'s circulation figures in the 1850s generally, see Isely, *Horace Greeley*, 337–338; "Aggregate Circulation Subscriptions to the Tribune," *NYDT*, April 10, 1860, 4. For a remarkably detailed description of the *Tribune*'s complex operations, see "An American Newspaper," *Troy (NY) Daily Times*, June 1, 1853, 2–3.

15. As a *Tribune* subeditor and correspondent, the abolitionist James Redpath noted in a pseudonymous piece that "Greeley would not enjoy one-fiftieth part of the fame he now has, if the name of the real writer were attached to every article attributed to him," before going on to name the real writers of *Tribune* content. See ["Berwick"], "Our New York Correspondence," *(Savannah) Daily Morning News*, May 23, 1854, 1. Redpath, a Scot, hailed originally from Berwick. Also see John McGivigan, *Forgotten Firebrand: James Redpath and the Making of Nineteenth-Century America* (Ithaca, NY: Cornell

University Press, 2008), 5. During Greeley's brief time as a congressman, one Illinois representative protested that the *Tribune* editor spoke more directly to the legislator's own constituents than he himself could. See "Mileage and Sundries—the House," *NYDT*, December 29, 1848, 2.

16. Ralph Waldo Emerson to Thomas Carlyle, March 11, 1854, in Joseph Slater, ed., *The Correspondence of Emerson and Carlyle* (New York: Columbia University Press, 1964), 499; Mary Potter Thacher Higginson, *Thomas Wentworth Higginson: The Story of His Life* (Boston: Houghton, Mifflin, 1914), 133; Mark Twain, *Roughing It* (Hartford, CT: American, 1872), 150–156.

17. Herman Melville, *The Confidence-Man: His Masquerade* (New York: Penguin, 1990), 138–155. On Greeley as the man from the Philosophical Intelligence Office, see Helen Trimpi, "Three of Melville's Confidence Men: William Cullen Bryant, Theodore Parker, and Horace Greeley," *Texas Studies in Literature and Language* 21:3 (Fall 1979), 368–395. Also see Michael F. Conlin, "Dangerous Isms and the Fanatical Ists: Antebellum Conservatives in the South and the North Confront the Modernity Conspiracy," *Journal of the Civil War Era* 4:2 (June 2014), 205–233.

18. "To Our Friends," *New-Yorker*, March 13, 1841, 409. On the ideal of "Intelligence," see Richard D. Brown, *The Strength of a People: The Idea of an Informed Citizenry in America, 1650–1870* (Chapel Hill: University of North Carolina Press, 1996); Richard R. John, *Spreading the News: The American Postal System from Franklin to Morse* (Cambridge, MA: Harvard University Press, 1998), 25–63.

19. Parton, *Life of Horace Greeley*, 412; Horace Greeley, *The American Conflict: A History of the Great Rebellion in the United States of America, 1860–65*, 2 vols. (Hartford, CT: O. D. Case, 1864–1867).

20. *Frank Leslie's Illustrated Newspaper*, June 8 and July 13, 1872, clippings in Greeley Papers, NYPL.

21. "Greeley's American Conflict," *North American Review* 104 (January 1867), 244.

22. Above all, see Benedict Anderson, *Imagined Communities: Reflections on the Origins and Spread of Nationalism* (London: Verso, 1983).

23. "A Bad Man," *(Washington, DC) Confederation*, February 20, 1861, in Howard Cecil Perkins, ed., *Northern Editorials on Secession* (Gloucester, MA: Peter Smith, 1964), vol. 2, 1003. On print and the acceleration of sectional divisions, see Edward L. Ayers, "What Caused the Civil War?," in *What Caused the Civil War? Reflections on the South and Southern History* (New York: W. W. Norton, 2005), 131–144; Lorman Ratner and Dwight L. Teeter Jr., *Fanatics and Fire-Eaters: Newspapers and the Coming of the Civil War* (Urbana: University of Illinois Press, 2003); Craig Miner, *Seeding Civil War: Kansas in the National News, 1854–1858* (Lawrence: University Press of Kansas, 2008).

24. James Ford Rhodes, "Newspapers as Historical Sources," *Atlantic Monthly*, May 1909, 650–656. The relationship between the North and American nationalism has received comparatively less attention and treatment than Southern nationalism. See Susan-Mary Grant, *North over South: Northern Nationalism and American Identity in the Antebellum Era* (Lawrence: University Press of Kansas, 2000); Michael T. Bernath, "Nationalism," *Journal of the Civil War Era*, https://journalofthecivilwarera.org/forum-the-future-of-civil-war-era-studies/the-future-of-civil-war-era-studies-nationalism/, accessed May 2012; William R. Taylor, *Cavalier and Yankee: The Old South and Ameri-*

can National Character (New York: G. Braziller, 1961). On Southern perceptions of Northern media, see John Nerone, "Newspapers and the Public Sphere," in Scott E. Casper et al., eds., *A History of the Book in America* (Chapel Hill, NC: University of North Carolina Press, 2007), vol. 3, 238. For Greeley's role in this dynamic, see, e.g., "Our Washington Correspondence," *Charleston (SC) Mercury*, January 26, 1861, 1: "What horrid hypocrisy for Greeley to prate constantly about duty to humanity, while supporting a journal founded upon systematic mendacity. . . . Is it not monstrous that this depraved sheet should be the Bible—not the political, but the moral and religious Bible—of the mass of the rural population at the North, and a great number of city and town folks as well?"

25. On the Civil War and the consolidation of American nationalism, see James M. McPherson, *The Battle Cry of Freedom: The Civil War Era* (New York: Oxford University Press, 1988), 859; Melinda Lawson, *Patriot Fires: Forging a New American Nationalism in the Civil War North* (Lawrence: University Press of Kansas, 2002); Garry Wills, *Lincoln at Gettysburg: The Words That Remade America* (New York: Simon & Schuster, 1993); Susan-Mary Grant, "From Union to Nation? The Civil War and the Development of American Nationalism," in Susan-Mary Grant and Brian Holden Reid, eds., *Themes of the American Civil War: The War between the States*, rev. 2nd ed. (New York: Routledge, 2010), 295–316.

26. David W. Blight, *Race and Reunion: The Civil War and American Memory* (Cambridge, MA: Harvard University Press, 2001). A spate of recent work has challenged the "race and reunion" synthesis, emphasizing the persistence of sectional identities, divisions, and bitterness long after the end of Reconstruction. See, e.g., Nina L. Silber, "Reunion and Reconciliation, Reviewed and Reconsidered," *Journal of American History* 103:1 (June 2016), 59–83.

Chapter 1 • Oracle

1. Horace Greeley to Richard T. Jones, January 17, 1860, Horace Greeley Papers, NYPL. This was a standard response for an autograph request. Also see Horace Greeley to W. E. P., October 24, 1853, and Verplanck Martindale to Horace Greeley, September 14, 1847 (taking issue with editorial content), both in Greeley Papers, NYPL. On Greeley's handwriting, see Horace Greeley to Moses A. Cortland, April 14, 1845, Horace Greeley Papers, LOC.

2. Horace Greeley to Harvey Hubbard, April 12, 1844, Greeley Papers, NYPL. Hubbard appears to have heeded Greeley's advice, but only in part. He went on to become the editor of the *Chenango Union* in Norwich, New York, in 1847, and he published a poetry collection: Harvey Hubbard, *Ixion, and Other Poems* (Boston: Ticknor, Reed, & Fields, 1852).

3. Thomas Carlyle, *On Heroes, Hero-Worship, and the Heroic in History* (London: Chapman & Hall, 1840), 183–224. Greeley called the book "a glorious volume" in his *Hints toward Reforms in Lectures, Addresses, and Other Writings* (New York: Harper, 1850), 106. Also see Horace Greeley to Rufus Wilmot Griswold, January 15, 1841, Greeley Papers, LOC. On Thomas Carlyle's influence, see Horace Greeley to Obadiah Bowe, May 14, 1843, Greeley Papers, NYPL.

4. "'The Whigs' and Nativism," *NYDT*, April 6, 1847, 2. On the Yankee and Brother

Jonathan characters, see David Hackett Fischer, *Liberty and Freedom: A Visual History of America's Founding Ideas* (New York: Oxford University Press, 2005), 215–227; Constance Rourke, *American Humor: A Study of the National Character* (New York: Doubleday, 1931), 15–36, 91. Greeley was certainly familiar with these characters, as his use of Yankee slang demonstrated in his letters to Obadiah Bowe through the 1830s and '40s, Greeley Papers, NYPL.

5. Paul Starr, *The Creation of the Media: The Political Origins of Modern Communications* (New York: Free Press, 2004), 113–150; Michael Schudson, *Discovering the News: A Social History of American Newspapers* (New York: Basic Books, 1978), 12–60. Scholars disagree about the extent to which the emergence of the penny press constituted a "revolution." See John C. Nerone, "The Mythology of the Penny Press," *Critical Studies in Mass Communications* 4 (December 1987), 376–404, and, in the same issue, Michael Schudson's response, "A Revolution in Historiography?," 405–408. With high literacy rates and policies that amounted to de facto subsidies for newspapers going back to the country's founding, the United States had a substantially more vibrant print marketplace than European nations, well before the 1830s. A combination of new printing technologies, cheaper paper, new business models, and expanding urban populations, however, undoubtedly did make the 1830s an explosive decade in the history of American journalism.

6. [Untitled], *New-York Mirror*, April 5, 1834, 319. Also see David M. Henkin, *City Reading: Written Words and Public Spaces in Antebellum New York* (New York: Columbia University Press, 1998), 1–27. On questions of authenticity and truth in the penny press, see Andie Tucher, *Froth & Scum: Truth, Beauty, Goodness, and the Ax Murder in America's First Mass Medium* (Chapel Hill: University of North Carolina Press, 1994), 7–21, 46–62.

7. "The Public Press," *Jeffersonian*, March 31, 1838, 49; "The Literature of the Age," *New-Yorker*, August 1, 1835, 2.

8. [George Foster], "New-York in Slices: Slice XXVI . . . The Literary Soirees," *NYDT*, September 27, 1848, 1.

9. George Hiram Greeley, *Genealogy of the Greely-Greeley Family* (Boston: Frank Wood, 1905), 80–81, 153–154, 329, 671; Horace Greeley, *Recollections of a Busy Life* (New York: J. B. Ford, 1868), 17–28; Horace Greeley to Moses Cortland, April 14, 1845, Greeley Papers, NYPL; James Parton, *The Life of Horace Greeley, Editor of the New-York Tribune* (New York: Mason Bros., 1854), 20–28; Beman Brockway, *Fifty Years in Journalism* (Watertown, NY: Daily Times, 1891), 71–72.

10. Greeley, *Recollections*, 295.

11. Greeley, *Recollections*, 60–68; Parton, *Life of Horace Greeley*, 43–47, 82–98. On print culture and individuals, see notes 9 and 11 in the introductory chapter.

12. "Newspapers," *(East Poultney, VT) Northern Spectator*, October 18, 1826; "Dr. Franklin," *(East Poultney, VT) Northern Spectator*, April 28, 1828.

13. David Paul Nord, "The Evangelical Origins of Mass Media in America, 1815–1835," *Journalism Monographs* 88 (1984). Starr, *Creation of the Media*, 84–86, 113–130; Richard R. John, *Spreading the News: The American Postal System from Franklin to Morse* (Cambridge, MA: Harvard University Press, 1998), 25–61; Edwin G. Burroughs

and Mike Wallace, *Gotham: A History of New York City to 1898* (New York: Oxford University Press, 2000), 439–441.

14. "Rules of a Graham House," *Graham Journal of Health and Longevity*, 1:6 (May 9, 1837), 47; Sylvester Graham, *A Lecture on Epidemic Diseases Generally, and Particularly the Spasmodic Cholera* (New York, 1833); "For the Courier," *Norwich (CT) Courier*, October 3, 1832, 3. Graham boardinghouses enjoyed a brief vogue in New York City after the cholera epidemic of 1832. Sylvester Graham (1794–1851) believed that people could stave off cholera and other diseases by following a strict dietary regimen of water, raw fruits and vegetables, and "graham bread" (the forebear to graham crackers), made from home-milled, coarsely ground grain and flour. He also advised a well-ventilated living space, regular exercise and bathing, and abstinent sexual practices. Greeley met his wife in a Graham boardinghouse—and it was an unhappy marriage. On Graham and his comprehensive plan for health reform, see Steven Nissenbaum, *Sex, Diet, and Debility in Jacksonian America: Sylvester Graham and Health Reform* (Westport, CT: Greenwood, 1980). Charles Sellers is most convincing and concise, however, in placing Graham and his followers into the larger context of middle-class modes of self-regulation adapted to a market culture. See Sellers, *The Market Revolution: Jacksonian America, 1815–1846* (New York: Oxford University Press, 1991), 246–257.

15. Fredric Hudson, *Journalism in the United States, from 1690 to 1872* (New York: Harper & Bros., 1873), 344–352, 596–597; Gilbert H. Muller, *William Cullen Bryant: Author of America* (Albany: SUNY Press, 2008), 93–95.

16. James Gordon Bennett, "Prospectus for the New-York Globe," quoted in Hudson, *Journalism*, 409–410, 416–417; Parton, *Life of Horace Greeley*, 139–141; Greeley, *Recollections*, 91–95.

17. William E. Huntzicker, *The Popular Press, 1833–1860* (Westport, CT: Greenwood, 1999), 1–16; William G. Bleyer, *Main Currents in the History of American Journalism* (Boston: Houghton, Mifflin, 1928), 158; Starr, *Creation of the Media*, 113–133; Schudson, *Discovering the News*, 43–50; Day, quoted in Burroughs and Wallace, *Gotham*, 524; Tucher, *Froth & Scum*, 51–52.

18. James L. Crouthamel, *Bennett's* New York Herald *and the Rise of the Popular Press* (Syracuse, NY: Syracuse University Press, 1989). On Bennett and the Jewett murder, see Patricia Cline Cohen, *The Murder of Helen Jewett* (New York: Vintage, 1999), 20–38, 87–101; Tucher, *Froth & Scum*, 21–25; Hans Bergmann, *God in the Street: New York Writing from the Penny Press to Melville* (Philadelphia: Temple University Press, 1995), 23–30.

19. Henkin, *City Reading*, 13–28; Bergmann, *God in the Street*, 19–23; James W. Cook, *The Arts of Deception: Playing with Fraud in the Age of Barnum* (Cambridge, MA: Harvard University Press, 2001), 96–118.

20. "To Our Friends," *New-Yorker*, March 13, 1841, 409; *New-York Sun*, September 3, 1833, quoted in Huntzicker, *Popular Press*, 2.

21. "Publisher's Address," *New-Yorker*, March 22, 1834, 1.

22. Neil Harris, *Humbug: The Art of P. T. Barnum* (Boston: Little, Brown, 1973), 59–91; David Meredith Reese, *Humbugs of New York: Being a Remonstrance against Popular Delusion* (New York: J. S. Taylor, 1838), 17; Tucher, *Froth & Scum*, 46–62; Cook, *Arts of Deception*, 73–118.

23. "The March of Humbug," *New-Yorker*, June 28, 1834, 2.

24. Horace Greeley to B. F. Ransom, May 2, 1836, Greeley Papers, NYPL; "The Morals of Our City," *New-Yorker*, April 23, 1836, 73.

25. "Lyceums," *New-Yorker*, January 1, 1836, 2.

26. "The Literature of the Age," *New-Yorker*, August 1, 1835, 2.

27. Robert Fanuzzi, *Abolition's Public Sphere* (Minneapolis: University of Minnesota Press, 2003), i–iv; "To the Public," *Liberator*, January 1, 1831, 1; William Lloyd Garrsion, "Declaration of Sentiments of the American Anti-Slavery Society," in *Selections from the Writings of W. L. Garrison* (Boston: R. F. Wallcut, 1852), 71.

28. John, *Spreading the News*, 257–280; Leonard L. Richards, *Gentlemen of Property and Standing: Anti-Abolition Mobs in Jacksonian America* (New York: Oxford University Press, 1970), 47–81. On the gag rule, see Sean Wilentz, *The Rise of American Democracy: Jefferson to Lincoln* (New York: W. W. Norton, 2005), 470–477.

29. "The Question," *New-Yorker*, June 7, 1834, 2.

30. Ibid.

31. "The Freedom of the Press," *New-Yorker*, June 14, 1834, 2. Similar criticisms and responses from Greeley were typical in other instances in which the *New-Yorker* waded into the controversy over slavery, e.g., "Friendly Admonition," *New-Yorker*, April 9, 1836, 45.

32. "The Spirit of the Press," *New-Yorker*, August 30, 1834, 2. On the New York anti-abolition riots, see Burroughs and Wallace, *Gotham*, 542–562.

33. "Colonization and Abolition," *New-Yorker*, July 25, 1835, 2.

34. "The Tragedy at Alton," *New-Yorker*, November 25, 1837, 569. Also see "Mobocracy," *New-Yorker*, September 16, 1837, 413; "The Philadelphia Riot," *New-Yorker*, May 26, 1838, 153.

35. "The Tragedy at Alton," *New-Yorker*, November 25, 1837, 569.

36. "Report of the Postmaster General," *New-Yorker*, December 24, 1836, 219; "The Postmaster General's Report—Again," *New-Yorker*, January 14, 1837, 265; "Friendly Admonition," April 9, 1836, 45; "Postmaster General's Report," *Niles' Weekly Register*, December 24, 1836, 267–269. On the problem of abolitionist literature in the mails, see John, *Spreading the News*, 263, 269–272.

37. "The Question, No. II," *New-Yorker*, June 21, 1834, 2.

38. "A Handsome Compliment," *New-Yorker*, October 21, 1837, 4; "Woman as She Should Be," *New-Yorker*, February 3, 1838, 4.

39. Burroughs and Wallace, *Gotham*, 603–619; "The State of the Country," *New-Yorker*, March 4, 1837, 377; "The Sun Newspaper—the Flour Riots," *New-York Herald*, February 20, 1837, 2. On the Panic of 1837, see Jessica Lepler, *The Many Panics of 1837: People, Politics, and the Creation of a Transatlantic Financial Crisis* (Cambridge: Cambridge University Press, 2013); Alisdair Roberts, *America's First Great Depression: Economic Crisis and Political Disorder after the Panic of 1837* (Ithaca. NY: Cornell University Press, 2012).

40. "The Country and the Currency," *New-Yorker*, November 26, 1836, 153.

41. "A Specie Currency," *New-Yorker*, June 24, 1837, 217.

42. "The Spirit of the Press," *New-Yorker*, March 25, 1837, 9; "The State and Prospects of the Country," *New-Yorker*, May 27, 1837, 153.

43. Greeley, *Recollections*, 95; Horace Greeley to B. G. Ransom and S. Mears, January 14, 1838, Horace Greeley to O. A. Bowe, June 11 and June 17, 1838, and Horace Greeley to B. F. Ransom, August 6, 1838, all in Greeley Papers, NYPL.

44. Horace Greeley to Obadiah Bowe, December 14, 1839, Greeley Papers, NYPL: "I can't get rid of the 'Yorker. . . . O that it was in the bottom of the sea. Make your politicians support you, if you don't know, 'a man can't buy corn when he aint got none.'"

45. Greeley, *Recollections*, 125. On Whig party principles and origins, see Daniel Walker Howe, *The Political Culture of the American Whigs* (Chicago: University of Chicago Press, 1979), 1–42; Michael F. Holt, *The Rise and Fall of the American Whig Party: Jacksonian Politics and the Onset of the Civil War* (New York: Oxford University Press, 1999), 19–32.

46. The only extant biography of Thurlow Weed, a towering figure in the history of American party politics, is Glyndon G. Van Deusen, *Thurlow Weed: Wizard of the Lobby* (Boston: Little, Brown, 1947).

47. Thurlow Weed, *Life of Thurlow Weed, Including His Autobiography and a Memoir* (Boston: Houghton, Mifflin, 1883), vol. 1, 466. Also see Thurlow Weed to William Henry Seward, December 2, 1837, and December 24, 1837, both in Thurlow Weed Papers, University of Rochester; Horace Greeley to Obadiah Bowe, December 14, 1839, Greeley Papers, NYPL. On the importance of Weed's patronage to Greeley's finances, see Horace Greeley to Thurlow Weed, December 29, 1837, in Weed, *Life of Thurlow Weed*, vol. 2, 54–55; Horace Greeley to B. F. Ransom, January 26, 1839, Greeley Papers, NYPL.

48. Horace Greeley to William Henry Seward, February 12, 1840. Also see, e.g., Horace Greeley to Obadiah Bowe, June 17, 1838, and Horace Greeley to Schuyler Colfax, March 17, 1850, and October 2, 1848, all in Greeley Papers, NYPL; Horace Greeley to James K. Pike, April 28, 1850, in Pike, *First Blows of the Civil War: The Years of Preliminary Conflict in the United States from 1850 to 1860* (New York: American News, 1879), 49. On the social functions of antebellum party politics, see Glenn C. Altschuler and Stuart M. Blumin, *Rude Republic: Americans and Their Politics in the Nineteenth Century* (Princeton, NJ: Princeton University Press, 2000), 14–46.

49. Richard Smith Elliott, *Notes Taken in Sixty Years* (St. Louis: R. P. Studley, 1883), 121. Also see Arthur M. Schlesinger Jr., *The Age of Jackson* (Boston: Little, Brown, 1945), 304; Arthur M. Schlesinger Jr., *Orestes Brownson: A Pilgrim's Progress* (Boston: Little, Brown, 1966), 108; Robert Gray Gunderson, *The Log-Cabin Campaign* (Lexington: University of Kentucky Press, 1957), 123–134; Daniel Walker Howe, *What Hath God Wrought? The Transformation of America, 1815–1848* (New York: Oxford University Press, 2007), 571–588.

50. "Mr. Bond's Speech," *Jeffersonian*, May 19, 1838, 105; "Speech of Mr. Bond," *Jeffersonian*, June 9, 1838, 132; *Jeffersonian—Extra*, June 30, 1838; "Mr. Bond and His Reviewers," *Jeffersonian*, August 18, 1838, 209; "Mr. Bond and His Reviewers (Remarks Concluded)," *Jeffersonian*, August 25, 1838, 217; Horace Greeley to Obadiah Bowe, June 11, 1838, Greeley Papers, NYPL. On the role of the press in both shaping and disseminating political speeches, see John, *Spreading the News*, 57–58.

51. "The Log Cabin," *Log Cabin*, May 2, 1840, 3. Greeley noted the broad geographical reach of the *Log Cabin*, including the South, to Seward. See Horace Greeley to William Henry Seward, August 8, 1840, Greeley Papers, NYPL.

52. "The Public Expenditures," *Log Cabin*, August 1, 1840, 1; [untitled], *Log Cabin*, August 29, 1840, 3.

53. "The Right and Wrong of Politics," *Jeffersonian*, November 3, 1838, 1–2. On the depth of Whig campaigning in 1838 and 1840, see Howe, *What Hath God Wrought?*, 575–576; Holt, *Rise and Fall*, 76–87, 108–112. George Bancroft's 1835 address, "The Office of the People in Art, Government, and Religion," is an exemplary statement of the Democratic Party's faith in the sovereign people. See Joseph L. Blau, ed., *Social Theories of Jacksonian Democracy* (Indianapolis: Bobbs-Merrill, 1954), 263–273.

54. "To the Public," *Jeffersonian*, February 17, 1838, 1; Horace Greeley to William Henry Seward, August 8, 1840, Greeley Papers, NYPL.

55. "O! Van Buren!—a Currency Song," *Log Cabin*, August 1, 1840, 4; "Baltimore Hymn," *The Log Cabin & Hard Cider Melodies: A Collection of Popular and Patriotic Songs; Respectfully Dedicated to the Friends of Harrison and Tyler* (Boston: Charles Adams, 1840), 56.

56. O[restes] A B[rownson], "Chartism by Thomas Carlyle," *Boston Quarterly Review*, July 1840, 358–394; Schlesinger Jr., *Orestes A. Brownson*, 96; "The Tendencies of Loco-Focoism," *Log Cabin*, August 1, 1840, 2; Greeley to William Henry Seward, September 30, 1840, William Henry Seward Papers, University of Rochester. Even before his political work, Greeley had shown this faith in the superiority of his principles. At the beginning of 1837, he had attempted to draw William Leggett, editor of the Democratic weekly, the *Plaindealer*, into a debate over the question of the tariff. When Leggett declined, Greeley marveled that "a political essayist of conceded ability and no little popularity [could] establish a public journal for the express purpose of diffusing and enforcing certain broad principles of political economy" and not be willing to stand by those principles when challenged. In the *Jeffersonian*, Greeley similarly urged the editor of a "violent anti-bank journal" in New York City to defend its hard-money principles before the workingmen whose interests he claimed to represent. In Greeley's mind, the inevitable weakness of that defense could only be to the Whigs' benefit. See [untitled], *New-Yorker*, January 21, 1837, 281; "The Plaindealer," *New-Yorker*, February 18, 1837, 346; "Currency and Prices," *Jeffersonian*, March 17, 1838, 33.

57. "The New-York Tribune," *Log Cabin*, April 3, 1841, 2.

58. Horace Greeley to Rufus Wilmot Griswold, February 26, 1841, in Rufus W. Griswold, *Passages from the Correspondence of Rufus W. Griswold* (Cambridge, MA: W. M. Griswold, 1898), 60–61; Horace Greeley to Obadiah Bowe, December 20, 1840, Greeley Papers, NYPL.

59. "To Our Friends," *New-Yorker*, March 21, 1841, 1; Greeley, *Recollections*, 142, 137; "The New-York Tribune," *Log Cabin*, April 3, 1841, 2.

60. Horace Greeley to William Henry Seward, June 29 and July 7, 1841, Seward Papers, University of Rochester. The McElrath partnership was finalized and announced by the end of July. See [untitled], *NYDT*, July 31, 1841, 2; Parton, *Life of Horace Greeley*, 196. On Greeley's difficult relationship with Thurlow Weed and Seward and the problems of New York City and Albany Whigs, see Glyndon G. Van Deusen, *Horace Greeley: Nineteenth-Century Crusader* (Philadelphia: University of Pennsylvania Press, 1953), 53–58. Greeley remained bitter about the lack of support from Weed and Seward,

even after Thomas McElrath steadied the operation. See Horace Greeley to Thurlow Weed, December 7 and December 15, 1841, Weed Papers, University of Rochester.

61. "The New York Tribune," *Log Cabin*, April 3, 1841, 2; "To the Public," *NYDT*, May 6, 1841, 2 ("horrible prostitution"). On the *Tribune*'s treatment of theater versus that of rival newspapers, see, e.g., "The Rule of Advertising," *NYDT*, May 11, 1841; "Theatres vs. Churches," *NYDT*, May 20, 1842, 2; "The Moral Character of New York," *NYDT*, May 22, 1841, 2. On theatrical notices advertising, see "Theaters and the Tribune: Remarks," *NYDT*, May 16, 1850, 4. On patent medicine advertisements, see *NYDT*, May 20, 1842, 4. On the *Tribune*'s policies toward patent medicine advertising, see H. Greeley, "Settling an Account," *NYDT*, April 2, 1853, 4; "What Is Quackery?" *NYDT*, November 29, 1854. On the *Tribune*'s simultaneous coverage and condemnation of "shocking murders," see, e.g., "Peter Robinson and the Newspaper Press," *NYDT*, April 19, 1841, 2; "Colt's Trial," *New-York Weekly Tribune*, January 29, 1842, 2; "Most Horrible Murder," *NYDT*, September 27, 1841, 2. Also see the *Tribune*'s extensive coverage of the trial of John C. Colt, murderer of printer Samuel Adams, *NYDT*, January 18, 1842, to March 1, 1842; Tucher, *Froth & Scum*, 141–148.

62. "The Moral Character of New-York," *NYDT*, May 22, 1841, 2; [untitled], *NYDT*, May 5, 1841, 2.

63. [Untitled], *New-York Herald*, April 20, 1841, 2. On the battles between Greeley and James Gordon Bennett over murder coverage, see Tucher, *Froth & Scum*, 141–162. On the role of rivalry and editorial feuds in the newspaper business, see Augustus Maverick, *Henry J. Raymond and the New York Press for Thirty Years* (Hartford, CT: A. S. Hale, 1870), 39. On Greeley's attire, see William Harlan Hale, *Horace Greeley: Voice of the People* (New York: Harper & Bros., 1950), 77–78; "Personal Matters," *NYDT*, January 29, 1844, 2.

64. *New-York Courier and Enquirer*, January 27, 1844, referenced in "Personal Matters," *NYDT*, January 29, 1844, 2; "Cooperage of the Tribune," *NYDT*, December 12, 1842, 2–3. This was Greeley's humorous account of the Cooper libel trial. On the "Yankee" as a comic folk character, see Cameron C. Nickels, *New England Humor from the Revolutionary War to the Civil War* (Knoxville: University of Tennessee Press, 1993); Rourke, *American Humor*, 15–36.

65. "New-York Weekly Tribune: Prospectus," *NYDT*, September 14, 1841, 3; Ralph Waldo Emerson to Thomas Carlyle, March 11, 1854, in Joseph Slater, ed., *The Correspondence of Emerson and Carlyle* (New York: Columbia University Press, 1964), 499.

66. *New-York Herald*, May 6, 1835, quoted in Hudson, *Journalism*, 432–433.

67. "Poverty in Cities," *New-York Weekly Tribune*, November 20, 1841, 2; "Slavery and the North," *New-York Weekly Tribune*, January 22, 1853, 2.

68. Greeley, *Recollections*, 183; Fuller, quoted in Charles Capper, *Margaret Fuller: An American Romantic Life* (New York: Oxford University Press, 2007), vol. 2, 169. On Fuller, Greeley, and the *Tribune* generally, see Capper, *Margaret Fuller*, 165–177, 194–233; Catherine C. Mitchell, *Margaret Fuller's New York Journalism: A Biographical Essay and Key Writings* (Knoxville: University of Tennessee Press, 1995), 3–48; Judith Mattson Bean and Joel Myerson, eds., *Margaret Fuller, Critic: Writings from the* New-York Tribune, *1844–1846* (New York: Columbia University Press, 2000), xv–xxxvii.

69. "An American Newspaper," *Troy (NY) Daily Times*, June 1, 1853, 4–5; Greeley, quoted in Van Deusen, *Horace Greeley*, 65. Variations on the "horned cattle" line can be found as early as Horace Greeley to Rufus W. Griswold, February 20, 1841, in Griswold, *Passages from the Correspondence*, 58.

70. On Greeley's marriage generally, see Van Deusen, *Horace Greeley*, 35–36, 145–158; Robert C. Williams, *Horace Greeley: Champion of American Freedom* (New York: New York University Press, 2006), 48–52; esp. Henry Luther Stoddard, *Horace Greeley: Printer, Editor, Crusader* (New York: G. P. Putnam, 1946), 106–122, which contains a series of Greeley's letters to Fuller detailing his home life. Also see Horace Greeley to Mary and Arthur Greeley, February 23, 1845–46, Greeley Papers, LOC, which conveys the distance in the Greeley marriage; Horace Greeley to Emma Whiting, August 30, 1847, Greeley Papers, NYPL; Greeley, *Recollections*, 426–427.

71. S. M. Fuller to Messrs. Little and Brown, Monday, June 3, 1844, in Robert Hudspeth, ed., *The Letters of Margaret Fuller* (Ithaca, NY: Cornell University Press, 1984), vol. 3, 200; S. Margaret Fuller, *Woman in the Nineteenth Century* (New York: Greeley & McElrath, 1845); Capper, *Margaret Fuller*, 165–166; Emerson, quoted in Capper, *Margaret Fuller*, 166.

72. [Margaret Fuller], "A Few Words in Reply to Mr. U. C. Hill," *NYDT*, May 16, 1846, suppl. 1, 1, "Swedenborgianism," *NYDT*, July 3, 1845, 1, and "Headley's Napoleon," *NYDT*, May 4, 1846, 1, all quoted in Capper, *Margaret Fuller*, 198. On Fuller and anonymity, see Mitchell, *Fuller's New York Journalism*, 39–40; "New-York Tribune: Prospectus for 1845," *NYDT*, November 16, 1844, 2.

73. Margaret Fuller to Mary Rotch, January 15, 1845, in Hudspeth, *Letters of Margaret Fuller*, vol. 4, 46; Margaret Fuller to Samuel G. Ward, December 29, 1844, in Hudspeth, *Letters of Margaret Fuller*, vol. 3, 256. Also see "Death of Margaret Fuller," *NYDT*, July 23, 1850, 4; Greeley, quoted in Lurton Dunham Ingersoll, *The Life of Horace Greeley* (Chicago: Union, 1873), 171, 173 ("win the favor").

74. Greeley, *Recollections*, 175–176, 178.

75. Horace Greeley to Elizabeth Oakes Smith, March 1, 1851, Gilder Lehrman Collection, NYHS.

Chapter 2 • The Nation in the Balance

1. "The Magnetic Telegraph—Some of Its Results," *NYDT*, July 8, 1845, 2; John Higham, *From Boundlessness to Consolidation: The Transformation of American Culture, 1848–1860* (Ann Arbor, MI: William L. Clements Library, 1969); Russel B. Nye, *American Thought and Culture, 1830–1860* (New York: Harper & Row, 1974), 3–15; Merle Curti, *The Roots of American Loyalty* (New York: Columbia University Press, 1946).

2. David M. Potter, *The Impending Crisis, 1848–1861* (New York: Harper & Row, 1976), 6; Timothy Mason Roberts, *Distant Revolutions: 1848 and the Challenge of American Exceptionalism* (Charlottesville: University of Virginia Press, 2009).

3. Ralph Waldo Emerson to Margaret Fuller and Ralph Waldo Emerson to Lidian Emerson, both March 1, 1842, in Ralph Rusk, ed., *The Letters of Ralph Waldo Emerson* (New York: Columbia University Press, 1966), vol. 3, 17–20. Greeley's enthusiasm and regular notice of Emerson's writings were critical to the growth of Emerson's reputation nationally. See Richard Teichgraeber III, *Sublime Thoughts / Penny Wisdom:*

Situating Emerson and Thoreau in the American Market (Baltimore: Johns Hopkins University Press, 1995), 211.

4. "Stand by the Cause of Humanity," *New-York Weekly Tribune*, January 8, 1842, 2; Horace Greeley, "Introduction to the American Edition," in William Atkinson, *Principles of Political Economy* (New York: Greeley & McElrath, 1843), xii.

5. Horace Greeley to Obadiah Bowe, February 2, 1842, Horace Greeley Papers, NYPL; "The Heresies of the Tribune," *NYDT*, December 1, 1845, 2.

6. Adam Tuchinsky, *Horace Greeley's* New-York Tribune: *Civil War–Era Socialism and the Crisis of Free Labor* (Ithaca, NY: Cornell University Press, 2009), 18–58; Carl J. Guarneri, *The Utopian Alternative: Fourierism in Nineteenth-Century America* (Cambridge: Cambridge University Press, 1991), 25–34; Arthur E. Bestor Jr., "Albert Brisbane—Propagandist for Socialism in the 1840s," *New York History* 27 (April 1947), 143–147; 150–154.

7. Tuchinsky, *Horace Greeley's* New-York Tribune, 35–40.

8. Horace Greeley, *Hints toward Reforms in Lectures, Addresses, and Other Writings* (New York: Harper & Bros., 1850), 176, 45. *Hints* was a collection of lectures he gave between 1842 and 1848.

9. Horace Greeley to Thurlow Weed, May 14, 1846, Thurlow Weed Papers, University of Rochester. Greeley's debate with Henry Raymond was first published in the *Tribune* and the *New-York Courier and Enquirer* and was subsequently published as a book: Horace Greeley and Henry Jarvis Raymond, *Association Discussed; or, The Socialism of the Tribune Examined* (New York: Harper & Bros., 1847). On Greeley's battles with conservative Whigs, see, e.g., "Progress and Conservatism," *New-York Weekly Tribune*, May 2, 1846, 2; "The Whigs—Reform and Progress," *New-York Weekly Tribune*, May 9, 1846, 2; "Social Reform," *New-York Weekly Tribune*, May 23, 1846, 2; "Silk Stocking Whiggery," *New-York Weekly Tribune*, November 6, 1846, 2; "The Tribune and Nativism," *New-York Weekly Tribune*, August 27, 1846, 2; "The Express on Land Reform, Poverty, Fourierism, and the Tribune," *New-York Weekly Tribune*, July 4, 1846, 2; "The Whig Party in the State of New York—Its Divisions," *New-York Weekly Tribune*, July 31, 1847, 2; Michael F. Holt, *Rise and Fall of the American Whig Party: Jacksonian Politics and the Onset of the Civil War* (New York: Oxford University Press, 1999), 227–230, 239–243.

10. "The Magnetic Telegraph—Some of Its Results," *NYDT*, July 8, 1845, 2. Also see Daniel Walker Howe, *What Hath God Wrought? The Transformation of America* (New York: Oxford University Press, 2007), 1–3, 691–698. Wildly optimistic visions for harmony like the one articulated in the *Tribune* were not uncommon. Most were disconnected from the specifics of how the network would be created, or how it would be administered. See Richard R. John, *Network Nation: Inventing American Telecommunications* (Cambridge, MA): Harvard University Press, 2010), 18–63.

11. Horace Greeley, "River and Harbor Improvements," *De Bow's Review*, November 1847, 291–296. Also see Greeley's reports from the Chicago Rivers and Harbors Convention, *NYDT*, July 13–15, 1847, 1 (for each date).

12. Daniel Walker Howe, *The Political Culture of the American Whigs* (Chicago: University of Chicago Press, 1979), 123–149.

13. Abraham Lincoln, "Eulogy on Henry Clay, July 6, 1852," in Don E. Fehrenbacher,

ed., *Lincoln: Speeches and Writings, 1832–1858* (New York: Library of America, 1989), 270; Horace Greeley, *Recollections of a Busy Life* (New York: J. B. Ford, 1868), 166. On Clay as a national figure and symbol, see Sarah Bischoff Paulus, "America's Long Eulogy for Compromise: Henry Clay and American Politics, 1854–58," *Journal of the Civil War Era* 5:1 (March 2014), 28–31; Sarah J. Purcell, "All that Remains of Henry Clay: Political Funerals and the Tour of Henry Clay's Corpse," *Common-Place* 12:3 (April 2012), http://www.common-place.org/vol-12/no-03/purcell/; Mark E. Neely Jr., "American Nationalism in the Image of Henry Clay: Abraham Lincoln's Eulogy on Henry Clay in Context," *Register of the Kentucky Historical Society* 73:1 (January 1975), 31–60. On Clay's magnetic persona, see Amy S. Greenberg, *A Wicked War: Polk, Clay, Lincoln, and the 1846 U.S. Invasion of Mexico* (New York: Knopf, 2012), 3–7.

14. Horace Greeley to Obadiah Bowe, August 21, 1843, Greeley Papers, NYPL. On Henry Clay, the American System, and the "harmony of interests," see Howe, *What Hath God Wrought?*, 270–271, 582–584. On Clay and slavery, see Howe, *What Hath God Wrought?*, 584–588; Robert V. Remini, *Henry Clay: Statesman for the Union* (New York: W. W. Norton, 1991), 26–27, 179–180, 439–440; Henry Clay, "On Abolition," in *The Life and Speeches of Henry Clay* (New York: James B. Swain, 1843), 2, 395–414.

15. A. Patterson to Samuel F. Patterson, March 23, 1844, quoted in Holt, *Rise and Fall*, 162.

16. Greenberg, *A Wicked War*, 9–24; Howe, *What Hath God Wrought?*, 671–690; Holt, *Rise and Fall*, 176–183; Remini, *Henry Clay*, 600–635.

17. "The Presidency and Slavery—Mr. Clay Cannot Be Abandoned," *New-York Weekly Tribune*, January 14, 1843, 2; Horace Greeley to Obadiah Bowe, August 21, 1843, Greeley Papers, NYPL. On Greeley's broader criticism of abolitionist "one-ideaism," see "Letter from Horace Greeley to the Anti-Slavery Convention at Cincinnati," *NYDT*, June 20, 1845, 1. On the Liberty Party, anti-slavery, and threats to the Whig Party, see Holt, *Rise and Fall*, 156–157; Bruce Laurie, *Beyond Garrison: Antislavery and Social Reform* (New York: Cambridge University Press, 2005), 49–83.

18. Epes Sargent, *Life and Public Services of Henry Clay* (New York: Greeley & McElrath, 1844), 5–6; Cassius M. Clay letters, *New-York Weekly Tribune*, June to August 1844, collected as Cassius M. Clay, *The Letters of Cassius M. Clay* (New York: Greeley & McElrath, 1844); "Mr. Clay and Slavery," *New-York Weekly Tribune*, September 21, 1844, 2; "Polk and Birney," *New-York Weekly Tribune*, October 19, 1844, 2; "A Word to Anti-Slavery Whigs," *New-York Weekly Tribune*, October 26, 1844, 2. Greeley's desperation became intense enough that he was willing to promise support for nativist candidates in New York City in exchange for Clay votes there. See Glyndon G. Van Deusen, *Horace Greeley: Nineteenth-Century Crusader* (New York: Hill & Wang, 1951), 95; Holt, *Rise and Fall*, 192–194.

19. Vernon L. Volpe, "The Liberty Party and Polk's Election, 1844," *Historian* 53 (1991), 691–710.

20. Greeley, *Recollections*, 176; "Our Defeat in New-York," *NYDT*, November 11, 1844, 2. Greeley would continue to hold a grudge against James Birney and "Birneyism" as both the cause of Whig failure and as a shorthand for short-sighted "one-ideaism" in favor of a more pragmatic politics. See, e.g., "A Party Is Known by the Character of Its Leaders," *New-York Weekly Tribune*, September 13, 1845, 2; "The Whig Party and

Oregon," *New-York Weekly Tribune*, January 31, 1846, 2; and "Birneyism—Texas—Suffrage," *New-York Weekly Tribune*, March 25, 1846, 2. He was still talking about it in 1852, in "Birney and Clay," *New-York Weekly Tribune*, February 14, 1852, 2.

21. "Annexation," *United States Magazine and Democratic Review* 17:1 (July–August 1845), 5. Credit for the term "Manifest Destiny" has traditionally gone to John L. O'Sullivan, but subsequent studies have cast doubt on his authorship. See Howe, *What Hath God Wrought?*, 703n; Amy Greenberg, *Manifest Manhood and the Antebellum American Empire* (Cambridge: Cambridge University Press, 2005). On the West as a "safety valve," see Michael A. Morrison, "New Territory versus No Territory: The Whig Party and the Politics of Western Expansion, 1846–1848," *Western Historical Quarterly* 23:1 (February 1992), 29; Drew R. McCoy, *The Elusive Republic: Political Economy in Jeffersonian America* (Chapel Hill: University of North Carolina Press, 1980), 185–209.

22. Horace Greeley, *Why I Am a Whig: A Reply to an Inquiring Friend* (New York: Tribune Office, 1851), 6; Henry Clay, quoted in Howe, *What Hath God Wrought?*, 704. On Democratic Manifest Destiny expansionism versus Whig developmentalism generally, see Howe, *What Hath God Wrought?*, 701–708; Greenberg, *Manifest Manhood*, 11–17.

23. C. W. Holden, "Horace Greeley," *Holden's Dollar Magazine*, January 1849, 35; "Our Country, Right or Wrong!" *New-York Weekly Tribune*, May 16, 1846, 2; "The War and the Tribune," *New-York Weekly Tribune*, June 13, 1846, 2.

24. "What Means This War?" *NYDT*, May 13, 1846, 2.

25. "Soldiers—Recruiting—the Tribune and the Courier and Enquirer," *NYDT*, June 29, 1846, 2; "The War and the Tribune," *New-York Weekly Tribune*, June 13, 1846, 2. On the domestic scene and cultural expressions of the Mexican War, see Robert W. Johannsen, *To the Halls of the Montezumas: The Mexican War in the American Imagination* (New York: Oxford University Press, 1985), 7–144; Shelley Streeby, *American Sensations: Class, Empire, and the Production of Popular Culture* (Berkeley: University of California Press, 2002), 38–158.

26. "Our Country, Right or Wrong!" *NYDT*, May 12, 1846, 2.

27. "The Fourth of July," *NYDT*, July 4, 1846, 2; "Thistles and Pack Saddles," *NYDT*, July 14, 1846, 2; "Slavery Triumphs!," *NYDT*, March 4, 1847, 2; "Historical Parallels," *NYDT*, March 18, 1847, 2; "Character of the War," *NYDT*, October 5, 1847, 2.

28. "The South," *NYDT*, August 19, 1846, 2.

29. "The Wilmot Proviso," *NYDT*, February 22, 1847, 2. On slaveholders' imperial ambitions in the Caribbean and the Americas, see Walter Johnson, *River of Dark Dreams: Slavery and Empire in the Cotton Kingdom* (Cambridge, MA: Harvard University Press, 2013), 303–330. Greeley saw the Whig nationalist economic program as a counter to the imperial designs of slaveholders. He would speak, for instance, of the transcontinental railroad as "a bond of union not easily broken and a new spring to our national industry" that would "open new vistas to national and to individual aspiration, and crush out filibusterism by giving a new and wholesome direction to the public mind." See Horace Greeley, *An Overland Journey from New York to San Francisco in the Summer of 1859* (New York, 1860), 386.

30. "Glorious News from Delaware!," *New-York Weekly Tribune*, February 27, 1847, 2; "Anti-Slavery in Maryland," *New-York Weekly Tribune*, October 9, 1847, 2; "Just Views

of the Wilmot Proviso at the South," *New-York Weekly Tribune*, October 16, 1847, 2; "Mr. Clay and Slavery," *New-York Weekly Tribune*, October 23, 1847, 2; "Mr. Clay and Slavery," *New-York Weekly Tribune*, November 13, 1847, 2; "Progress of Public Opinion at the South Respecting Slavery," *New-York Weekly Tribune*, October 14, 1847, 2. Also see "The Whigs and the South," *New-York Weekly Tribune*, March 18, 1848, 2; "C. M. Clay's Writings," *New-York Weekly Tribune*, July 8, 1848, 2.

31. Greeley supported Thomas Corwin of Ohio over Henry Clay through the spring of 1847, after Corwin's angry antiwar harangue in the Senate, but had come back to Clay by the end of the summer. See Horace Greeley to Joshua R. Giddings, April 24, 1847, Joshua Giddings Papers, Ohio Historical Society, Columbus, quoted in Holt, *Rise and Fall*, 277; Horace Greeley to Schuyler Colfax, May 1, 1847, Greeley Papers, NYPL; "The Presidency in 1848—Slavery—Mr. Clay," *NYDT*, October 11, 1847, 2.

32. "1848," *NYDT*, January 1, 1848, 2. Greeley began talking about the critical importance of 1848 as early as September of 1847. See "The New-York Tribune," *New-York Weekly Tribune*, October 2, 1847, 2. On the *Tribune*'s broader coverage of 1848, see Adam Tuchinsky, " 'The Bourgeoisie Will Fall, and Fall Forever': The *New-York Tribune*, the 1848 French Revolution, and American Social Democratic Discourse," *Journal of American History* 92:2 (September 2005), 470–497.

33. Greeley helped orchestrate and distribute a speech by Henry Clay late in 1847 in which he declared his moral opposition to slavery and condemned the war. See "Mr. Clay's Speech at Lexington, Ky., November 13, on the Mexican War &c.," *NYDT*, November 15, 1847, 2; "Response of the People!" *NYDT*, November 19, 1847, 2. Also see Holt, *Rise and Fall*, 278–279.

34. Holt, *Rise and Fall*, 284–330.

35. William Henry Seward to Thurlow Weed, January 30, 1848, Weed Papers, University of Rochester; "The Presidency and the Whigs—Mr. Clay and Gen. Taylor," *New-York Weekly Tribune*, January 29, 1848, 2; "Gen. Worth on Gen. Politics," *NYDT*, May 16, 1848, 2; Horace Greeley to Alvah Hunt, November 17, 1847, Bernhard Knollenberg Collection, Yale University; Horace Greeley to Alexander H. Wells, May 23, 1848, Horace Greeley Collection, NYHS.

36. Horace Greeley to Henry Clay, April 28 and May 29, 1848, Henry Clay Papers, LOC; Horace Greeley to Schuyler Colfax, April 3, 1848, Greeley Papers, NYPL. Greeley had been predicting more or less this outcome since 1847, claiming that the Whigs would be "Tylerized" (i.e., again let down by a false Whig, as John Tyler had been) should Taylor win the nomination. See Horace Greeley to Schuyler Colfax, May 1, 1847, Greeley Papers, NYPL. On Greeley's flirtations with other candidates (Justice John McLean and Senator Thomas Corwin, both of Ohio), see Van Deusen, *Horace Greeley*, 119–120.

37. Horace Greeley is often misquoted, without an ellipsis, as calling the convention a "slaughterhouse of Whig principles." The actual quote reads, "the late National Slaughter-House at Philadelphia, of everything approaching a frank and manly avowal of cardinal Whig principles." See "Whig Principles at Philadelphia," *NYDT*, June 14, 1848, 2.

38. "Henry Clay," *NYDT*, June 13, 1848, 2. On the Whig convention, see Holt, *Rise and Fall*, 320–333; Henry Luther Stoddard, *Horace Greeley: Printer, Editor, Crusader*

(New York: G. P. Putnam, 1946), 125–127; "Whig Principles at Philadelphia," *NYDT*, June 14, 1848, 2.

39. On the United States and the 1848 revolutions generally, see Roberts, *Distant Revolutions*, 3–11. On the revolutions and American reform, see Roberts, *Distant Revolutions*, 81–104; Lucretia Mott, quoted in Roberts, *Distant Revolutions*, 92; Theodore Parker, "Some Thoughts on the Free Soil Party and the Election of General Taylor, December 1848," in Frances Power Cobbe, ed., *The Collected Works of Theodore Parker* (London: Trubner, 1863), 4, 113.

40. "Signs of Progress," *New-York Weekly Tribune*, April 15, 1848, 2. On Greeley, the *Tribune*, and 1848, see Tuchinsky, *Horace Greeley's* New-York Tribune, 82–107.

41. "The Nomination," *NYDT*, June 10, 1848, 2; Horace Greeley to Joshua Giddings, June 20, 1848, Greeley Collection, NYHS.

42. Richard H. Sewell, *Ballots for Freedom: Anti-Slavery Politics in the United States, 1837–1850* (New York: Oxford University Press, 1976), 142–151, quotes on 149, 150.

43. "The Tribune and the Presidency," *NYDT*, July 31, 1848, 2; "The Buffalo Convention," *NYDT*, August 12, 1848, 2; "The Buffalo Platform," *NYDT*, August 16, 1848, 2.

44. Horace Greeley to Schuyler Colfax, September 15, 1848, Greeley Papers, NYPL.

45. Horace Greeley to Schuyler Colfax, October 2, 1848, Greeley Papers, NYPL.

46. Horace Greeley to Joshua R. Giddings, June 20, 1848, Greeley Collection, NYHS. Greeley would claim vindication for these suspicions in 1849, when the Free Soil organization in New York State melted away and the warring "Barnburner" and "Hunker" factions reunited. See Van Deusen, *Horace Greeley*, 134–135. On the Free Soil Party and its Democratic origins, see Jonathan Earle, *Jacksonian Anti-Slavery and the Politics of Free Soil, 1824–1854* (Chapel Hill: University of North Carolina Press, 2004), 163–180; Sewell, *Ballots for Freedom*, 142–169; Sean Wilentz, *The Rise of American Democracy: Jefferson to Lincoln* (New York: W. W. Norton, 2005), 614–628. On the Whig response, see Holt, *Rise and Fall*, 338–345.

47. Horace Greeley to Schuyler Colfax, September 15, 1848, Greeley Papers, NYPL; Horace Greeley to Thurlow Weed, September 18 and 22, 1848, Greeley Collection, NYHS; "The Choice," *NYDT*, September 29, 1848, 2.

48. Bayard Tuckerman, ed., *The Diary of Philip Hone, 1828–1851* (New York: Dodd, Mead, 1889), vol. 2, 351; "After the Battle," *NYDT*, Thursday, November 9, 1848, 2.

49. *Congressional Globe*, 30th Congress, 2nd Session, vol. 20, 13, 83, 605, 608–610 (1849). Early in the session, Greeley told a friend that the controversies relating to slavery in the territories would be "satisfactorily adjusted" before March. See Horace Greeley to J. B. Wilcox, December 11, 1848, quoted in Robert C. Williams, *Horace Greeley: Champion of American Freedom* (New York: New York University Press, 2006), 114.

50. [Untitled], *New London (CT) Democrat*, December 16, 1848, 3. Greeley referred to Congress as the "embodied scoundrelism of the nation" in a later reflection. See Horace Greeley to Schuyler Colfax, June 5, 1854, Greeley Papers, NYPL.

51. Much of the controversy stirred by Greeley's presence stemmed from the perception that Greeley used his journalistic stature in unfair ways. One colleague complained that Greeley spoke "to an audience to which members of this House could not speak." Another said that his exposés were prejudicial in districts where people knew Greeley and the *Tribune* better than their own representative. In debate, members

expressed confusion as to how they should distinguish between "Mr. Greeley, a member of Congress, and Mr. Greeley, the editor of the Tribune." See Mileage and Sundries—the House," *NYDT*, December 29, 1848, 2; *Congressional Globe*, 30th Congress, 2nd Session, 111; "Mileage of Members of Congress," *Trenton (NJ) State Gazette*, December 29, 1848, 2.

52. "Congress and Its Doings in Print," *NYDT*, December 9, 1848, 2; Greeley, *Recollections*, 222.

53. "A Day in Congress," *NYDT*, December 8, 1848, 2; "Waste of Time in Congress," *NYDT*, December 25, 1848, 2. For a useful compendium of Greeley's dispatches from Congress, see James Parton, *The Life of Horace Greeley, Editor of the New-York Tribune* (New York: Mason Bros., 1854), 288–319.

54. "The Mileage of Congress," *NYDT*, December 22, 1848, 2; Greeley, *Recollections*, 218–220; *Whig Almanac and United States Register for 1850* (New York: Greeley & McElrath, 1850), 44–45.

55. "Mileage and Sundries—the House," *NYDT*, December 29, 1848, 2.

56. *Congressional Globe*, 30th Congress, 2nd Session, 108–112; "The Mileage Report—a Side-Blow," *NYDT*, January 19, 1849, 2. On Greeley's belief that his efforts would cast out crooked members of Congress, see Horace Greeley to Schuyler Colfax, January 2 and January 24, 1849, Greeley Papers, NYPL.

57. Greeley, *Recollections*, 229–233; *Congressional Globe*, 30th Congress, 2nd Session, 694. On the final battles and brawls of the session, see Allan Nevins, *Ordeal of the Union: A House Dividing* (New York: Scribner, 1947), vol. 1, 225–229; "The Mileage Report—a Side-Blow," *NYDT*, January 19, 1849, 2.

58. "Free Territory—How to Be Preserved—My Proposition," *New-York Weekly Tribune*, September 29, 1849, 2; "The Late Session of Congress," *NYDT*, March 9, 1849, 2.

59. See the introductory chapter.

Chapter 3 • *Making the Yankee Nation*

1. "The Extension of Slavery," *New-York Weekly Tribune*, April 28, 1854, 2, published originally under the same title in the *NYDT*, April 24, 1854, 4.

2. "Freedom and Slavery, and the Coveted Territories," in *The Border Ruffian Code in Kansas* (New York: Tribune Office, 1856). New Yorker John Jay (grandson of a framer of the Constitution) drew the pamphlet version of the map. It was probably based on a large-scale version that thrilled a crowd of 3,000 at a New York City meeting "in defence [*sic*] of the Missouri Compromise" in January of 1854. Prepared by George Colton, it was meant to illustrate the profound impact repealing the compromise had on the Kansas-Nebraska Bill. See "Nebraska Territory!" *NYDT*, January 31, 1854, 1; "The Missouri Compromise Meeting," *NYDT*, January 31, 1854, 5; Susan Schulten, *Mapping the Nation: History and Cartography in Nineteenth-Century America* (Chicago: University of Chicago Press, 2012), 128–130.

3. "A Few Figures," *NYDT*, December 22, 1855, 4; James Parton, *The Life of Horace Greeley, Editor of the New-York Tribune* (New York: Mason Bros., 1854), 54, 119–120, 412. On the *Tribune*'s circulation figures in the 1850s generally, see Jeter Allen Isely, *Horace Greeley and the Republican Party, 1853–1861* (Princeton, NJ: Princeton University Press,

1947), 337–338; "Progress—Vol. XX: Aggregate Circulation Subscriptions to the Tribune," *NYDT*, April 10, 1860, 4.

4. Michael F. Holt, "Making and Mobilizing the Republican Party, 1854–1860," in Robert F. Engs and Randall M. Miller, eds., *The Birth of the Grand Old Party: The Republicans' First Generation* (Philadelphia: University of Pennsylvania Press, 2002), 29–59; William Gienapp, *The Origins of the Republican Party, 1852–1856* (New York: Oxford University Press, 1987); Heather Cox Richardson, *To Make Men Free: A History of the Republican Party* (New York: Basic Books, 2014), 1–24.

5. Historians disagree over the extent to which sectional issues surrounding slavery drove the creation of the Republican Party. Some argue that party realignment had less to do with sectional issues than is typically imagined. These "revisionist" scholars (notably William Gienapp and Michael F. Holt) emphasize ethnocultural issues (e.g., religion, temperance, and immigration), in addition to the actions of political leaders and the events they drove. Others (most notably Eric Foner) see the sectional clash over slavery as fundamental to the creation of the Republican Party. The story of Greeley, the *Tribune*, and, by implication, the press, that I tell in this chapter suggests a way to bridge these perspectives. Greeley's struggles to bring the Republican Party together around a Northern sectional identity, in opposition to the South, suggest that there was work involved in drawing sectional politics to the forefront. Though these categories and identities existed, it took effort to mobilize them politically. The press in general, and Greeley and the *Tribune* in particular, were important in the process, because party organizations were weak and less effectual during this period of transition. For the "revisionist" perspective, see Holt, "Making and Mobilizing"; Gienapp, *Origins*; Michael F. Holt, *The Political Crisis of the 1850s* (New York: W. W. Norton, 1978). Eric Foner provides a classic "fundamentalist" take on the Republican Party in his *Free Soil, Free Labor, Free Men: The Ideology of the Republican Party before the Civil War* (New York: Oxford University Press, 1969). I follow Edward L. Ayers, both in identifying the "revisionist" and "fundamentalist" camps and in his suggestions for understanding the links between the two perspectives. See Edward L. Ayers, "What Caused the Civil War?," in *What Caused the Civil War? Reflections on the South and Southern History* (New York: W. W. Norton, 2005), 131–144.

6. On Northern identity and the Republican Party, see Susan-Mary Grant, *North over South: Northern Nationalism and American Identity in the Antebellum Era* (Lawrence: University Press of Kansas, 2000), 130–152. Northern identity and its place in American nationalism have not received nearly as much treatment as Southern identity before and during the Civil War. See, e.g., Paul Quigley, *Shifting Ground: Nationalism and the American South, 1848–1865* (New York: Oxford University Press, 2014); Robert E. Bonner, *Mastering America: Southern Slaveholders and the Crisis of American Nationhood* (Cambridge: Cambridge University Press, 2009); Michael T. Bernath, *Confederate Minds: The Struggle for Intellectual Independence in the Civil War South* (Chapel Hill: University of North Carolina Press, 2010).

7. Eugen Weber, *Peasants into Frenchmen: The Modernization of Rural France, 1870–1919* (Palo Alto, CA: Stanford University Press, 1976), 67–94. On print and nationalism, see Benedict Anderson, *Imagined Communities: Reflections on the Origin and*

Spread of Nationalism (London: Verso, 1983). I follow Edward Ayers in suggesting these connections between the press, the making of sectional identities, and the coming of the Civil War. See Edward Ayers, "What Caused the Civil War?," 140–141. On links between the rise of a mass press in the United States and the problems of American nationalism, see Richard John, *Spreading the News: The American Postal System from Franklin to Morse* (Cambridge, MA: Harvard University Press, 1998); Lorman Ratner and Dwight L. Teeter Jr., *Fanatics and Fire-Eaters: Newspapers and the Coming of the Civil War* (Urbana: University of Illinois Press, 2003). Many of these suggestions have been casual and have not made a strong dent in the broader narrative of the coming of the war.

8. Horace Greeley to Schuyler Colfax, January 13, 1853, Horace Greeley Papers, NYPL.

9. "Politics for 1853," *NYDT*, November 30, 1852, 4; "The Future of Politics," *NYDT*, April 20, 1853, 4.

10. Glyndon G. Van Deusen, *Horace Greeley: Nineteenth Century Crusader* (Philadelphia: University of Pennsylvania Press, 1953), 173–175; Horace Greeley to William Henry Seward, January 27 and April 15, 1853, both in William Henry Seward Papers, University of Rochester; [untitled], *Albany (NY) Evening Journal*, September 6, 1853, 2.

11. "A Neighborly Word," *NYDT*, April 14, 1852, 4; Horace Greeley to Thurlow Weed, August 16, 1854, Horace Greeley Collection, NYHS; Horace Greeley to Schuyler Colfax, April 21, 1853, Greeley Papers, NYPL. In his letter to Colfax, Greeley described Raymond's *Times* as being "conducted with the most folly and the least principle of any paper ever started. It is ever trimming for the popular side of any question that turns up, and has made lots of friends by ultra abuse of Abolitionists, Women's Rights, and Spirit Rappers &c., which I cannot." Also see Beman Brockway, *Fifty Years in Journalism* (Watertown, NY, 1891), 152.

12. David M. Potter, *The Impending Crisis, 1846–1848* (New York: Harper & Row, 1976), 160–177.

13. Alvan Bovay to Horace Greeley, February 26, 1854, in Frank A. Flower, *History of the Republican Party, Embracing Its Origin, Growth, and Mission* (Springfield, IL: Union Publishing, 1884), 160–163; Eli Thayer to Horace Greeley, February 2, 1854, Greeley Papers, NYPL. In its full context, Bovay's letter suggests the importance of the *Tribune* in recasting sectional identities: "Your paper is now a power in the land. Advocate calling together [in] every church and school-house in the free States all the opponents of the Kansas-Nebraska Bill, no matter what their party affiliation. Urge them to forget their previous political names and organizations, and to band together under the name I suggested to you at Lovejoy's Hotel in 1852. I mean the name Republican. It is the only one that will serve all purposes, present and future, the only one that will live and last. The people of the South stand shoulder to shoulder; the North must align itself or be engulfed by Slavery."

14. "The Neb-Rascal Bill in Massachusetts," *NYDT*, February 16, 1854, 5; "Traitors and Doughfaces," *NYDT*, February 6, 1854, 4.

15. *The Republican Scrapbook, Containing the Platforms etc.* (Boston: John P. Jewett, 1856), 66.

16. C[harles] K. W[hipple], "Horace Greeley's Lecture on Slavery," *Liberator*, March 17, 1854, 44; "Lecture by Hon. Horace Greeley," *Boston Evening Transcript*, March 10, 1854, 2; "Lecture on the Slavery Question," *Boston Herald*, March 10, 1854, 4.

17. Horace Greeley to Schuyler Colfax, March 12, 1854, Greeley Papers, NYPL; Horace Greeley to Alvan Bovay, March 7, 1854, in Flower, *History of the Republican Party*, 163; "Is It a Fraud?" *NYDT*, February 15, 1854, 4.

18. "Newspaper Fabrications," *New-York Herald*, March 7, 1854, 4.

19. Horace Greeley to Alvan Bovay, March 7, 1854, in Flower, *History of the Republican Party*, 163; [untitled,] *NYDT*, March 2, 1854, 4; "THE VOICE OF THE NORTH—NO SLAVERY EXTENSION," *NYDT*, February 18, 1854, 7; [untitled,] *NYDT*, March 15, 1854, 4.

20. James S. Pike to William Pitt Fessenden, February 10, 1854, James Shepherd Pike Papers, LOC.

21. E. B. Washburne to James Pike, May 24, 1854, I. Washburn Jr. to James Pike, May 13, 1854, and L. D. Campbell to James Pike, May 14, 1854, all in James S. Pike, *First Blows of the Civil War: The Ten Years of Preliminary Conflict in the United States, from 1850 to 1860* (New York: American News, 1879), 233, 226, 229–230.

22. "The Shame and Disgrace of America," *NYDT*, March 7, 1854, 4.

23. "A Peep into the Future," *NYDT*, March 10, 1854, 4; "A Word to Working Men," *NYDT*, March 23, 1854, 4.

24. "Slavery and the Union," *NYDT*, April 12, 1854, 4; A Citizen of Virginia [Muscoe R. H. Garnett], *The Union, Past and Future: How It Works, and How to Save It* (Charleston, SC, 1850).

25. "Slavery and the Union," *NYDT*, April 12, 1854, 4; "Relative Power of the North and South," *NYDT*, April 14, 1854, 4; "The South," *NYDT*, April 15, 1854, 4; "The Commerce of North and South," *NYDT*, April 18, 1854, 4; "The Cost of the Union," *NYDT*, April 19, 1854, 4; "The Great Struggle," *NYDT*, April 21, 1854, 4; "North and South," *NYDT*, April 25, 1854, 4; "How the Case Stands," *NYDT*, April 29, 1854, 4; "The Navy and the Country," *NYDT*, April 1, 1854, 4. Also see Henry Charles Carey, *The North and the South* (New York: Greeley & McElrath, 1854).

26. [Untitled], *NYDT*, March 15, 1854, 4; "Mechanics Bought and Sold," *NYDT*, February 14, 1854, 4.

27. "Party Names and Public Duty," *NYDT*, June 16, 1854, 4. On Greeley and the name "Republican," see Robert C. Williams, *Horace Greeley: Champion of American Freedom* (New York: New York University Press, 2006), 175–176.

28. For comments on an anti-slavery meeting broken up by a mob of drunken taverngoers, led by a "notorious rumseller" of the neighborhood, see, e.g., "Anti-Slavery in Maryland," *New-York Weekly Tribune*, October 9, 1847, 2. On Greeley's ambitions for political office, see Glyndon G. Van Deusen's very pro-Seward account of Greeley's life having cast a long shadow, in *Horace Greeley*, 178–192. Also see "Prohibitory Law," *NYDT*, October 8, 1853, 4; "Will It Hurt the Party?," July 18, 1854, 4. To the extent that personal ambition did enter into Greeley's vision of fusion, he certainly would have welcomed a nomination, not just to win, but also perhaps to extend his own influence and that of the *Tribune*. When he urged Schuyler Colfax to run for office (US Congress) in Indiana, he wrote, "I don't think it much object to be elected, but running at such a

time will enable you to extend your acquaintance, your influence, and your circulation. I decidedly would do it if I were asked to do so." See Horace Greeley to Schuyler Colfax, July 7, 1854, Greeley Papers, NYPL.

29. "The Saratoga Convention," *NYDT*, July 24, 1854, 4; "The Saratoga Convention," *NYDT*, August 15, 1854, 4.

30. Greeley had successfully predicted precisely this outcome when he called for fusion in the first place: "Those who fear their party standing, so laboriously achieved, will suffer by any disruption . . . [and] will of course labor to keep things as nearly as may be in the old ruts, and make the Saratoga movement as aimless and insignificant as possible." See "Will It Hurt the Party?" *NYDT*, July 18, 1854, 4. On the failures of "fusion" in New York in the summer of 1854, see Michael F. Holt, *The Rise and Fall of the American Whig Party* (New York: Oxford University Press, 2003), 893–898; Gienapp, *Origins*, 149–160.

31. Horace Greeley to Schuyler Colfax, November 6, 1854, Greeley Papers, NYPL.

32. "After the Battle," *NYDT*, November 9, 1854, 4; Horace Greeley to Schuyler Colfax, November 6, 1854, Greeley Papers, NYPL; "Fusion—Our State," *NYDT*, October 3, 1854, 4; "Fusion and the Future," *NYDT*, October 16, 1854, 4; "The 'Know-Nothing' Conspiracy," *NYDT*, October 23, 1854, 4; Horace Greeley to William Henry Seward, October 25, 1854, Seward Papers, University of Rochester.

33. "After the Battle," *NYDT*, November 9, 1854, 4; "The Lesson of the Day," *NYDT*, November 11, 1854, 4.

34. Horace Greeley to William Henry Seward, November 11, 1854, in Greeley, *Recollections of a Busy Life* (New York: J. B. Ford, 1868), 315–320; William Henry Seward to Thurlow Weed, November 21, 1854, Thurlow Weed Papers, University of Rochester; Horace Greeley to George E. Baker, February 8, 1855, in Thurlow Weed Barnes, *Memoir of Thurlow Weed* (Boston: Houghton, Mifflin, 1884), vol. 2, 232.

35. "The Rising Cloud," *NYDT*, April 12, 1855, 4; "Tribulations of the Wicked," *NYDT*, June 2, 1855, 4; [Samuel Bowles], "The K.N. National Convention: Eighth Day—Wednesday," *NYDT*, June 14, 1855, 4; "The Bolters' Address," *NYDT*, June 15, 1855, 4; Gienapp, *Origins*, 182–187; Tyler Anbinder, *Nativism and Slavery: The Northern Know-Nothings & the Politics of the 1850s* (New York: Oxford University Press, 1992), 165–174.

36. "The Prospect," *NYDT*, November 3, 1855, 5; "The Moral," *NYDT*, November 8, 1855, 4; Horace Greeley to Schuyler Colfax, November 13, 1855, Greeley Papers, NYPL; Artemas Carter to Charles Sumner, November 16, 1855, quoted in Gienapp, *Origins*, 235. On the nativist victories of 1855 more generally, see Gienapp, *Origins*, 223–237. Following the fall elections, Greeley suggested that Republicans take a friendlier approach to nativists, in hopes of luring them into party ranks. See, e.g., "The Republican Movement," *NYDT*, November 21, 1855, 4.

37. "The Abolition Fusionists at the Tabernacle—a Poor Concern," *New-York Herald*, September 20, 1855, 4; "Young Africa on a Spree," *New-York Herald*, August 2, 1855, 4; "Whig and Abolition State Convention—Amalgamation into an Abolition League," *New-York Herald*, September 30, 1855, 2.

38. "UNPALATABLE COUNSEL," *NYDT*, September 22, 1855, 4; "The Idleness and Improvidence of the Free Blacks," *NYDT*, September 26, 1855, 5. For a response, see "The New-York Tribune and Its 'Unpalatable Counsel': Our Political Rights and

Duties," *Frederick Douglass' Paper*, September 28, 1855, 2; [untitled], *NYDT*, September 29, 1855, 5.

39. David M. Potter, *The Impending Crisis, 1848–1861* (New York: Harper, 1976), 217. For an exhaustive study of Kansas newspaper coverage, see Craig Miner, *Seeding Civil War: Kansas in the National News, 1854–1858* (Lawrence: University Press of Kansas, 2008). I differ from Miner in suggesting a more central role for Greeley and the *Tribune* and in drawing closer connections between the political expediencies of the Republican Party and the content of the coverage.

40. Nicole Etcheson tells the larger story of territorial conflict in Kansas as, fundamentally, a struggle for white liberty in an age of conflict over slavery. See Nicole Etcheson, *Bleeding Kansas: Contested Liberty in the Civil War Era* (Lawrence: University Press of Kansas, 2004), 5–8. This fits with a larger sense in which, for many, antislavery politics revolved less around the immorality and horrors of slavery than its implications for white men. As Larry Gara put it, "Some abolitionists were indignant at the slave system and what it did to black men, many more northerners became anti-Southern and antislavery because of what the slave system did or threatened to do to them." See Larry Gara, "Slavery and the Slave Power: A Crucial Distinction," *Civil War History* 15:1 (March 1969), 5–18.

41. William Henry Seward perhaps best captured this sentiment when, just before the passage of the Kansas-Nebraska Bill in May of 1854, he announced in the US Senate, "Come on then, Gentlemen of the Slave States, since there is no escaping your challenge, I accept it in behalf of the cause for freedom. We will engage in competition for the virgin soil of Kansas, and God give the victory to the side which is stronger in numbers as it is in right." Quoted in Horace Greeley, *A History of the Struggle for Slavery Extension or Restriction in the United States* (New York: Tribune Office, 1856), 79.

42. Eli Thayer to Horace Greeley, February 2, 1854, and Horace Greeley to James Hall, February 24, 1854, both in Greeley Papers, NYPL. On Greeley and Thayer's collaborations, see Eli Thayer, *A History of the Kansas Crusade: Its Friends and Its Foes* (New York: Harper & Bros., 1889), 36–52; "The New Territories," *NYDT*, June 30, 1854, 4; [untitled], *NYDT* May 30, 1854, 4; "The Kansas Emigrants," *NYDT*, July 31, 1854, 4. Also see, e.g., "A Plan for Freedom: Report," *NYDT*, May 29, 1854, 4; "The New Territories: Nebraska," *NYDT*, June 20, 1854, 6; "Kansas: Its Forts, Settlements, and Missions," *NYDT*, June 22, 1854, 6.

43. J[ames] S. P[ike], "Kansas and Slavery," *NYDT*, February 13, 1855, 5; O. B. Matteson, "The Advantages of Kansas," *NYDT*, June 30, 1854, 6.

44. Etcheson, *Bleeding Kansas*, esp. 34–42; Gunja SenGupta, *For God and Mammon: Evangelicals and Entrepreneurs, Masters and Slaves in Territorial Kansas, 1854–1860* (Athens: University of Georgia Press, 1996).

45. W. H. Isely, "The Sharps Rifle Episode in Kansas History," *American Historical Review* 12:3 (April 1, 1907), 546–558; Jonathan Earle, "Beecher's Bibles and Broadswords: Paving the Way for the Civil War in the West, 1854–1859," in Virginia Scharff, ed., *Empire and Liberty: The Civil War and the West* (Berkeley: University of California Press, 2015), 50–65.

46. Allan Nevins, *Ordeal of the Union: A House Dividing* (New York: Scribner, 1947), vol. 2, 410; *(Lawrence, KS) Herald of Freedom*, December 15, 1855, quoted in SenGupta,

For God and Mammon, 106. On the "Wakarusa War" generally, see Etcheson, *Bleeding Kansas*, 82–88; SenGupta, *For God and Mammon*, 101–109; Nevins, *Ordeal of the Union*, vol. 2, 408–411.

47. Horace Greeley to Charles Dana, December 1, 1855, in Joel Benton, ed., *Greeley on Lincoln* (New York: Baker & Taylor, 1893), 88.

48. Gienapp, *Origins*, 244.

49. It was a measure of Greeley's power that several of those exposed by his dispatches (which one hapless victim complained "went abroad on the wings of lightning") took to the House floor to vindicate their reputations. George Dunn of Indiana, whom Greeley said "made Judas exemplary, [and] Benedict Arnold a Patriot," assured his colleagues and constituents he would "not turn his back upon his country or her cause, upon true manliness or his own honor, though the devil or Horace Greeley himself . . . should bid him do it. [Laughter and applause]." Lewis Campbell of Ohio, who only a year earlier had conspired with the *Tribune*'s James Pike to rally pro-Northern sentiment, felt it necessary to state on the record that he was "regarded as an extreme northern man" and not the "doughface" Greeley claimed he was. See *Congressional Globe*, 34th Congress, 1st Session, 31–32, 174–175, 230 (1856); H[orace] G[reeley], "From Washington: How Dunn Is Done," *NYDT*, December 19, 1855, 4.

50. "Matters in Washington," *(Worcester) Massachusetts Spy*, December 19, 1855, 2; [untitled], *Weekly St. Louis Pilot*, December 15, 1855, 3; "Horace Greeley a White Man," *(Milwaukee) Wisconsin Free Democrat*, December 26, 1855, 3.

51. H[orace] G[reeley], "From Washington," *NYDT*, January 28, 1856, 4.

52. "How Mr. Rust of Arkansas Served Philosopher Greeley," *(Savannah) Daily Morning News*, February 4, 1856, 1; "The Recontre between Messrs. Greeley and Rust," *(Savannah) Daily Morning News*, February 4, 1856, 2; "Personalities and Their Consequences," *Baltimore Sun*, February 5, 1856, 2; "Congress," *Fayetteville (NC) Observer*, February 11, 1856, 3.

53. "Border Ruffianism at Washington," *NYDT*, January 31, 1856, 4; "Why the South Fears War," *NYDT*, January 31, 1856, 4; "The New Power," *NYDT*, January 31, 1856, 4. According to the *Tribune*, "We have no doubt that our [Southern] kinsmen are fond of sanguinary delights, but they prefer to take them in the form of assaults on peaceable, unarmed men, chasing timid, weaponless blacks, and slaughtering their antagonists generally with the least possible danger to their own persons" ("Why the South Fears War").

54. *York (PA) Democratic Press*, June 24, 1856, quoted in Elizabeth Varon, *Disunion! The Coming of the American Civil War, 1789–1859* (Chapel Hill: University of North Carolina Press, 2008), 275.

55. H[orace] G[reeley], "Republican National Convention," *NYDT*, February 25, 1856, 4; George Julian, "The First Republican National Convention," *American Historical Review* 4:2 (January 1899), 313–319.

56. Horace Greeley to Charles A. Dana, February 6, 1856, and Horace Greeley to Charles A. Dana, April 2 and April 11, 1856, all in Horace Greeley Papers, LOC. Also reprinted in Benton, *Greeley on Lincoln*, 111–117, 138–142.

57. Horace Greeley to Schuyler Colfax, May 16, 1856, Greeley Papers, NYPL.

58. Varon, *Disunion!*, 283–285; Amy S. Greenberg, *Manifest Manhood and the Antebellum American Empire* (Cambridge: Cambridge University Press, 2005), 135–169.

59. Horace Greeley to Schuyler Colfax, May 21, 1856, Greeley Papers, NYPL.

60. [William F. Bartlett], *Life of John Charles Frémont* (New York: Greeley & McElrath, 1856), 29, 30; Horace Greeley to Schuyler Colfax, June 20, 1856, Greeley Papers, NYPL. Upon seeing Greeley after the Republican convention in June, William Henry Seward described the *Tribune* editor as "exultant that he has done the very best thing in the rightest way." See Frederick W. Seward, *Seward at Washington: Senator and Secretary of State* (New York: Derby & Miller, 1891), 279.

61. Greeley, *History of the Struggle*, 1–3.

62. *Congressional Globe*, 34th Congress, 1st session, 496 (1856); [Horace Greeley], "The Latest News," *NYDT*, February 29, 1856, 4; [Horace Greeley], "Kansas in the Senate—Hale—Toombs," *NYDT*, March 3, 1856, 4.

63. Horace Greeley to Charles A. Dana, January 30, 1856, Greeley Papers, LOC, reprinted in Benton, *Greeley on Lincoln*, 106–108.

64. Nevins, *Ordeal of the Union*, vol. 2, 413–431. On the continued, if strained, cross-regional relationships between national politicians, see Rachel Shelden, *Washington Brotherhood: Politics, Social Life, and the Coming of the Civil War* (Chapel Hill: University of North Carolina Press, 2013).

65. J[ames] S. P[ike], "From Washington: The Incoherence of the Slavery Extension Party," *NYDT*, May 12, 1856, 4.

66. Nevins, *Ordeal of the Union*, vol. 2, 434–450; [untitled], *NYDT*, May 26, 1856, 4.

67. [Untitled], *NYDT*, May 24, 1856, 6.

68. The *Tribune*'s report on John Brown's Pottawatomie killings went down as a daring rescue against a group of pro-slavery men who were about lynch a Free Settler. See "Later from Kansas," *NYDT*, June 3, 1856, 3: "The last serious difficulty occurred on the Pottowatomie [*sic*] Creek. A gang of Border Ruffians attempted to drive a Free-State man from his claim. He resisted when they seized him and were about to hang him. But some of his neighbors came to his rescue, and in the fight that occurred some of the Border Ruffians were shot." On the sectional contrast in modes and practices of violence, see "Killing in Kansas," *NYDT*, May 5, 1856, 4: "Such is the contrasted course of the two adverse parties in Kansas with respect to the shedders of blood among them."

69. Various articles, *NYDT*, June to October 1856.

70. "Departure of the Connecticut Colony for Kansas," *NYDT*, April 4, 1856, 5.

71. "The Tribune Fund for Kansas," *NYDT*, July 19, 1856, 5; "Kansas Fund," *NYDT*, September 9, 1856, 2; "The Tribune Kansas Fund," *NYDT*, October 1, 1856, 5.

72. Thomas Shankland, "To The Free North," *NYDT*, June 13, 1856, 5; [untitled], *NYDT*, September 26, 1856, 4.

73. "Free Homes," *NYDT*, February 18, 1854, 4; "The Cost of Living," *NYDT*, February 21, 1854, 4; "Going West," *NYDT*, February 23, 1854, 4.

74. [Bartlett], *Life of John Charles Frémont*; [untitled], *NYDT*, May 29, 1856, 4.

75. See, e.g., [untitled], *NYDT*, May 24, 1856, 4; "The Carolinians in Kansas," *NYDT*, October 1, 1856, 6.

76. [Untitled], *Charleston (SC) Courier*, September 27, 1856, 1.

77. Lydia Maria Child, *Autumnal Leaves: Tales and Sketches in Prose and Rhyme* (New York: C. S. Francis, 1857), 302–364. The novella ran in the *Tribune* between October 23 and November 4, 1856. On the novella and the broader gendered meanings of Kansas conflict, see Kristen Tegtmeier Oertel, *Bleeding Borders: Race, Gender, and Violence in Pre–Civil War Kansas* (Baton Rouge: Louisiana State University Press, 2013), 94–97. Also see Brie Anna Swenson Arnold, "Competition for the Virgin Soil of Kansas," PhD dissertation, University of Minnesota, 2008.

78. [Untitled], *NYDT*, November 5, 1856, 4; [untitled], *NYDT*, November 10, 1856, 4; Geo. Weston, "Who Are and Who May Be Slaves in the United States: Facts for the People," *NYDT*, November 5, 1856, 2–3; [untitled], *NYDT*, June 4, 1856, 4.

79. [Untitled], *NYDT*, November 7, 1856, 4; [untitled], *NYDT*, November 10, 1854, 4.

80. "Greeley-Phobia," *(Worcester) Massachusetts Spy*, December 5, 1855, 1.

81. *Norfolk Daily News*, December 15, 1855, quoted in "Fools Legislative and Editorial," *NYDT*, December 18, 1855, 4; *Petersburg (VA) Intelligencer*, quoted in "The Voice of the Ancient Dominion," *NYDT*, May 27, 1856, 5; [untitled], *NYDT*, April 3, 1860, 4.

82. "The Interesting Event," *Young America*, February 9, 1856, 87; "From Albany Atlas and Argus: Important from Kansas! Intercepted Correspondence!!" *Daily (Columbus) Ohio Statesman*, May 25, 1856, 1.

83. Jeremiah Black to J. Reynolds, June 9, 1856, quoted in Isely, *Horace Greeley*, 160; [Jeremiah Black, John W. Forney, and W. B. Reed], *Short Answers to Reckless Fabrications, against the Democratic Candidate for President, James Buchanan* (Philadelphia: William Rice, 1856), 3; Nevins, *Ordeal of the Union*, vol. 2, 496.

84. "A Bad Man," *(Washington, DC) Confederation*, February 20, 1861, reprinted in Howard Cecil Perkins, ed., *Northern Editorials on Secession* (Gloucester, MA: Peter Smith, 1964), vol. 2, 1003.

85. James Ford Rhodes, "Newspapers as Historical Sources," *Atlantic Monthly*, May 1909, 654.

Chapter 4 • Horace Greeley's American Conflict

1. The entire work was published as Horace Greeley, *The American Conflict: A History of the Great Rebellion in the United States of America, 1860–'64; Its Causes, Incidents, and Results; Intended to Exhibit Especially Its Moral and Political Phases, with the Drift and Progress of American Opinion Respecting Human Slavery from 1776 to the Close of the War for the Union*, 2 vols. (Hartford: O. D. Case, 1864–1866). On that era's market for early Civil War histories, see Alice Fahs, *The Imagined Civil War: Popular Literature of the North & South, 1861–1865* (Chapel Hill: University of North Carolina Press, 2001), 287–301.

2. Horace Greeley, *Recollections of a Busy Life* (New York: J. B. Ford, 1868), 417–424; "Later News from New York Riot," *Cleveland Plain Dealer*, July 16, 1863, 3; "The New-York Riot: Continued Depredations," *Portland (ME) Daily Advertiser*, July 17, 1863, 2; "Important from the North," *Richmond Examiner*, July 18, 1863, 2.

3. Robert C. Williams, *Horace Greeley: Champion of American Freedom* (New York: New York University Press, 2006), 245–246.

4. William Vermilion to Mary Vermilion, November 7, 1862, Mary Vermilion to William Vermilion, December 9, 1862, Mary Vermilion to William Vermilion, October

27, 1863, and William Vermilion to Mary Vermilion, November 8, 1864, all in Donald C. Elder, ed., *Love amid the Turmoil: The Civil War Letters of William and Mary Vermilion* (Iowa City: University of Iowa Press, 2003), 14, 25, 254, 295. Private Wilbur Fisk from Vermont considered going AWOL to see a Greeley lecture in Washington, DC, early in 1862, after his commanding officer "not appreciating my literary taste refused to grant me a pass. . . . I certainly should have lost a month's pay, such was my infatuation." See Wilbur Fisk to the *Green Mountain (VT) Freeman*, February 12, 1862, in Emil Rosenblatt and Ruth Rosenblatt, eds., *Hard Marching Every Day: The Civil War Letters of Private Wilbur Fisk* (Lawrence: University Press of Kansas, 1983), 6. Also see "New Publications," *Arthur's Home Magazine*, December 1864, 294–295; "The American Conflict," *Liberator*, March 18, 1864, 46; "Books, Catalogues, &c. Received," *Prairie Farmer*, February 13, 1864, 104; "The American Conflict," *Independent*, January 7, 1864, 3.

5. On Greeley's finances, see Williams, *Horace Greeley*, 269–271, 310–311.

6. Greeley, *American Conflict*, vol. 1, 10 and vol. 2, 8; Horace Greeley, "The Sunlight of Victory," *Independent*, July 9, 1863, 1; Horace Greeley, "The Alternative of War," *Independent*, August 18, 1864, 1.

7. Oliver Wendell Holmes, "Bread and the Newspaper," *Atlantic Monthly*, September 1861, 347.

8. Horace Greeley to O. D. Case, May 1, May 3, and November 20, 1864, all in Horace Greeley Papers, NYPL. Ever conscious of his own symbolic importance, Greeley spurned Case's suggestion to reprint advertising circulars for the second volume of *The American Conflict*, telling him, "I wish the public to believe the truth that I <u>expect</u> an early result."

9. "'H. G.' and the President," *(Worcester) Massachusetts Spy*, August 10, 1864, 2; Adam Gurowski, *Diary: 1863–'64–'65* (Washington, DC: W. H. & O. H. Morrison, 1866), 243–246.

10. Francis Lieber, *No Party Now, but All for Our Country* (New York: C. S. Wescott, 1863), 3.

11. Holmes, "Bread and the Newspaper," 346; Menahem Blondheim, "'Public Sentiment Is Everything': The Union's Public Communications Strategy and the Bogus Proclamation of 1864," *Journal of American History* 89:3 (December 2002), 869–899; Louis M. Starr, *Bohemian Brigade: Civil War Newsmen in Action* (New York: Knopf, 1954); Frank Luther Mott, *American Journalism: A History of Newspapers in the United States through 250 Years, 1690 to 1940* (New York: Macmillan, 1941), 324–359; Richard Kluger, *The Paper: The Life and Death of the New-York Herald Tribune* (New York: Vintage Books, 1989), 97–131.

12. Greeley, *Recollections*, 424; Samuel Wilkeson to Horace Greeley, January 4, 1865, Greeley Papers, NYPL.

13. "NEW-YORK WIDE AWAKE; THE FLOWER OF OUR YOUTH FOR FREEDOM," *NYDT*, October 4, 1860, 5–6; "Grand Wide-Awake Demonstration in New-York," *Boston Daily Advertiser*, October 5, 1860, 2.

14. "Going to Go," *NYDT*, November 9, 1860, 4; Thomas N. Bonner, "Horace Greeley and the Secession Movement, 1860–1861," *Mississippi Valley Historical Review* 38:3 (December 1951), 425–444; Greeley, *Recollections*, 396–399.

15. George Weston, "The Poor Whites of the South," *NYDT*, February 5, 1856, 5;

George Weston, "Who Are and Who May Be Slaves in the United States," *NYDT*, November 5, 1856, 2.

16. Hinton Rowan Helper, *The Impending Crisis of the South* (New York: Burdick Bros., 1857). Greeley promoted the less dense version of this book, *Compendium of the Impending Crisis of the South* (New York: Burdick Bros., 1860). Also see George M. Fredrickson, "The Anti-Slavery Racist: Hinton Rowan Helper," in *The Arrogance of Race: Historical Perspectives on Slavery, Racism, and Social Inequality* (Middleton, CT: Wesleyan University Press, 1988), 28–53.

17. [Untitled], *NYDT*, December 4, 1858, 4–5; "A Homely Talk," *NYDT*, November 19, 1859, 4. On Greeley's promotion of *The Impending Crisis*, which coincided closely with John Brown's raid, see "The Helper Bugaboo," *NYDT*, December 7, 1859, 4. Greeley parried charges that promotion of Helper's book would spark further insurrections, stating that the book was "an appeal to Free Whites—to Legal Voters—urging them to use their rightful power to free themselves from the blight of Slavery." Also see "Helping Helper," *NYDT*, December 26, 1859, 4; "Helper's Crisis," *NYDT*, December 27, 1859, 4.

18. V., "Letter from a 'Poor White' of the South," *NYDT*, August 22, 1860, 7; J. R. S., "Prospects in Tennessee," *NYDT*, July 19, 1860, 5; "From Texas," *NYDT*, August 11, 1860, 3. Also see Danell, "Politics in Kentucky," *NYDT*, October 26, 1860, 6; Horace Greeley, "A Truthful Letter: To the Hon. Washington Hunt," *NYDT*, July 23, 1860, 4.

19. [Untitled], *NYDT*, July 10, 1860, 4; "Tragedy Subsiding into Farce," *NYDT*, July 11, 1860, 4; Horace Greeley, "The Menaces of Disunion," *Independent*, August 16, 1860, 1; Horace Greeley, "The Changes of Four Years," *Independent*, July 12, 1860, 1. No doubt aided by Hinton Rowan Helper's book and letters to the *Tribune*, Greeley's interpretations of white Southern political, economic, and social dynamics were fairly accurate. He erred mostly in predicting what outcomes those dynamics would produce. See Keri Leigh Merritt, *Masterless Men: Poor Whites and Slavery in the Antebellum South* (Cambridge: Cambridge University Press, 2017), 1–11, 251–322.

20. "The Republicans of the Slave States," *NYDT*, October 12, 1860, 4.

21. "How the Union Is to Be Dissolved," *NYDT*, November 2, 1860, 4; "Going to Go," *NYDT*, November 9, 1860, 4; Greeley, *American Conflict*, vol. 1, 357. Greeley would continue to debate and defend his ideas through the course of the war, e.g., H[orace] G[reeley], "Monsieur Tonson Again!" *NYDT*, February 2, 1863, 4.

22. "Prospects in South Carolina," *NYDT*, November 10, 1860, 5; "Waiting for the Republicans to Strengthen Them," *NYDT*, February 18, 1861, 6; "The Carnival of Treason," *NYDT*, December 24, 1860, 4; [untitled], *NYDT*, December 22, 1860, 4; Horace Greeley to Abraham Lincoln, December 22, 1860, and Horace Greeley to William Henry Herndon, December 26, 1860, both in Abraham Lincoln Papers, LOC. Political and professional calculations may well have influenced Greeley's opposition to compromise through the secession crisis. Greeley's ally-turned-rival William Henry Seward was deeply involved in compromise efforts, and to oppose compromise was to oppose Seward, Thurlow Weed, and their branch of the New York State Republican Party. Greeley's opposition to compromise. however, should not be seen solely in this light, as that opposition was perfectly consistent with his understanding of secession since the summer of 1860.

23. "The Attitude of the North," *NYDT*, January 7, 1861, 4. Also see Greeley's open

letters to John L. O'Sullivan: "Mr. O'Sullivan on the Crises," *NYDT*, January 14, 1861, 4; "To Mr. John L. O'Sullivan," *NYDT*, January 21, 1861, 4. Greeley wrote about his distaste for compromise and his dogged belief in Republican victory in his history of the war: "The North, in the full flush of a long awaited and fairly achieved triumph, did not see fit to repudiate the cherished and time-honored principle for which it had patiently, ardently struggled. No other successful party was ever before required, at such a moment, to surrender its principle, its consistency, its manhood, on peril of National disruption and overthrow" (*American Conflict*, vol. 1, 405–406).

24. "Are We Going to Fight!" *NYDT*, November 30, 1860, 4; Horace Greeley to W. H. Herndon, December 26, 1860, Lincoln Papers, LOC.

25. Horace Greeley, "Civil War in Our Country," *Independent*, April 18, 1861, 1.

26. [Untitled], *NYDT*, December 29, 1860, 6; "WHAT CONGRESS MIGHT AND SHOULD DO TO SAVE THE UNION," *NYDT*, January 11, 1861, 4; Horace Greeley, "The Old and the New," *Independent*, April 4, 1861; Horace Greeley, "Southern Unionism and Its Fruits," *Independent*, April 25, 1861, 1; "The War and Slavery," *NYDT*, May 14, 1861, 4.

27. Horace Greeley to Abraham Lincoln, December 22, 1860, Lincoln Papers, LOC; Horace Greeley, "Civil War in Our Country," *Independent*, April 18, 1861, 2; Horace Greeley, "Has the Nation a Right to Be?," *Independent*, May 16, 1861, 1; "Are We Going to Fight?" *NYDT*, November 30, 1860, 4; Horace Greeley, "Southern Unionism and Its Fruits," *Independent*, April 25, 1861, 1; Horace Greeley, "The Spirit of the South," *Independent*, May 9, 1861, 1; Horace Greeley, "Is the American Republic Lost?," *Independent*, May 23, 1861, 1; Horace Greeley, "The Old Dominion," *Independent*, May 30, 1861, 1; Horace Greeley, "A Nation Based on Theft," *Independent*, June 20, 1861, 1; Horace Greeley, "What Is There to Compromise?" *Independent*, June 27, 1861, 1.

28. Greeley, "Spirit of the South," *Independent*, May 9, 1861, 1; "The Result," *NYDT*, April 15, 1861, 4.

29. "Will the Government Stand by the People?" *NYDT*, April 22, 1861, 4; "No Half Measures," *NYDT*, May 1, 1861, 4.

30. Horace Greeley, "The Duty of Hating Evil," *Independent*, May 2, 1861, 1; Horace Greeley, "War and Its Lessons," *Independent*, July 18, 1861, 1. Greeley also believed that war presented opportunities to purge the nation of its baser elements and, in the process, achieve a more complete nationhood. Greeley joined a host of Northern intellectuals in welcoming the conflict as a moral winnowing for Yankees who had lost their souls in the pursuit of gain. See George Fredrickson, *The Inner Civil War: Northern Intellectuals and the Crisis of the Union* (New York: Harper, 1965), 65–78.

31. "To Richmond! To Richmond! Onward!" *NYDT*, May 30, 1861, 6. Charles Dana began running the "Forward to Richmond" banner in the *NYDT*, June 28, 1861, 4. Greeley told friends that he did not wish for the war to be "hurried," but instead hoped that it would be "quietly pressed on to a righteous conclusion." See Horace Greeley to Margaret Allen and Mrs. A. Daury, June 17, 1861, Horace Greeley Papers, LOC. Also see Starr, *Bohemian Brigade*, 30–37.

32. "Beaten for a Day—How to Conquer for All Times," *NYDT*, July 23, 1861, 4. On perceptions of Greeley's responsibility, see, e.g., "Greeley on the Administration," *Cincinnati Enquirer*, July 25, 1861, 2. Also see "Field-Marshal Greeley, the Mischief Maker," *Harper's Weekly*, August 3, 1861, 496; William F. Thompson, *The Image of War: The*

212 Notes to Pages 124–128

Pictorial Reporting of the American Civil War (Baton Rouge: Louisiana State University Press, 1959), 101–102.

33. Horace Greeley, "Just Once," *NYDT*, July 25, 1861, 4; "Massa Greeley in a Flood of Tears," *New-York Herald*, July 26, 1861, 4. Greeley was not the only journalist under fire in the wake of the Bull Run debacle. William Howard Russell of the London *Times* was also criticized sharply for his battle account that accused Union soldiers of shameful cowardice. *Tribune* editors may have fanned this line of attack to distract from the opprobrium of the "Forward to Richmond" episode. See Harold Holzer, *Lincoln and the Power of the Press: The War for Public Opinion* (New York: Simon & Schuster, 2014), 318–322.

34. Horace Greeley to Abraham Lincoln, July 29, 1861, Lincoln Papers, LOC; Holzer, *Lincoln and the Power*, 330–331.

35. Moncure Daniel Conway, *Autobiography: Memories and Experiences* (London: Cassell, 1904), vol. 1, 294.

36. Horace Greeley, "The Prayer of Twenty Millions," *NYDT*, August 20, 1862, 4.

37. "A Letter from the President," *(Washington, DC) Daily National Intelligencer*, August 24, 1862, 5. On Lincoln's letter, see Eric Foner, *The Fiery Trial: Abraham Lincoln and American Slavery* (New York: W. W. Norton, 2010), 227–231; James Oakes, *Freedom National: The Destruction of Slavery in the United States, 1861–1865* (New York: W. W. Norton, 2013), 309–313; Holzer, *Lincoln and the Power*, 399–405; "President Lincoln's Letter," *NYDT*, August 25, 1862, 4.

38. Horace Greeley to Gerrit Smith, August 14 and August 21, 1861, both in Gerrit Smith Papers, Syracuse University. Also see Horace Greeley to Beman Brockway, August 14, 1861, Greeley Papers, LOC.

39. "LET US END THIS WAR!" *NYDT*, December 16, 1861, 4. The presence of a pro-Union majority in the South was also a central claim of his. See Greeley, "Prayer of Twenty Millions," *NYDT*, August 20, 1862, 4.

40. Horace Greeley to Rebecca M. Whipple, April 1860, Greeley Papers, LOC.

41. "LET US END THIS WAR!" *NYDT*, December 16, 1861, 4; Horace Greeley, "Out from the House of Bondage," *Independent*, April 24, 1862, 1; Horace Greeley, "Southern Treason and Northern Sympathy," *Independent*, April 3, 1862, 1.

42. "The Vital Question," *NYDT*, November 1, 1861, 4; "Slaves and Slavery in the War for the Union," *NYDT*, December 6, 1861, 4; "The London Times on Union and Slavery," *NYDT*, October 17, 1861, 4; Horace Greeley, "The President's Emancipation Message," *Independent*, March 13, 1862, 1; Horace Greeley, "Southern Treason and Northern Sympathy," *Independent*, April 3, 1862, 1; Horace Greeley, "Out From the House of Bondage," *Independent*, April 24, 1862, 1; Horace Greeley, "Is Negro-Hate an Anglo-Saxon Instinct? Why Is It?" *Independent*, July 3, 1862, 1.

43. Holzer, *Lincoln and the Power*, 376–379; Williams, *Horace Greeley*, 224–225; Glyndon G. Van Deusen, *Horace Greeley: Nineteenth Century Crusader* (Philadelphia: University of Pennsylvania Press, 1953), 258–261; Abraham Lincoln to Robert J. Walker, November 21, 1861, in James R. Gilmore, *Personal Recollections of Abraham Lincoln and the Civil War* (London: 1899, 54).

44. "LET US END THIS WAR!" *NYDT*, December 16, 1861, 4.

45. Clipping of an anonymous opinion piece by John Hay, quoted in Holzer, *Lincoln and the Power*, 376–377.

46. William A. Croffut, "Lincoln's Washington: Recollections of a Journalist Who Knew Everybody," *Atlantic Monthly*, January 1930, 56–58; "Mr. Greeley's Lecture," *NYDT*, January 4, 1862, 5; "Greeley in Washington," *(Sandusky, OH) Daily Commercial Register*, January 9, 1862, 2. This is the lecture Private Wilbur Fisk considered going AWOL for, in order to attend it after his colonel denied his request. See note 4 above.

47. "General Hunter's Order," *NYDT*, May 19, 1862, 4; "General Hunter Overruled," *NYDT*, May 20, 1862, 4; "Wanted: A Policy," *NYDT*, December 23, 1861, 4; "'Support Arms and Advance!,'" *NYDT*, July 19, 1862, 4; "Confiscation!," *NYDT*, June 19, 1862, 4; Horace Greeley, "War and Its Delays," *Independent*, January 14, 1862, 1; Horace Greeley, "What and For What We Are to Pay," *Independent*, January 23, 1862, 1; Horace Greeley, "Slavery and Freedom in the Union That Is To Be," *Independent*, February 27, 1862, 1; Abraham Lincoln to Horace Greeley, March 24, 1862, and Horace Greeley to Abraham Lincoln, March 24, 1862, both in Roy P. Basler, ed., *Collected Works of Abraham Lincoln* (New Brunswick, NJ: Rutgers University Press, 1953), 5, 169.

48. "Opening the Presidential Canvass for 1864," *NYDT*, February 23, 1864, 4; Horace Greeley, "The Presidency in Prospect," *Independent*, February 25, 1864, 1. Tension between Greeley and Abraham Lincoln reached back to the 1858 senate campaign and was magnified by Greeley's treatment of the president-elect in 1860–1861. See Van Deusen, *Horace Greeley*, 258–260; "President Lincoln's Letter," *NYDT*, August 25, 1862, 4.

49. "The Message of Freedom," *NYDT*, March 8, 1862, 4; Horace Greeley, "The President's Emancipation Message," *Independent*, March 13, 1862, 1.

50. Horace Greeley, "The National Promise of 1863," *Independent*, January 1, 1863, 1; Horace Greeley, "The President's Plan of Colonization," *Independent*, August 21, 1862, 1. This represented a reversal from his earlier embrace of colonization. See "The Slavery Question," *NYDT*, September 21, 1861, 4.

51. Horace Greeley, "National Unity," *Continental Monthly*, September 1862, 357–360; Horace Greeley, "Southern Hate of the North," *Continental Monthly*, October 1862, 448–451; Horace Greeley, "Aurora," *Continental Monthly*, November 1862, 622–625.

52. Horace Greeley, "Southern Hate of the North," *Continental Monthly*, October 1862, 448–451. On Greeley's faith in the power of Free Labor to remake the South, see "Slanderous Piety," *NYDT*, November 25, 1862: "General Emancipation will immensely increase and speedily benefit the South . . . after ten years' experience of Free Labor, it will never return to slavery."

53. Abraham Lincoln, "Annual Message to Congress, December 1, 1862," in Don E. Fehrenbacher, ed., *Lincoln: Speeches and Writings, 1859–1865* (New York: Library of America, 1989), 415.

54. Horace Greeley, "The Collapse at Hand," *Independent*, December 4, 1862, 1; Horace Greeley to Abraham Lincoln, December 12, 1862, Lincoln Papers, LOC.

55. "Rejoicings over the Proclamation," *Independent*, January 8, 1863, 1; Horace Greeley, "The National Promise of 1863," *Independent*, January 1, 1863, 1.

56. "Rejoicings over the Proclamation," *Independent*, January 8, 1863, 1; "Peace at

the South," *NYDT*, January 3, 1863, 4; James W. White to Horace Greeley, February 13, 1863, Greeley Papers, NYPL.

57. Greeley, "Dark and Bright Hours," *Independent*, May 14, 1863; 1; "Letter of the Hon. Horace Greeley," *North American Review*, April 1867, 674; Gideon Welles and Edgar Thaddeus Welles, eds., *Diary of Gideon Welles* (Boston: Houghton, Mifflin, 1911), vol. 2, 112.

58. Horace Greeley to Sydney Howard Gay, August 22, 1861, Sydney Howard Gay Papers, Columbia University: "I have no faith in wholesale bloodshed to no definite end. It is our duty to fight so long as we may with a rational hope of success—no longer." Quoted in Starr, *Bohemian Brigade*, 289.

59. Horace Greeley to Salmon Chase, January 31, 1863, Salmon Chase Papers, Historical Society of Pennsylvania, Philadelphia; "A Copperhead Peace," *NYDT*, March 10, 1863, 4; "Prospects of Peace," *NYDT*, March 11, 1863, 4; Horace Greeley, "A CARD," *NYDT*, March 11, 1863, 4; "The Conditions of Peace," *NYDT*, March 26, 1863, 4. To some degree, Greeley's peace efforts in 1863 were exaggerated by his enemies within the New York State Republican Party. The extent to which Greeley embraced peace (and collaborated with Clement Vallandigham) became a source of an extended fight with Thurlow Weed and, to a lesser extent, Henry Raymond in the first half of 1863 and again during the 1872 presidential election. On Greeley, peace, and politics, see Van Deusen, *Horace Greeley*, 297–298.

60. Horace Greeley to Abraham Lincoln, December 12, 1862, Lincoln Papers, LOC.

61. Warren F. Spencer, "The Jewett-Greeley Affair: A Private Scheme for French Mediation in the American Civil War," *New York History* 51 (1970), 238–268.

62. Walter Stahr, *Seward: Lincoln's Indispensable Man* (New York: Simon & Schuster, 2012), 363–364.

63. Greeley seemed to reverse all of this in August 1863. See Greeley, "European Intervention in America," *Independent*, August 6, 1863, 1.

64. Horace Greeley, "The Conduct of the War," *Independent*, April 9, 1863, 1; Horace Greeley to Edwin D. Morgan, June 14, 1864, Edwin D. Morgan Papers, NYSL.

65. Horace Greeley, "A Great War in Winter," *Independent*, January 15, 1863, 1; Horace Greeley, "The Conduct of the War," *Independent*, April 9, 1863, 1; Horace Greeley, "Dark and Bright Hours," *Independent*, May 14, 1863, 1; Horace Greeley, "Protection to Black Soldiers," *Independent*, May 21, 1863, 1; "Is It Prejudice?" *NYDT*, March 13, 1863, 4; "Negro Troops," *NYDT*, March 28, 1863, 4; "The Negro Influx," *NYDT*, April 16, 1863, 4. On the causes and impact of racial violence and riots, see "Copperhead Machinations to Inaugurate Civil War," *NYDT*, March 8, 1863, 4; all editorial pages of the *NYDT*, July 14–20, 1863, esp. "The Conscription—the Riot," July 14, 1863, 4, "Our Peril," July 16, 1863, 4, and "The Animus of the Mob," July 17, 1863, 4. On broader Republican charges about George McClellan and other Democratic military leaders' deliberate efforts to sabotage the war, see Thomas Harry Williams, *Lincoln and the Radicals* (Madison: University of Wisconsin Press, 1972), 246–254.

66. James R. Gilmore, *Personal Recollections of Abraham Lincoln and the Civil War* (Boston: L. C. Page, 1898), 103. Horace Greeley, "The Lessons of Invasion," *Independent*, July 2, 1863, 4; "The Rebel Offensive," *NYDT*, June 17, 1863, 4; "Last Ditch Heroics," *NYDT*, June 22, 1863, 4. For criticisms of the *Tribune*'s apparent defeatism, see, e.g.,

"The Weak-Kneed Tribune," *New-York Times*, June 18, 1863, 4; "Greeley Denying His Panic," *New-York Herald*, July 12, 1863, 4.

67. Theodore Tilton, "Shall the President Break His Covenant with the Slaves?," *NYDT*, April 1, 1863, 4; Horace Greeley, "Reply [to Theodore Tilton]," *NYDT*, April 1, 1863, 4. Tilton referenced the editorial "An Instructive Precedent," *NYDT*, March 30, 1863, 4. Also see James W. White to Horace Greeley, February 13, 1863, Greeley Papers, NYPL.

68. Horace Greeley, "Reply [to Theodore Tilton]," *NYDT*, April 1, 1863, 4. On slave uprisings and black military service, see, e.g., "Negro Troops," *NYDT*, March 28, 1863, 4; "Our Notion of the War," *NYDT*, January 22, 1863, 4; Horace Greeley, "Protection to Black Soldiers," *Independent*, May 21, 1863, 1. Other exchanges with critics include [Oliver Johnson], "THE UNION—THE STATES—HUMAN RIGHTS—EMANCIPATION," *NYDT*, April 18, 1863, 4; Horace Greeley, "Reply [to Oliver Johnson]," *NYDT*, April 18, 1863, 4.

69. Horace Greeley to Lemuel Smith, August 16, 1864, and Horace Greeley to W. O. Bartlett, August 30, 1864, both in Greeley Papers, NYPL.

70. Horace Greeley to Abraham Lincoln, July 7, 1864, in Basler, *Collected Works of Lincoln*, 435. Greeley had already substantially laid out such peace terms (and criticisms of the administration) by the turn of 1864. See Horace Greeley to Edwin D. Morgan, January 8, 1864, Morgan Papers, NYSL: "We could have peace on these terms (substantially) tomorrow, if we had men of real capacity at the head of affairs. Or rather, I should conclude that we have not such men if nothing is effected."

71. Abraham Lincoln to Horace Greeley, July 9, 1864, in Basler, *Collected Works of Lincoln*, 7, 435; Horace Greeley to Abraham Lincoln, July 10 and 13, 1864, both in Basler, *Collected Works of Lincoln*, 7, 440–442.

72. The Confederates—Clement C. Clay and James P. Holcombe—turned over the entire correspondence to the press, and it ran widely. See, e.g., "Peace Negotiations: The Correspondence on the Subject: The President's Note," *(Philadelphia) Daily Age*, July 23, 1864, 1.

73. "WHAT DID HE MEAN?" *Daily Eastern Argus* (Portland, ME), July 28, 1864, 2.

74. "Mr. Greeley—Fiasco—Niagara," *Albany (NY) Evening Journal*, July 23, 1864, 3.

75. Welles and Welles, *Diary of Gideon Welles*, vol. 2, 112. Greeley was not done with Lincoln and continued to hound the president with unsolicited advice and commentary on war and peace. See Horace Greeley to Abraham Lincoln, August 29, September 16, and November 23, 1864, all in Lincoln Papers, LOC. As embarrassing as the moment was for Greeley, it was also politically damaging to Lincoln, who was facing criticism for his handling of the war, Reconstruction, and peace plans. See "To the Supporters of the Government," *NYDT*, August 5, 1864, 5; Adam I. P. Smith, *No Party Now: Politics in the Civil War North* (New York: Oxford University Press, 2006), 112–114.

76. Horace Greeley, "The Alternative of War," *Independent*, August 18, 1864, 1. Note also Greeley's promotion of a nationalist tract by Tayler Lewis, an obscure Union College theologian. See Tayler Lewis, *State Rights: A Photograph from the Ruins of Ancient Greece* (Albany, NY: Weed, Parsons, 1865), 7; Horace Greeley, "Dr. Lewis on State Sovereignty," *Independent*, December 8, 1864, 1. Also see "The Dawn of Peace," *NYDT*, April 14, 1865, 4; "The Fundamental Error," *NYDT*, April 29, 1865, 4. Even in the depths of the

war, Greeley struck similar notes. See, following the battles of Gettysburg and Vicksburg, "The Sunlight of Victory," *Independent*, July 9, 1863, 1.

77. "Sectionalism," *NYDT*, April 27, 1865, 4; Horace Greeley, "Our Next Fourth of July," *Independent*, June 15, 1865, 1; "Terms of Reconstruction—Letter from O. A. Brownson," *NYDT*, November 19, 1866, 4.

78. "Trial of Jeff. Davis," *NYDT*, May 17, 1865, 4; "The Trial of Davis," *NYDT*, May 15, 1866, 4; "The Prisoner of State," *NYDT*, June 16, 1866, 4; Varina Davis to Horace Greeley, September 2, October 16, November 21, 1866, and [n.d., 1867], all in Greeley Papers, NYPL.

79. "Jefferson Davis," *NYDT*, November 9, 1866, 4.

80. "Speech Delivered by Horace Greeley at the African Church, Richmond, Virginia, May 15, 1867," appended to Lurton Dunham Ingersoll, *Life of Horace Greeley* (Philadelphia: John E. Potter, 1874), 637–644.

81. Ibid.

82. Wendell Phillips, "Treason Made Easy and Respectable," *New-York Times*, May 23, 1867, 5; "Horace Greeley and Jefferson Davis," *Nation*, May 23, 1867, 414; "Greeley among the Farmers—Inquiries about 'Jeff,'" *Albany (NY) Argus*, June 18, 1867, 2; Horace Greeley to Messrs. George W. Blunt, John A. Kennedy, John O. Stone, Stephen Hyatt, and thirty others, members of the Union League Club, May 23, 1867, reprinted in Ingersoll, *Life of Horace Greeley*, 432–436. Also see Horace Greeley to Joseph Harley, May 15, 1867, Greeley Papers, NYPL.

83. Horace Greeley to Messrs. Blunt et al., May 23, 1867, reprinted in Ingersoll, *Life of Horace Greeley*, 432–436; O. D. Case to Horace Greeley, February 11, 1870, Greeley Papers, NYPL; Fahs, *Imagined Civil War*, 298–299. Robert C. Williams, in *Horace Greeley*, suggests that *The American Conflict* should be considered a success, even with the Davis affair, which O. D. Case estimated cost the project 30,000–40,000 subscribers. The book sold around 225,000 copies by 1870, beating several competitors.

84. Greeley, *American Conflict*, vol. 2, 9–10.

85. F. B. Carpenter, *Six Months at the White House with Abraham Lincoln: The Story of a Picture* (New York: Hurd & Houghton, 1866), 152–153; Holzer, *Lincoln and the Power*, 517–518; Greeley, *American Conflict*, vol. 2, 249–251. In its review of volume 2, the *North American Review* cited Greeley's critical account of Lincoln as one of the book's consistent shortcomings. See "Greeley's American Conflict," *North American Review*, March 1867, 246.

86. "Greeley's American Conflict," *North American Review*, March 1867, 238–247.

Chapter 5 • The Most American of Americans

1. Charles F. Wingate, *Sketch of the Celebration of the Sixty-First Birthday of the Hon. Horace Greeley, LL.D.* (New York: 1872).

2. On the postwar theme of rebirth, see Jackson Lears, *Rebirth of a Nation: The Making of Modern America, 1877–1920* (New York: Harper Perennial, 2009), 1–2, 13–18. Though Greeley did not use religious language, he was working in a vein of millennial nationalism that developed during the war and remained in place in its aftermath. See Edward J. Blum, *Reforging the White Republic: Race, Religion, and American Nationalism* (Baton Rouge: Louisiana State University Press, 2015), 5–7, 20–50; David W. Blight,

Frederick Douglass's Civil War: Keeping Faith in Jubilee (Baton Rouge: Louisiana State University Press, 1989), 111; George M. Frederickson, *The Inner Civil War: Northern Intellectuals and the Crisis of the Union* (New York: Harper & Row, 1965), 184–189.

3. "Official Notice to Mr. Greeley of the Liberal Republican Nomination [with Greeley's reply]," *NYDT*, May 22, 1872, 4; *New-York Times*, November 5, 1872, quoted in Mark Wahlgren Summers, *The Ordeal of Reunion: A New History of Reconstruction* (Chapel Hill: University of North Carolina Press, 2014), 308–314.

4. "Magnanimity in Triumph," *NYDT*, April 10, 1865, 4; "Peace—Punishment," *NYDT*, April 13, 1865, 4. On the meanings of "peacetime" versus "wartime," see Gregory P. Downs, *After Appomattox: Military Occupation and the Ends of War* (Cambridge, MA: Harvard University Press, 2015), 1–10.

5. "THE QUESTION OF THE HOUR: Comments by the Tribune," *NYDT*, December 31, 1864, 4; "Reconstruction," *NYDT*, February 23, 1865, 4.

6. "THE INAUGURAL," *NYDT*, March 6, 1865, 4; "Reconstruction," *NYDT*, February 23, 1865, 4; "Peace Overtures," *NYDT*, March 27, 1865, 4; "PEACE PROSPECTS," *NYDT*, March 11, 1865, 4.

7. "Peace Movement," *NYDT*, January 2, 1865, 4; "Reconstruction," *NYDT*, February 23, 1865, 4; "The Press—Reconstruction—The President's Speech," *NYDT*, April 14, 1865, 4.

8. "Respectable Labor," *NYDT*, May 24, 1866, 4. In it, Greeley expressed his belief that Delaware would provide the earliest favorable results of the moral, material, and political revival brought by free labor: "[The state's] Democratic majority knows it owes its ascendancy to Slavery, and to nothing else—that, but for Slavery, this old Federal and Whig State would not pretend to be Democratic. Never mind: the next election will bring her out right: and Delaware will find her population, industry, intelligence, and wealth so rapidly and vastly increased by it that her people will be amazed that they could have been kept so long in the toils of Slavery and Sham Democracy." Also see Horace Greeley, "The Future of the South," *Independent*, April 6, 1865, 1; Horace Greeley, "From Out of the Furnace," *Independent*, April 27, 1865, 1.

9. "Sectionalism," *NYDT*, April 27, 1865, 4; "An Appeal to the Statesmen of the South," *NYDT*, June 20, 1865, 4; "Let Us Clearly Understand Each Other," *NYDT*, June 30, 1865, 4; "Appeal to Conservatives North and South," *NYDT*, July 10, 1865, 4.

10. "A White Man's Government, *NYDT*, February 12, 1866, 4; "Fate of the Freedmen's Bureau," *NYDT*, February 21, 1866, 4; "The Irrepressible Conflict," *NYDT*, February 23, 1866, 4; "Civil Rights," *NYDT*, April 9, 1866, 4; "Shall We Greatly Dare," *NYDT*, May 30, 1866, 4. For Theodore Tilton on Greeley as the "author of the Civil Rights Bill," see "The Tribune Banquet," *Independent*, April 26, 1866, 2; Horace Greeley to Schuyler Colfax, February 25, 1866, Horace Greeley Papers, NYPL. On the amendments and "Universal Amnesty, Impartial Suffrage," see esp. "Terms of Reconstruction—Letter from O. A. Brownson," *NYDT*, November 19, 1866, 4; Eric Foner, *Reconstruction: America's Unfinished Revolution, 1863–1877* (New York: Harper, 1988), 243–247.

11. "The Convention," *NYDT*, July 11, 1867, 1. On Greeley and suffrage at the New York State convention, see Glyndon G. Van Deusen, *Horace Greeley: Nineteenth Century Crusader* (Philadelphia: University of Pennsylvania Press, 1953), 362–363; "An Appeal to the Statesmen of the South," *NYDT*, June 20, 1865, 4; "Let Us Clearly Be Understood

by Each Other," *NYDT*, June 30, 1865, 4. On the Fifteenth Amendment, see "The Suffrage Amendment," *NYDT*, February 18, 1869, 4; "The Policy of Proscription," *NYDT*, June 9, 1869, 4; "Negro Suffrage—Two Faces," *NYDT*, July 20, 1869, 4; "Close the Books!," *NYDT*, April 8, 1870, 4. On the violent backdrop for Greeley's equivocal reflections on the Fifteenth Amendment, see "Letter from a Freedman," *NYDT*, February 20, 1869, 2. At the same moment, Greeley was writing that "the Colored People of this country are called to evince Self-Reliance." See "The Future of the Blacks in America," *Independent*, February 25, 1869, 1.

12. Horace Greeley to Janice Griffing, September 7, 1870, in Elizabeth Cady Stanton et al., eds., *History of Woman Suffrage, 1861–1876* (New York: Fowler & Wells, 1882), vol. 2, 36.

13. "Speech Delivered by Horace Greeley at the African Church, Richmond, Virginia, May 15, 1867," appended to Lurton Dunham Ingersoll, *Life of Horace Greeley* (Philadelphia: John E. Potter, 1874), 641.

14. Horace Greeley, "The Future of the South," *Independent*, April 6, 1865, 1. Greeley returned to the image of blacks as a "docile peasantry" more than once during the postwar years. See "Black Labor and White Capital—Comments by the Tribune," *NYDT*, May 28, 1866, 4; "The New South," *NYDT*, April 4, 1867, 4.

15. Horace Greeley, "The Future of the Blacks in America," *Independent*, February 25, 1869, 1; "WHAT SHALL BE DONE WITH THE NEGROES?" *NYDT*, May 25, 1865, 4; "Coddling the Blacks," *NYDT*, September 16, 1869, 4.

16. Horace Greeley, *Mr. Greeley's Letters from Texas and the Lower Mississippi* (New York: Tribune Office, 1871), 37.

17. "Amnesty—Personal Security," *NYDT*, March 16, 1871, 4.

18. "MR. ELLIOTT ON THE KU-KLUX OUTRAGES," *NYDT*, March 21, 1871, 4.

19. "Let Us Clearly Understand Each Other," *NYDT*, June 30, 1865, 4.

20. Horace Greeley, *Essays Designed to Elucidate the Science of Political Economy: While Serving to Explain and Defend the Policy of Protection to Home Industry as a System of National Cooperation for the Elevation of Labor* (Boston: Fields, Osgood, 1870). Also see Horace Greeley to Schuyler Colfax, January 16, 1870, Greeley Papers, NYPL, in which he confessed to Colfax that such "books are often hard reading, and the subject is not bewitching." Even the friendliest publications described Greeley as of "the old class of Protectionists," e.g., "Mr. Greeley's Essays on Political Economy," *Independent*, January 27, 1870, 6. As a measure of Greeley's engagement with the past, one of his political economy essays that ran in the *Tribune* in 1869 was still lamenting Henry Clay's defeat in the 1844 presidential election. See Horace Greeley, "Political Economy," *NYDT*, July 10, 1869, 8–9.

21. Horace Greeley, *Essays*, vii.

22. Ibid.

23. Ibid., 108–119, 133–145.

24. Ibid., 199, 213. On Henry Carey, see Howe, *Political Culture*, 109–122; Henry C. Carey, *The Harmony of Interests* (Philadelphia: J. S. Skinner, 1851); "The Coal Miners," *NYDT*, June 15, 1869, 4; "The Crispins," *NYDT*, June 17, 1869, 4. Greeley's magical thinking on *The Harmony of Interests* shaped a rather jaundiced view of the labor movement

and strikes in the mounting clashes of the Gilded Age. See Van Deusen, *Horace Greeley*, 331–333, 379–380.

25. Horace Greeley, *Essays*, 1–25. Also see Daniel T. Rodgers, *The Work Ethic in Industrial America, 1850–1920* (Chicago: University of Chicago Press, 1979), 4–25.

26. "The Laborers' Congress," *NYDT*, August 27, 1866, 4; Horace Greeley, "The Future of the Temperance Cause," *Independent*, December 9, 1869, 1; Horace Greeley, "Present Aspects and Needs of the Temperance Cause," *Independent*, April 7, 1870, 1.

27. Greeley, *Letters from Texas*, 9.

28. Horace Greeley, *What I Know of Farming: A Series of Brief and Plain Expositions of Practical Agriculture as an Art Based upon Science* (New York: G. W. Carleton, 1871), ix; Thomas Jefferson, *Notes on the State of Virginia*, in Adrienne Koch and William Peden, eds., *The Life and Selected Writings of Thomas Jefferson* (New York: Library of America, 1984), 280. The "What I Know of" line would become a fertile field for political attacks during the 1872 elections. See Constance Mayfield Rourke, *Trumpets of Jubilee: Henry Ward Beecher, Harriet Beecher Stowe, Lyman Beecher, Horace Greeley, P. T. Barnum* (New York: Harcourt Brace, 1927), 350–351.

29. Greeley, *What I Know of Farming*, 96, 124, 183–189, 195–200, 254.

30. "An American Idea," *NYDT*, March 6, 1871, 4.

31. "A Western Colony," *NYDT*, December 4, 1869, 11; "Co-Operation: Horace Greeley on Co-Operative Manufactures and Land Companies," *NYDT*, February 10, 1871, 8.

32. "Emigration to the West," *NYDT*, December 4, 1869, 6; H[orace] G[reeley], "The Union Colony," *NYDT*, November 5, 1870, 11; "The Mid-West," *NYDT*, January 21, 1871, 4; "Systematic Colonization," *NYDT*, March 3, 1871, 4; "Colonizing by Method," *NYDT*, March 7, 1871, 4; "National Emigration," *NYDT*, April 12, 1871, 1. Also see Robert C. Williams, *Horace Greeley: Champion of American Freedom* (New York: New York University Press, 2006), 284–290.

33. Horace Greeley to ——, July 22, 1870, in Joel Benton, ed., *Greeley on Lincoln* (New York: Baker & Taylor, 1893), 161 ("I actually begin to feel old"); Horace Greeley to Whitelaw Reid, September 10, 1870, in Royal Cortissoz, *The Life of Whitelaw Reid* (London: Thornton Butterworth, 1921), 201–202.

34. [Untitled,] *Cincinnati Commercial*, November 28, 1870, 4; "Greeley for President," *Cincinnati Commercial*, December 29, 1870, 4.

35. Ulysses S. Grant to John Russell Young, November 15, 1870, and Ulysses S. Grant to Horace Greeley, December 10, 1870, both in John Y. Simon, ed., *The Papers of Ulysses S. Grant* (Carbondale: Southern Illinois University Press, 1998), 21, 8–9, 84; "Radicalism in the City," *Albany (NY) Argus*, February 2, 1871, 2; Horace Greeley to Schuyler Colfax, November 1, 1869, and January 8, 1870, Greeley Papers, NYPL.

36. See, e.g., "Greeley Goes Back on Grant," *(Macon) Georgia Weekly Telegraph*, January 3, 1871, 4; "Washington," *New-York Herald*, January 4, 1871, 7; "What Horace Thinks of Ulysses," *Weekly Eastern Argus* (Portland, ME), January 12, 1871, 4.

37. [Untitled], *NYDT*, December 21, 1870, 4.

38. "An Invitation to Mr. Greeley," *Galveston Tri-Weekly News*, January 30, 1871, 2.

39. "Greeley for President," *Cincinnati Commercial*, December 29, 1870, 4; Logan

Reavis, quoted in "St. Louis Democrat, Horace Greeley for President," *Cincinnati Commercial*, April 15, 1871, 1.

40. "The Greeley Demonstration," *Cincinnati Commercial*, June 18, 1871, 2; [untitled], *Springfield (MA) Republican*, September 8, 1871, 4.

41. "Horace Greeley in Texas—the Trip from New Orleans to Galveston," *(New Orleans) Daily Picayune*, May 21, 1871, 15; "Greeley in Texas," *Cincinnati Commercial*, May 20, 1871, 8; "Invitation to Mr. Greeley," *Houston Daily Union*, May 23, 1871, 2; "Honors to Horace Greeley: Excursion up the Central Railroad," *Houston Daily Union*, May 23, 1871, 2.

42. "Horace Greeley in Texas," *Cincinnati Commercial*, May 30, 1871, 1.

43. "The South—Its Sins and Its Sufferings," *NYDT*, May 17, 1871, 4; "Greeley's Journey," *Cincinnati Commercial*, May 24, 1871, 2.

44. ["Galveston News—Mr. Greeley—State—Texas"], *Houston Daily Union*, May 20, 1871, 2; "Horace Greeley in Texas," *Cincinnati Commercial*, May 30, 1871, 1.

45. "Why Not?" and "Mr. Greeley's Visit," both in *(New Orleans) Weekly Louisianian*, May 21, 1871, 2.

46. [Galveston News; Mr. Greeley; State; Texas], *Houston Daily Union*, May 20, 1871, 2; "Horace Greeley in Texas: Opinions of the Press and Opinions of the People of Galveston," *New Orleans Times-Picayune*, May 23, 1871, 2.

47. [Untitled], *New-York Herald*, May 22, 1871, 2; [untitled], *Providence (RI) Evening Press*, May 20, 1872, 2; [untitled], *Cleveland Plain Dealer*, May 20, 1871, 2.

48. Greeley, *Letters from Texas*, 35–42.

49. Ibid., 43–53. On the appreciation of military valor across sectional lines, see David W. Blight, *Race and Reunion: The Civil War and American Memory* (Cambridge, MA: Harvard University Press, 2001).

50. "Greeley and the Presidency," *Cincinnati Commercial*, May 30, 1871, 1; [untitled], *Cincinnati Commercial*, June 4, 1871, 4; [untitled], *Golden Age*, June 5, 1871, 5.

51. On the Liberal Republican movement, see Andrew L. Slap, *The Doom of Reconstruction: The Liberal Republicans in the Civil War Era* (New York: Fordham University Press, 2006); Richard White, *The Republic for Which It Stands: The United States during Reconstruction and the Gilded Age* (New York: Oxford University Press, 2017), 172–208; Foner, *Reconstruction*, 488–500.

52. "The Conspiracy to Destroy the Republican Party," *NYDT*, September 1, 1870, 4; "Mr. Greeley's Essays on Political Economy," *Independent*, January 27, 1870, 6; Horace Greeley to Schuyler Colfax, January 16, 1870, and October 6, 1870, both in Greeley Papers, NYPL; "The Moral in Missouri: Comments by the Tribune," *NYDT*, September 26, 1870, 4; Horace Greeley, "The Issue that Looms on Our Horizon," *Independent*, April 22, 1869, 1.

53. D. A. Wells to Francis Blair, December 22, 1871, article in the *Springfield (MA) Republican*, March 18, 1872, and K. Prime to Lyman Trumbull, March 29, 1872, all quoted in Slap, *Doom of Reconstruction*, 142–145.

54. Horace Greeley to Beman Brockway, March 13, 1872, Horace Greeley Papers, LOC; "One Presidential Term," *NYDT*, December 11, 1872, 4; "Civil Service," *NYDT*, December 19, 1871, 4; "A New Broom," *NYDT*, December 21, 1871, 4; "A Chance for Retrenchment," *NYDT*, January 19, 1872, 4; "The Shadow of Coming Events," *NYDT*,

January 29, 1872, 4; "A Demand for Reform" and "Amnesty at Washington," both in *NYDT*, February 9, 1872, 4; "The Arms Scandal," February 15, 1872, 4; "The Decay of Official Conscience," *NYDT*, February 16, 1872, 4; "Civilization at the South," *NYDT*, March 23, 1872, 4; "The Grant Meeting," *NYDT*, April 18, 1872, 6.

55. "The Cincinnati Convention," *NYDT*, March 16, 1872, 4; "About Cincinnati," *NYDT*, April 4, 1872, 4.

56. On the role of newspapers and the "Quadrilateral" group of editors (Samuel Bowles, Horace White, Murat Halstead, and Henry "Marse" Watterson) who supported Greeley at the convention (along with his managing editor, Whitelaw Reid), see Mark W. Summers, *The Press Gang: Newspapers and Politics, 1865–1878* (Chapel Hill: University of North Carolina Press, 1994), 233–250.

57. Carl Schurz, "The Aims of the Liberal Republican Movement," May 2, 1872, in Frederic Bancroft, ed., *Speeches, Correspondence, and Political Papers of Carl Schurz* (New York: G. P. Putnam's Sons, 1913), 359.

58. *Springfield (MA) Republican*, May 1, 1872, quoted in Matthew T. Downey, "Horace Greeley and the Politicians: The Liberal Republican Convention in 1872," *Journal of American History* 53:4 (March 1967), 741 ; Marcus Morton to John Van Buren, October 4, 1852, quoted in Downey, "Horace Greeley," 749; *(St. Louis) Missouri Democrat*, October 17, 1872, quoted in Downey, "Horace Greeley," 749. On the convention generally, Downey offers a compelling case that Greeley's nomination was the result of his popularity. Also see John Greenleaf Whittier to Edwin Morton, May 10, 1872, in John B. Pickard, ed., *The Letters of John Greenleaf Whittier* (Cambridge, MA: Harvard University Press, 1975), vol. 3, 267–268.

59. Carl Schurz to Horace Greeley, May 6, 1872, Greeley Papers, NYPL; Horace Greeley's responses to Carl Schurz, May 8 and 10, 1872, both in Carl Schurz Papers, LOC; Slap, *Doom of Reconstruction*, 163; Allan Nevins, *The Evening Post: A Century of Journalism* (New York: Boni & Liveright, 1922), 396; "Some Lessons of the Cincinnati Convention," *Nation*, May 16, 1872, 317. Thomas Nast mocked Schurz's piano playing in his cartoon "Played Out," *Harper's Weekly*, June 15, 1872, 468.

60. Gideon Welles, quoted in Van Deusen, *Horace Greeley*, 406; W. O. Duvall to Gerrit Smith, July 19, 1872, quoted in Ralph Volney Harlow, *Gerrit Smith: Philanthropist and Reformer* (New York: Henry Holt, 1937), 477.

61. Van Deusen, *Horace Greeley*, 407–408; Horace Greeley to Samuel Sinclair, June 4 and June 5, 1872, both in Greeley Papers, NYPL.

62. "Official Notice to Mr. Greeley of the Liberal Republican Nomination; Mr. Greeley's Reply," *NYDT*, May 22, 1872, 4; Horace Greeley, "A Card," *NYDT*, May 15, 1872, 4.

63. Theodore Tilton, quoted in Joseph Bucklin Bishop, *Notes of Many Years* (New York: Scribner's, 1925), 26; clippings from *Frank Leslie's Illustrated Newspaper*, June 8 and July 13, 1872, both in Greeley Papers, NYPL; *One Hundred Reasons Why General Grant Should Not Be Re-Elected President of the United States* (Philadelphia: J. C. Thompson, 1872); *One Hundred Reasons Why Horace Greeley Should Be Elected President of the United States* (Philadelphia: J. C. Thompson, 1872); "The White Hat Infection," *Galveston Tri-Weekly News*, May 27, 1872, 1; *Farmer of Chappaqua Songster* (New York: Robert M. DeWitt, 1872). Also see Van Deusen, *Horace Greeley*, 410–412.

64. [Untitled], *Nation*, August 8, 1872, 83. According to Henry Morton Stanley, the

joke originated with Mark Twain in the *Hartford (CT) Courant*. See Henry Morton Stanley, "Twenty-Five Years' Progress in Equatorial Africa," *Atlantic Monthly*, October 1897, 472.

65. "Official Notification of Mr. Greeley's Nomination at Baltimore; Mr. Greeley's Acceptance," *NYDT*, July 24, 1872, 4; Horace Greeley to ——, July 16, 1872, in Benton, *Greeley on Lincoln*, 226–229.

66. Charles Sumner, *The Interest and Duty of Colored Citizens in the Presidential Election: Letter to Colored Citizens, July 29, 1872* (Washington, DC: F & J. Rives & Geo. Bailey, 1872), 8. Sumner's old abolitionist allies savaged his decision to endorse Greeley. See *Grant or Greeley—Which? Facts and Arguments for the Consideration of the Colored Citizens of the United States: Being Extracts from Letters, Speeches, and Editorials by Colored Men and Their Best Friends; Sumner's Mistake, Greeley's Surrender, and Grant's Faithfulness; Opinions in Brief of Wm. Lloyd Garrison, Wendell Phillips, Prof. J. Mercer Langston, R. H. Dana, Jr., Judge Hoar, Fred. Douglass, Speaker Blaine, Wm. D. Forten, Prof. Wm. Howard Day* (Washington, DC: Republican Congressional Committee, 1872); James M. McPherson, "Grant or Greeley? The Abolitionist Dilemma in the Election of 1872," *Journal of American History* 71:1 (October 1965), 55–58; Blight, *Race and Reunion*, 127–128.

67. "Democracy and Vice: Comments by the Tribune," *NYDT*, January 7, 1868, 4. Also see James Ford Rhodes, *History of the United States: From the Compromise of 1850*, in vol. 6, *1862–1864* (New York: Macmillan, 1917, 430n. A full compendium of similar characterizations of Democrats by Greeley and the *Tribune* can be found in *What Horace Greeley Knows about the Democratic Party, from 1841 to 1872 Inclusive* (n.p., [1872]).

68. Summers, *Ordeal of Reunion*, 308–314; Benjamin Butler, quoted in Blight, *Race and Reunion*, 127.

69. Frederick Douglass, "Speech in New York City, September 25, 1872," *New-York Times*, September 26, 1872, reprinted in Brooks Simpson, ed., *Reconstruction: Voices from America's First Great Struggle for Racial Equality* (New York: Library of America, 2018), 428–434. On Wendell Phillips and William Lloyd Garrison, see McPherson, "Grant or Greeley," 57–59; *Grant or Greeley—Which?*, 1–4.

70. "Red Hot!" *Harper's Weekly*, July 13, 1872, 560; "Let Us Clasp Hands over the Bloody Chasm," *Harper's Weekly*, September 21, 1872, 732; "The Next in Order," *Harper's Weekly*, September 14, 1872, 713; "H. G.: Let Us Clasp Hands over the Bloody Chasm," *Harper's Weekly*, October 19, 1872, 804. An excellent online resource for Thomas Nast's cartoons of Horace Greeley can be found at http://nastandgreeley .harpweek.com/default.asp/. Also see Fiona Deans Halloran, *Thomas Nast: The Father of Modern Political Cartoons* (Chapel Hill: University of North Carolina Press, 2013), 145–176.

71. Horace Greeley, *Recollections*, dedication; J. Bowker, *Wreck-Elections of a Busy Life* (Hartford, CT: Kellog & Bulkeley, n.d.); Horace Greeley paper fan, ca. 1872, General Artemas Ward House Museum, HU3408, https://curiosity.lib.harvard.edu/artemas -ward-house-and-its-collections/catalog/7-W387768_urn-3:HPREWARD:1186819, accessed March 20, 2019; *The Comic Life of Horace Greeley* (New York: Winchell & Small, 1872), 7. Also see *'H. G.' at Chappaqua: An Epic by a Farmer Poet* (New York: John P. Jewett, 1872); *Political Oats: A Kernel or Two for Everybody* (New York: Winchell &

Small, 1872), 6; "Chappaquackery: A Sample of the Fun that's Being Poked at Horace," *(Little Rock) Daily Republican*, May 25, 27, and 28, 1872, 3 (for each date).

72. *The True Issues of the Presidential Campaign: Speeches of Horace Greeley during His Western Trip and at Portland* (n.p., 1872), 7–9.

73. Summers, *Ordeal of Reunion*, 314–315; "Who Is the Traitor Now?" *Harper's Weekly*, October 12, 1872, 792; *Evening Post*, quoted in *Mr. Greeley and the Reformers*, broadside, 1872.

74. Summers, *Ordeal of Reunion*, 314; Blight, *Race and Reunion*, 126–128; Foner, *Reconstruction*, 501–504.

75. Foner, *Reconstruction*, 509–511; Blight, *Race and Reunion*, 127–129.

Epilogue • A Union Printer

1. Allan Nevins and Milton Halsey Thomas, eds., *The Diary of George Templeton Strong*, vol. 4, 453; Horace Greeley to Col. Tappan, quoted in O. J. Hollister, *Life of Schuyler Colfax* (New York: Funk & Wagnalls, 1886), 387n. Also see Horace Greeley to Margaret Allen, October 25 and November 4, 1872, both in Horace Greeley Papers, LOC. On Greeley's physical appearance in his final days, see Josiah Bushnell Grinnell, *Men and Events of Forty Years* (Boston: D. Lothrop, 1891), 226–227.

2. Horace Greeley, "A Card," *NYDT*, November 7, 1872, 4.

3. "Re-enter H. G.," *New-York Times*, November 8, 1872, 4; "Crumbs of Comfort," *NYDT*, November 7, 1872, 4; "Mr. Greeley's Card," *Independent*, November 14, 1872, 4.

4. "Our Artist's Occupation Gone," *Harper's Weekly*, November 23, 1872, 920; Mark Twain and James Parton, quoted in Albert Bigelow Paine, *Thomas Nast: His Period and His Pictures* (New York: Macmillan, 1904), 263–264.

5. Horace Greeley to [unknown], November 8, 1872, in Joel Benton, ed., *Greeley on Lincoln* (New York: Baker & Taylor, 1893), 234–235; "Mr. Greeley's Health," *NYDT*, November 27, 1872, 5; Horace Greeley to Cornelius Vanderbilt, November 13, 1872, and Greeley testimonial, November 13, 1872, both in Horace Greeley Papers, NYPL; "Horace Greeley," *Cincinnati Daily Gazette*, November 30, 1872, 2.

6. "A Man Who Deserves a Testimonial," *Yankton (Dakota Territory [SD]) Press*, December 4, 1872; "Death of Horace Greeley," *Yankton (Dakota Territory [SD]) Press*, December 4, 1872, 2.

7. Henry Ward Beecher, quoted in "Funeral of Horace Greeley," *Lowell (MA) Daily Citizen and News*, December 5, 1872, 2; Charles Sumner, quoted in "News of the Day," *Charleston (SC) News*, December 7, 1872, 2; "Horace Greeley," *Boston Daily Advertiser*, December 4, 1872, 1; "Honors to the Dead: The Remains of Mr. Greeley Viewed by Vast Throngs of People," *Cincinnati Daily Gazette*, December 4, 1872, 1.

8. "Mr. Greeley's Life and Services," *Albany (NY) Evening Journal*, December 4, 1872, 2; *New-York Herald* reflections, printed in "Horace Greeley," *Pittsfield (MA) Sun*, December 4, 1872, 2; "Death of Mr. Greeley," *(New Orleans) Daily Picayune*, December 1, 1872, 2; "Horace Greeley," *(New Orleans) Weekly Louisianian*, December 7, 1872, 2; "Where is Nast?," *(San Francisco) Daily Evening Bulletin*, February 21, 1873, 4; Paine, *Thomas Nast*, 264–266.

9. Constance Mayfield Rourke, *Trumpets of Jubilee: Henry Ward Beecher, Harriet Beecher Stowe, Lyman Beecher, Horace Greeley, P. T. Barnum* (New York: Harcourt

Brace, 1927), 70; Nevins and Thomas, *Diary of George Templeton Strong*, vol. 4, 459–460, 444.

10. "The Tribune," *NYDT*, December 23, 1872, 4; Richard Kluger, *The Paper: The Life and Death of the New-York Herald Tribune* (New York: Vintage Books, 1989), 131–135; Harry William Baehr, *The New-York Tribune since the Civil War* (New York, Dodd, Mead, 1936), 119–123. One faction had sought to install outgoing vice president Schuyler Colfax as Greeley's replacement. Doing so would have immediately put the *Tribune* back into the good graces of the Republican Party.

11. Baehr, *New-York Tribune*, 126–128; editorial, "The New Tribune," *NYDT*, April 10, 1875, 4; "The New Tribune: Opening of the Great Building," *NYDT*, April 10, 1875, 9–10.

12. "The New Tribune," *NYDT*, April 10, 1875, 4; "The New Tribune: Opening of the Great Building," *NYDT*, April 10, 1875, 9–10; Baehr, *New-York Tribune*, 127; Kluger, *The Paper*, 134.

13. Fred A. Palmer, "A Centennial Retrospect," in Frederick Saunders, ed., *Our National Jubilee: Orations, Addresses, and Poems Delivered on the Fourth of July, 1876* (New York: E. B. Treat, 1877), 238. On the decline of antebellum national idealism in the 1870s, see Paul C. Nagel, *This Sacred Trust: American Nationality, 1798–1898* (New York: Oxford University Press, 1971), 197–213.

14. Rutherford B. Hayes, "Letter of Acceptance of the Republican Nomination for President of the United States, July 8, 1876" and "Inaugural Address, March 5, 1877," both in *Letters and Messages of Rutherford B. Hayes, President of the United States* (Washington, DC, 1881), 5–8, 11–15. Hayes used much of the same language verbatim in his letter of acceptance and the inaugural. On Hayes and the contested election of 1876, see Richard White, *The Republic for Which It Stands: The United States during Reconstruction and the Gilded Age* (New York: Oxford University Press, 2017), 325–337. On feelings of national failure in 1876, see Nagel, *This Sacred Trust*, 213.

15. George A. Stevens, *New York Typographical Union No. 6: Study of a Modern Trade Union and Its Predecessors* (Albany, NY: J. B. Lyon, 1913), 626–632. I would like to thank the staff at the Bowne & Co. print shop at the South Street Seaport Museum in New York City for an informative conversation about how types were made in the nineteenth century.

16. Amos Cummings, quoted in Lurton Dunham Ingersoll, *Life of Horace Greeley* (Philadelphia: John E. Potter, 1874), 475; Stevens, *New York Typographical Union*, 630.

17. Stevens, *New York Typographical Union*, 636, 383–396 (on the strike); Baehr, *New-York Tribune*, 183–192.

The initials HG in this index refer to Horace Greeley. Page numbers followed by *f* indicate a figure.

Case, O. D., 114, 142, 209n8, 216n83
Cass, Lewis, 70–72
Channing, William Ellery, 155
Chase, Salmon, 100, 133
Cheever, George B., 131
Child, Lydia Maria, 106, 208n77
Civil Rights Bill, 150
Civil War: Confiscation Act and, 126, 128–29;
Draft Riots of, 113–14, 135; emancipation
debates of, 125–33, 136–37, 213n52; Fort
Sumter attack of, 121–23; HG's faith in
Southern white yeomen and, 65–66, 118–20,
122, 148–49, 210n17, 210n19, 212n39; HG's
national unity vision and, 13, 114–17, 121,
130–32, 208–9n4, 210n21; HG's peace and
reconciliation plans and, 132–40, 148–53,
171–72, 179–80, 214n59, 214n63, 215n70,
215n72, 215nn75–76, 216n2; outbreak of,
122–25, 211n23, 211nn30–31; press coverage of, 116; secession crisis and, 117–22,
210–11nn22–23; Union advances and victory
in, 137–40, 148; Union defeats in, 116, 123–25,
133, 136, 212n33. See also *American Conflict,
The*; Reconstruction era; US sectionalism
Clay, Cassius M., 60, 66
Clay, Clement C., 215n72
Clay, Henry, 13, 58–61, 153–54; American
System of, 59–61, 68; Baillie's cartoon of, 52*f*,
53; Compromise of 1850 of, 77; presidential
candidacy of, 59–61, 66–68, 69*f*, 196n18,
196n20, 198n31, 198n33; Whig Party vision
of, 36, 54, 64
Clinton, DeWitt, 36
Colfax, Schuyler, 71–72, 76, 84, 104, 203n28,
224n10
colonization movement, 32, 130, 213n50
Columbian Orator (Bingham), 6, 21
Comic Life of Horace Greeley, The, 172
Confidence-Man (Melville), 9–10
Confiscation Act, 126, 128–29
Congress, 1, 13–14, 73–77, 158, 185n15; debates
of Northern values in, 97–99, 107–8, 206n49;
HG's critiques of, 74–77, 199–200nn49–51;
HG's legislative proposals in, 73, 76–77;
travel reimbursements for, 75. *See also* US
sectionalism
Conkling, Roscoe, 158–59, 166

Cooper, James Fenimore, 44–45, 193n64
cooperative settlements, 156–57
Copperhead movement, 133–36, 214n65
Corwin, Thomas, 198n31, 198n36
Crittenden, John J., 120
Cummings, Amos, 181
"Currency Song, The" (Whig songbook), 41

Dana, Charles A., 47*f*, 69, 93, 102; on HG's
writing, 45–46; on Kansas, 97; on the
outbreak of the Civil War, 123, 211n31
Davis, David, 167
Davis, Jefferson, 138; HG's posting of bail for,
5, 11, 15, 140–43, 147, 157, 216n83; postwar
imprisonment of, 140
Davis, Varina, 140
Day, Benjamin, 10, 23–25
Democracy in America (Tocqueville), 8, 185n12
Democratic Party, 38–42; anti-slavery factions
of, 70, 84, 199n46; Copperhead peace movement of, 133–36, 214n65; election of 1840
and, 39–42; election of 1844 and, 60–61;
election of 1848 and, 70–72; election of 1872
and, 169–74; Free Soil factions of, 71–72, 97,
199n57; Jacksonian populism of, 36, 40,
192n53; penny dailies and, 44; publications
of, 192n56
Dickens, Charles, 106
Douglas, Stephen A., 83–84, 88
Douglass, Frederick, 49, 171, 185n11
Draft Riots, 113–14, 125, 135
Dunn, George, 206n49

Eggleston, Edward, 145–46
Elliott, Richard Smith, 38
Elliott, Robert Brown, 152–53
emancipation, 125–33, 136–37, 148–49; Confiscation Act and, 126, 128–29; HG's calls for,
116, 125–26, 128–29, 143, 213n52; legislative
efforts for, 66; Northern racism and opposition to, 93–94, 126–28, 135–36
Emancipation Proclamation, 125, 130–31,
136–37, 143
Emerson, Ralph Waldo, 49; on HG, 9, 45,
55–56; national reputation of, 194n3; on the
US-Mexican War, 62
English Reader (Murray), 6